10: PERSPECTIVES IN CRITICISM

PERSPECTIVES IN CRITICISM

1: *Elements of Critical Theory*

2: *The Disinherited of Art*

3: *Stream of Consciousness in the Modern Novel*

4: *The Poet in the Poem*

5: *Arthurian Triptych*

6: *The Brazilian Othello of Machado de Assis*

7: *The World of Jean Anouilh*

8: *A New Approach to Joyce*

9: *The Idea of Coleridge's Criticism*

10: *Introduction to the Psychoanalysis of Mallarmé*

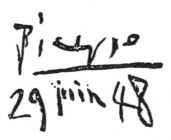

PORTRAIT OF MALLARMÉ BY PABLO PICASSO

Engraved by Angladon. From the Flandreysy-Espérandieu Collection, Archives of the Palais du Roure, Avignon.

10:

Charles Mauron

Translated from the French by
Archibald Henderson, Jr., and Will L. McLendon

Introduction
to the Psychoanalysis
of Mallarmé

UNIVERSITY OF CALIFORNIA PRESS
Berkeley and Los Angeles
1963

University of California Press
Berkeley and Los Angeles, California
Cambridge University Press
London, England

L'Introduction à la psychanalyse de Mallarmé,
FIRST PUBLISHED IN NEUCHÂTEL, SWITZERLAND, BY
LES EDITIONS DE LA BACONNIÈRE À BOUDRY, 1950

PUBLISHED WITH THE ASSISTANCE OF A GRANT
FROM THE UNIVERSITY OF HOUSTON

LIBRARY OF CONGRESS CATALOG CARD NUMBER: 63-8918
Printed in the United States of America
Designed by Ward Ritchie

Contents

	Introduction	1
1.	*Maria Mallarmé*	23
2.	*Poetic Alienation*	53
3.	*Before* Hérodiade	81
4.	*Anxiety This Midnight*	111
5.	*The Prisoner*	150
6.	*The Spectator*	167
7.	*Orpheus*	193
8.	*From the Youthful Poems to the* Livre	217
	Notes	251
	Index	273

Introduction to
the American Edition

THOUGH THE *Introduction to the Psychoanalysis of Mallarmé* was written in French ten years ago, it is still, in my opinion, scientifically valid, and that is why I have authorized its translation. Indeed, it is made up not of mere impressions or personal interpretations but of objective results, uncontested as to the essentials and—doubtless more important—as to the method which led to these results. As this method has developed, it has laid the basis for what I have called "psychocriticism," and even "comparative psychocriticism." Slowly, experimentally, we are beginning to understand what creative imagination is. Since I have never ceased to study Mallarmé as well as other writers and artists, I should now like to complete my study of Mallarmé by drawing the reader's attention to a number of new works of research and their contributions. In chapter 8[1] I shall analyze the works of Mallarmé's youth which have been published since 1949. The introduction I shall reserve for the examination of questions of methodology.

First, a bit of history. The ideas contained in *L'Introduction à la psychanalyse de Mallarmé* have had a curious fate. They sprang from the application of a method to given materials, and these two elements must be dealt with separately.

1

The method goes back to my first book on this subject, *Mallarmé l'obscur* (written in 1939, published in 1941).[2] Psychoanalytic in inspiration but voluntarily limited as to scope, the method at first consisted of searching in the poems for groups of obsessive associations which form underlying networks necessarily linked to the unconscious. Results were immediate: there did indeed exist autonomous groups of metaphors forming complexes and structuring the creative imagination of Mallarmé. However, in 1939, certain critical materials (unpublished works, variants, biographical documents, correspondence) were still inaccessible. Dr. Mondor's biography,[3] published in 1941, revealed to me the event which was lodged—at least this was the way it appeared at first glance—at the center of the network of associations which had been experimentally revealed. It was the death of Maria, the poet's sister. In the preface (1941) to *Mallarmé l'obscur*, which was then about to appear, I connected this death with that of his mother and pointed out the great importance of these events for any explanation of the poet's work:

> This double death and double childish love, with the probable unconscious fusion of the two, largely account for the irresistible nostalgia of the first poems, this longing for Paradise Lost and musician angel. All Mallarmé's eroticism continued to be marked, or rather impregnated, with them. An ardent sensuality drew him to women, but soon in the women he had to love the sister. Thence no doubt his taste on the one hand for ambiguous forms of chastity, fierce, intangible but naked and very close to desire, precisely the chastity of a Hérodiade; on the other hand for beloveds who have turned maternal and to whom one can "whisper" the name "sister." This ambiguity constitutes in fact a magnificent keyboard passing

2

from the most carnal sensuality to the most subtle ideality.[4]

Mallarmé l'obscur enjoyed a certain success in France, but the small discovery tucked away thus in its preface passed almost unnoticed. The edition of the poet's *Oeuvres complètes*, published four years later, gives obvious proof of the fact (see p. 27 of the present work). In my own investigations, however, a connecting link between the biographical event (that is, the death of the young sister Maria) and the "personal myth" just emerging at the center of the networks of obsessive associations was still missing.[5] For a phantasm is not determined by a current incident; it proceeds from earlier phantasms whose origin is, in the last analysis, very early; it is only *applied* to the current incident. Fairbairn,[6] among others, has observed that these imaginative fantasies reflect at each instant the acquired psychic structure and strive to assimilate and integrate the new event into their dynamic equilibrium. Here the missing link was furnished to me by the free composition,[7] *Les trois Cigognes*, published for the first time by Dr. Mondor in *Mallarmé plus intime* in 1944. It is presented therein as an odd, though in no way essential, text.[8] In this same work the erudite biographer indeed admits, though with many reservations, the thesis of *Mallarmé l'obscur*. It is clear, moreover, that what he rejects throughout my thesis is psychoanalysis as he understands it. His attitude may be listed in the general history of resistances to this science. Thus, to any suspicion of incestuous inclination, Mondor opposes the purity of the tenderness expressed in the childhood correspondence between Stéphane and Maria.[9] Dr. Mondor could not therefore have guessed that in publishing the free composition he would confirm in the most startling fashion the relationship between the image of the dead girl and the totality of Mallarmé's work, a relationship which does not explain everything

3

(this I have never claimed) but which is everywhere present. All that remained for me to do then was to connect the free composition to Maria, on one side, and to the poems, on the other. This was no new subjective interpretation of Mallarmé's obscurities, like so many others which have appeared after great expenditures of talent and often of reason. It was rather the simple blazing of a trail which was at once obsessive and creative. I immediately drew several general conclusions as to the psychology of poetic creation, which will be found gathered below, especially in the chapter "Orpheus."

Thus, with a certain method and with the materials which were granted us, we were arriving at certain results. What danger was there that these results would be outmoded by future works? As early as 1949 my mind was made up on this score.

1. The new materials which Dr. Mondor or others would surely reveal would no doubt complete, but not modify, the fundamental relationship. The *personal myth* of an author resembles a sort of funnel or filter through which his psychic energy must necessarily pass. The free composition gives us the state of this myth for the Mallarmé of sixteen.

2. Much was still to be discovered in the field of literary influences. But these variations would not modify our idea of the inner source, whose determination is distinct from these influences and anterior to them.

3. On the other hand, an improvement of the psychocritical method and thus a more precise interpretation of the free composition and the analysis of new texts which might be turned up would doubtless lead to a deepening of the results which had already been obtained.

Ten years have passed, and a number of works have been published. Certain of these have but a distant connection with my own research, and I shall refrain from discussing them here despite their interest. On the other

4

hand, in 1955 Mme Ayda published a work called *Le Drame intérieur de Mallarmé*, the subject of which partially overlapped my own; and, indeed, when I had read well into her volume, I felt like the man who passes, as the poet says,

 . . . through forests of symbols
 Which gaze at him familiarly.[10]

Everywhere I came upon my own views, which (with or without reason) I had thought were disdained, presented as anonymous and, as it were, self-evident ideas. Maria's death *was* significant; the free composition *was* the open sesame to the poet's work; the network of associations *did* run from poem to poem. At almost the same time (1954) Dr. Mondor published in *Mallarmé lycéen* a newly found notebook containing works of the poet's youth, the reading of which had visibly increased Mondor's interest, if not in psychoanalysis, at least in its problems![11] Finally, quite recently (April, 1959), M. Cellier, professor in the Faculté des Lettres at Grenoble, published an original work, *Mallarmé et la morte qui parle*,[12] whose subject leads him to make frequent references to Mme Ayda's book and to my own. M. Cellier's erudition appears as profound as his intellectual honesty. I therefore had confidence in his evidence, which led me to two conclusions:

 1. *L'Introduction à la psychanalyse de Mallarmé* remained quite valid, on the whole, and could serve as a basis for, or as adjuvant to, other works.

 2. My own findings, on the other hand, ran the greatest risk of being twisted and becoming a source of errors in the mind of non-psychoanalytic researchers.

 What had happened? Let us note first a fact whose methodological importance I shall stress later. If the results obtained by a psychocriticism based on psychoanalysis have been largely adopted, psychoanalysis itself—its essential conceptions and its works—has been repudiated. "No need to follow the teaching of Freud," declares M. Cellier, who nonetheless draws a distinct

5

benefit—quite successfully, too—from his personal study of myths, the very sense of the imaginative "material" which the psychoanalyst acquires from the practical study of dreams and fantasies in general (myths included). Mme Ayda believes, as many others do today, in a vague, expurgated sort of psychoanalysis. Her revision is apparently based far more on personal resistances than on an experimentally informed criticism.[13] She speaks of the unconscious but oufits it with conscious content. Thus the least one can say is that Mallarméan criticism is traveling ambiguous paths, which may lead to syntheses or to confused thinking. I therefore believe that we must take stock of our methods.

Subjective criticism, with its decipherings and its diverse interpretations, had at least achieved most of the word-by-word literal interpretation and elucidated the syntactical structure of many Mallarméan texts. M. Cellier accuses me of undue optimism on this point. Perhaps he is right. But does he realize what reading Mallarmé was like for the generation of, say, Mauclair?[14] We read the *Faune* today much as we listen to Debussy. The assimilation has been made, except for a few details which still delight our quibblers. Twenty years ago Mallarméan criticism entered a new phase: the study of exterior and interior sources. These are two distinct areas of research, each boasting its own province and method. However, they complete one another and therefore have a common boundary or, better, a common ground of ambiguities. *L'Introduction à la psychanalyse de Mallarmé* was by choice concerned only with the interior source. M. Cellier's work studies primarily the exterior sources, especially Gautier. However, he carries out his study with the notion that there was a determining interior source, in which respect his research becomes exciting, for it comes near to achieving a synthesis. The trouble is, he borrows from Mme Ayda his conception of the inner source, which in my opinion is not synthetic but confused.

6

This present status of the problem and the consequences it entails for the development of psychocriticism persuade me to formulate at this point a series of observations in which neither the reader nor Mme Ayda should envision any lack of courtesy. It is a question, let it be repeated, of clarification of methodology, and not of polemics.

I shall group my observations under three headings:
A. In the first place, Mme Ayda did not realize how dangerous it was to pass from the plane of psychocriticism to that of psychology. I limited myself to an *Introduction* to the psychoanalysis of Mallarmé; I related texts to other texts. She has tried to explain Mallarmé himself, to reveal his interior drama. She undertakes the formidable task of connecting the work of a writer to his individual psychology. In a general way this assumes that the quality of this relationship is known and that the psychological problem of aesthetic creation is resolved. But, more specifically, the case in question is that of an adolescent orphan in full pubertal crisis, suffering from a recent sorrow and groping for social or spiritual sublimations. Here is quite a complicated case, if one takes into account the mass of works on the psychology of the orphan, of adolescence, of the crisis of puberty, of mourning and sublimation. Literary genius, plus readings, plus influences, plus biographical events, do not make things any simpler.
B. Mme Ayda's thesis is brilliantly summed up in the metaphor which unfolds on the last page of her book. The author has first compared the hermetic symbols of Mallarméan poetry to gems with many facets. The poet, as it were, threaded them on the strands of a curtain whose surface the work presents us.

But this curtain . . . is a magic screen, which hides in its folds, or rather in its reflections, a coded language. The fires the gems throw out are signals.

7

These signals tend to bring back to life the phases of a personal and intimate human drama. . . .[15] There is thus a human drama, and a symbolic work which at one and the same time masks and reveals it. The a priori simplicity of this relationship between the human being and the work is what I have criticized in A above: it would be good to know whether this explication of literary creation holds for Mallarmé alone or applies to hermetic poets generally, or to all writers. However, let us go on to point B: interior drama.

I will summarize here the way Mme Ayda sees the situation. Stéphane was piously reared by his mother till his fifth year. After her death he believed his mother was in heaven—in accord with his family's teaching— quite near a beneficent God. Thus, till he reached the age of fifteen he lived in a security and happiness which turned to mystic ecstasy. Several shocks in succession destroyed this faith. After the death of his sister Maria, he no longer believed in the *wisdom* of God. After the death of his friend Harriet Smyth, he no longer believed in the *goodness* of God. His grandparents' death in 1865 and 1869 brought on a final atheism. However, this loss of faith, caused by painful shocks, remained an incurable wound. He always longed to talk of it, to confide his pain to someone else, but through diffidence he wished to say nothing about it. He would therefore speak of it in the form of hermetic symbols.

Mme Ayda puts the crux of the drama between the years 1857 and 1859. Her thesis necessarily implies that she thinks it possible, by interpreting five or six literary texts dated from 1858 to 1864,[16] to define what actually took place in the mind of the youthful Stéphane. A psychoanalyst would call this a rash effort. It differs greatly from mine, which was simply to follow a network of associations of ideas from the poems to the free composition, which was itself very probably connected with the double death of Maria and the mother. I brought together and organized verifiable facts. Mme Ayda reads Mallarmé's heart. If, following her example, I ask myself about this new problem, the psychic evolution of the adolescent Mallarmé, I should think it more prudent to limit myself to a few hypotheses based on psychoanalytic experience. What will these hypotheses be?

Here is an orphan who has lost his mother at five and whose father has remarried a year later. The child is brought up with his sister Maria, two years his junior, by their grandparents, pious bourgeois Parisians, who take tender care of him. From ten on he is in a pension in Paris. At fourteen he is sent to the *lycée* at Sens (the town where his father lives). When Maria dies, one year later (August 31, 1857), the adolescent brother must face a triple crisis, which emerges in October, 1857: puberty (re-evoking the Oedipus complex); new bereavement (re-evoking his mother's death); choice of social and spiritual sublimations.

I shall lay down the following hypotheses. In early childhood Stéphane probably extricated himself only with difficulty from the normal experience which Melanie Klein calls the "depressive position."[17] The defense mechanisms of that period reappear in all the signs which Dr. Fretet used to make a diagnosis which seems to me more accurate, clinically speaking, than Mme Ayda's: "schizoid base with depressive crises."[18] We also come close here to Bergler's conclusions, which are based on his psychoanalysis of numerous living authors.[19] An Oedipus complex has much more chance of being inadequately resolved if the mother's death happens at the time of the Oedipal crisis. At this point of the argument all the psychoanalytic works on the process of mourning, its affinities with the normal "depressive position," the restoration of lost objects, and the analogies between mourning, its cure, and aesthetic creation, should come into play. In any case, the loss of a parent of the opposite sex leads to a fantastic idealization of his image. Elizabeth Mallarmé's image under-

9

went this fate. Let us guard against confusing this sort of interior and unconscious idol with the "mother in heaven" of consciousness and familial piety. Idealization is accompanied with a violent denial of all that has become evil in the lost object. It is in this very way that grief itself, implying the emotional recognition of the loss, is not tolerated in consciousness. This tallies with the only symptom we have from this period, reported by Mallarmé himself.[20] Mme Ayda designates as "bashfulness" this (unconsciously terrified) refusal of reality and grief. The first significant text is *Ange gardien,* written by Stéphane in September, 1854. From the mass of later documents published by Dr. Mondor in *Mallarmé lycéen,* it seems Mme Ayda has greatly exaggerated young Stéphane's piety when she speaks of "rapture" [*ivresse*], of "continuous mystic joy," of "heart overflowing with love for the Creator," and of "incomparable intoxication" on the "peaks of mystic joy" (p. 28). The letters reveal normal childhood preoccupations. Dr. Mondor takes just note of the fact, but at once draws the conclusion that there was therefore no repression.[21] But a repression that works is, by definition, invisible. Was Mallarmé's completely successful? Mondor himself speaks of "essential emotional frustration" (p. 23) and specifies that the rigors of boarding school made the child feel cruelly the absence of his mother: "This absence of his mother, which was so little felt by Stéphane till age ten that he at times felt obliged to shed false tears . . ." (p. 30). There was thus indeed repression of the normal emotions of grief and, under the impact of a new frustration (boarding school life and the separation from Maria), the resurgence of the mother in a form which was idealized and charged with affect in the fantasy of *Ange gardien.* Thus, to confine ourselves to Stéphane's piety, we can without great risk conjecture that in the youth's unconscious: (1) the guardian angel is a maternal figure, (2) the communion is a communion with the mother,

10

(3) God himself is largely maternal. The apparent piety must thereby have been reinforced, especially on the occasion of family communions. But I cannot say so much for the security of the infant boy and for the reality of his religious sentiment. Psychic health demands that we love objects outside ourselves. True religious feeling is addressed to an objective God that the mystic recognizes to be very different from himself, and to whom he voluntarily sacrifices himself. On the contrary, adoration of the self, or of the images one bears within one, constitutes a mechanism of manic defense, the sign of a profound insecurity. Mme Ayda recognizes in Mallarmé's religious revolt after the crisis this character of egocentrism. This same character holds equally true for the religious feeling of Stéphane *before* the crisis. The childhood piety of the young communicant must not therefore be confused with a true mysticism. It seems to have been accentuated by the shock experienced at his mother's death, a shock not cured by a normal process of mourning. In my opinion, therefore, Mme Ayda runs a great danger of deceiving herself when she makes the twelve-year-old Mallarmé a true mystic and a normally happy child.[22] His true childhood happiness is located in the period of the "beautiful dreams of a spoiled child," hence before his mother's death. As for his religious sentiment, it matured only very slowly in the course of his adult life.

In my view, therefore, the hypothetical outline of young Stéphane's personality could be briefly traced as follows: at the center, the ego of an orphan who refuses mourning; above, the guardian angel representing, in consciousness, the beneficent part of the lost and internalized mother; below, in the unconscious, the lost and internalized mother, in its ideal part beneficent, but also with its maleficent and terrifying part, the death-object one has perhaps killed, who can kill one, with the whole complex of repressed images and emotions. It is

the unconscious existence of this ambivalent and powerfully charged image that constitutes the sickness of having lost the beloved object, a sickness that will be cured
slowly in the course of mourning. I use as a working
hypothesis, let me repeat, the idea that Mallarmé never
recovered from the death of his mother. This judgment
is based on (1) all the facts bearing out Fretet's diagnosis, (2) the denial of sorrow after the shock, (3) the
egocentric religiosity and the fantasy of *Ange gardien*,
(4) the nonresolution of the later grief, with all its traces
in the poet's work (that is, latent obsession and not suffering or conscious memory). To this picture it is necessary to add the vigorous efforts which, all the same,
the child's ego made to recover, that is, to reëstablish
contact with external reality and its living objects. He
transferred from mother to sister, and doubtless to the
grandparents, a good share of his affection. He sought
a social compromise between the religious ideal and
earthly life (becoming a bishop would have been one
such compromise). Let us say then that the ego, at the
center, refused the suffering, healed poorly but sought
out new objects and viable sublimations. Of this schema,
Mme Ayda (in her no less hypothetical construction)
maintains only a divine protection and an ego she deems
happy; but the rest she rejects—that is, specifically, the
unconscious and its effect on consciousness.

Then came Stéphane's adolescence and Maria's death.
What happened then? Certainly an attack of anxiety
against which the ego had to defend itself.[23] The defense mechanisms recur, but in a different context—
puberty. The denial of death takes the form of a desire
for resurrection, at least in the imagination. The idealization, on the other hand, is now no longer religious
but is musical and poetic. Finally, the ego isolates itself
from the social milieu, vigorously expels internal images
which have become evil (crisis with family and teach-
ers) but seeks new real love-objects, replacing Maria by

Em. Sul., Harriet, Ettie, and Marie, as he had replaced his mother with his sister.

To these mechanisms of mourning, however, must be added those of puberty. The erotic drive contributes heavily to bringing his sister's phantom to life (see the free composition). It helps the ego to dissociate poetic sublimation from the previous religious one.[24] Further, the erotic drive obviously orients the ego toward the search for real love-objects. For its part the aggressive impulse, the classic revolt of the adolescent, renewed by the Oedipal struggle, intervenes in the break with the milieu (family, school, morals and ethics)—isolation, moreover, instead of rupture—and in the vigorous expulsion of evil internal objects (personal religious crisis).

This complex yet intelligible picture is reflected in the fantasies of the works of Mallarmé's youth. I shall analyze them below (see Appendix), since there we properly enter the sphere of psychocriticism. For the moment let us continue with Mme Ayda's thesis. Why out of this totality does she isolate one process: the loss of faith? And why does she make it an incurable wound? The free composition shows quite clearly what the ego, from 1857 on and perhaps as the consequence of an earlier evolution, expels from its circle of warmth and light. All the objects outside the hut are rejected together: night, cold, death, cemetery, church, owl, angel (maternal figure), and the storks (paternal figures by association with the three magi). Moreover, the angel and storks obey the desires of the ego and therefore have lost the parental omnipotence. What was going on inside the hut? We already know: memory, joyful resurrection, and poetry. The religious crisis fits into this picture and cannot be detached from it. Nor does anything suggest that it should be called a wound. I much prefer to think of it as an attempt to heal. The whole fantasy appears as a splitting: the ego picks out what it wants

13

to keep or restore and rejects everything else as dead. In this second group stands the angel, who does not (as we have seen) represent a true mystic faith but a childish idealization which is largely bound up with an unresolved mourning situation. Moreover, everything seems childish in this "drama" Mme Ayda presents to us, both Mallarmé's initial belief and Mme Ayda's explanation of its disappearance. A poor objective faith indeed which could not bear up under the discovery that men are mortal! The Mallarmé who blasphemes "within four walls" is simply making a negative transfer: the accusations he brings against God are in reality addressed—in his unconscious—to a parental figure which is probably a composite of both parents. I look at it as merely an episode in the whole story of Stéphane's uneasy adaptation to reality.

It is not a question, then, of drama, but of molting. We have schematized its initial state: the ego and its real love-objects, midway between the guardian angel above him (conscious sublimation) and, below, in the unconscious, the ambivalent divinity, the dead mother, half-ideal, half-evil. After the molting this schema turns into that of the free composition. We find the ego in its protective enclosure. It insists on keeping a real sister nearby and will find her (in Marie or Méry). On the level of sublimation, poetic communion has replaced the guardian angel. The angel has gone to rejoin (in the direction of the unconscious, that is, somewhere outside the cabin) the old complex of idealized death. This repression "pays for" the birth of poetry. The religious crisis is reduced to this exchange: an infantile faith is replaced by art, while the erotic pursuit of real objects goes on. Here, let us admit, is the truth or rather the truism which is at the bottom of Mme Ayda's thesis: the adolescent Mallarmé ceases to be pious and turns poet. What we have here is not "drama"; it is adolescent molting. We must remember, too, that the adolescent was a genius. For a birth attends the molting: "horrible birth," indeed, a bit of life snatched out of death. Mallarmé's orphic ego seems to be born in Nick Parrit's hut, and the three stork-king magi have come to greet it. Each poem from then on will be born in the same way and will tell of its own ascent toward the light. It will be more or less anxious according to the pressure of the repressed evil, which can always try to retrieve what the ego has snatched from it. Each depressive trough of his subsequent life is marked by a hostile threat of cold, shadow, whiteness, inhibition, death, or madness. Therefore we shall replace the drama played out between years fifteen and seventeen and repeatedly avowed afterwards, by a birth again and again relived, alike and yet different with each poem.

C. We have now said enough of the adolescent Mallarmé's "drama." Let us come to his "symbolic veil." This "manifest content," designing and masking a "latent" one, at once of course reminds the reader of dream analysis. We expect to see Mme Ayda copy from it her decoding of Mallarmé's symbols, since this is the goal of her endeavor. Her use of a psychoanalytic vocabulary ("unconscious," "repression," "complex," and so on) bears out our expectation. But we soon realize that such an impression is misleading.

As a matter of fact, Mme Ayda thinks only in terms of conscious ideas, relations, and feelings. For instance, she quotes Mallarmé: "The Poet draws more from his secret, previous Individuality than from circumstances." I understand this statement as follows: "The poet is able to read in his own unconscious, which is the most secret and chronologically the remotest part of himself"—and I cannot refrain from noting that the poet himself came to my conclusion long before I did.[25] Mme Ayda, however, wondering at the fact that no Mallarméan has ever pondered on this text, offers the following commentary, splitting what is secret (latent content, "drama") from what is previous (manifest content, "symbols"):

It is indeed obvious that by "secret Individuality"

must be understood the totality of intimate personal feelings which the poet "conceals" behind the images, and that by "previous Individuality" should be understood the totality of the conceptions which made up his vision of the world, "prior" to the shock or shocks that led to the formation of complexes and symbols in his soul (p. 94).

Thus we learn that the "secret" is a conscious content Mallarmé knows. It is not secret, because it has been forgotten, swallowed in the unconscious. It is kept for one's self, voluntarily unsaid. In the same way, "previous" would not mean dating from the poet's individual prehistory, but previous to a perhaps recent shock. Latent and manifest contents are thus held to be equally conscious. It is through delicacy that Mallarmé wants to conceal drama—and through a desire for confession, that he wants to speak of it. Symbolic expression with its no less voluntary hermeticism provides the sought-for solution: to conceal and confess at the same time. Here is a conception which many passages in Mme Ayda's book appear to confirm.[26]

In reality, Mme Ayda seems to limit the action of the unconscious to the genesis of symbols. These, she thinks, would emerge under the stimulus of the painful shock —hence, at a specific moment of time—and would then remain, as it were, "on tap" for ulterior conscious uses. Thus Mme Ayda calls the 1857–1859 period a receptacle out of which Mallarmé later on was able to draw his symbols. It is the jewel box with its precious stones. The symbols themselves would belong to the period preceding the shock. Here is the key sentence summing up the theory of this genesis:

> As we know, the more powerful has been the repression, the more complicated is the system of symbolic images which characterizes an individual's unconscious; and the closer the feelings or occurrences which determined the repression, the greater the energy commanding them (p. 95).[27]

Isolating what may remain of psychoanalysis in such a sentence was not, I must confess, an easy task for me. Here, honestly, is my conclusion: Mme Ayda calls mere associations "symbols." Thus:

purple is associated with Maria's burial, which took place at the hour when the sun sets;
thunder is associated with the image of an angered God;
white is associated with the "memory of the white creature," Maria crowned with white roses in her casket;
the clock is associated with Harriet, whose foreseeable death Stéphane awaited.

A reading of the lists in which Mme Ayda classifies these associations shows that some of them are authenticated by texts, some are merely inferred, and some are deduced by a mental process which is peculiar to Mme Ayda.[28] But all of them lead back to memories that Mallarmé can scarcely have forgotten after several months or even several years—hence to the preconscious. The connection with the unconscious (which is necessary to explain the dynamic and persistent obsession of the "ensemble" of the associative network) implies the connection of the whole network with the phantasms of first infancy, and thus with the Oedipus complex and the mother. Now this is just what Mme Ayda eliminates.

Her use of a psychoanalytic vocabulary therefore introduces a confusion. But this confusion at once leads the reader into a far more serious one, since it concerns method. My own work was conceived along psychoanalytic lines. Mme Ayda, on nearly every page of her book, makes use of concepts and conclusions borrowed from my work. What happens to these ideas when they are transposed into a non-psychoanalytic framework?

They are so twisted that the reader can no longer find his way among them. Let us give a specific example. When I analyze the *Triptyque* (*Tout Orgueil, Surgi de la croupe et du bond, Une dentelle s'abolit*) and once more find the fireplace, the rose, and the musical instrument, I propose, in fact, the following hypothetical explication: a network of associations—entirely or almost entirely unconscious in the poet's mind when he wrote the *Triptyque*—binds these three images to the corresponding images of the free composition (fireplace, rose, and tambourine in Nick Parrit's hut) and from there slips back into unconscious images of the dead sister, the dead mother, and last, the nursing mother. In view of this I am not surprised that a mysterious metaphor should have appeared in the poet's conscious mind, comparing the musical instrument to a dead woman, and to a woman giving birth to a son.[29] If I now adopt Mme Ayda's thesis, shall I say that Mallarmé in composing the *Triptyque* chose voluntarily from his casket of precious stones these three symbols (fireplace, rose, musical instrument) in order to hide from us and confess to us at the same time the memory of his religious crisis of 1859 (ever-present in his consciousness)?

The reader may try to reconcile the two theses. He may feel that I am exaggerating the role of consciousness in Mme Ayda's explication. I have already said that I would concede ambiguities at the boundary lines but only on condition that the reality of the two domains be conceded, and that their frontier be seen as a passageway, not as a simple and soon-dismissed fringe of consciousness alone. Actually, the arbitration of the reader would lead to suppressing the constant presence and action of the unconscious in the creation of imaginative fantasies, dreams, myths, or aesthetic creations, whereas all clinical experience proves, to the contrary, that this role is the determining one. Mme Ayda then comes back to the criticism of "external" sources (conscious or preconscious), and this is why she so readily obtains the approval of M. Cellier and so many others. But this is why also, much against my will, I choose to quarrel with her method, for the reduction of the internal source to external ones is today a fundamental error.

And M. Cellier seems well aware of the fact, since his own study of myths induces him to modify the classic notion of influence: he comes close to the idea that, when all is said and done, the inner source may "choose" the external sources.

Our very example of the *Triptyque* will illustrate nicely this little war over methods. The chain of unconscious associations which I personally believe to be traceable in Mallarmé led him and leads us to the deepest and most stabilizing image of the mother, watching over the "beautiful dreams of a spoiled child." There, for me, is the source of the associative knot: food—music —light (breast—voice—eyes); and, behind my conviction, there are the works of Melanie Klein, Spitz,[30] Bergler, and many others. Mme Ayda's explanation of these same metaphors in the *Triptyque* leads, not to the mother of 1842 but to the Harriet of 1859. The symbols "breast" and "musical instrument" are, indeed, connected by Mme Ayda to the memory of this dead friend, in my view an episodic double of Maria. At this point we must make a choice. Mme Ayda rests her case on the following facts: (1) Harriet is called "angelic," (2) she sang, (3) she died of tuberculosis (so that Mme Ayda proposes the associative sequence "breast—chest —lungs"). Let us note in passing the very conscious precision of the symbols—angelic face, musical talent, sickness of a girl clearly remembered—which implies, moreover, the voluntary use of symbols as masks. But if we come back to the point, the angel was of course already present in the fantasy of 1858 (in an earlier one as well, 1854), already associated with music, feeding, communion, melodious light. No sound method would allow us to give a concrete, conscious event in 1859 as the cause of a group of associations in a text as early as 1857–1858 or even earlier. Nor are we allowed to ignore the maternal character of the associative group in question; a number of texts affirm it, among them *Apparition:*

la fée au chapeau de clarté

[the fairy with the cap of light]
and *Don du poème:*
Et ta voix rappelant viole et clavecin
Avec le doit fané presseras-tu le sein
Par qui coule en blancheur sybilline la femme

[and your voice recalling viola and clavichord
With the faded finger you will press the bosom
Whence in sibylline whiteness woman flows]
and *Une dentelle s'abolit:*
Mais, chez qui du rêve se dore
Tristement dort une mandore
Au creux néant musicien
Telle que vers quelque fenêtre
Selon nul ventre que le sien,
Filial on aurait pu naître.

[But, with him of the gilded dream
Sadly a mandolin sleeps
Musician of hollow nothingness
Such as through what window
According to no womb but its,
Filial one might be born.]
How could we give Harriet's image as the origin of this
undeniably maternal character which is prior to 1859?
It is not a question of a single instance. The choice
between the suckling mother and Harriet is crucial. It
implies the choice between (1) the individual prehistory, the childhood genesis of affective structures, their
symbolic expression in the fantasies of the imagination
—in brief, psychoanalysis on the one hand; and (2) the
history, the biographical facts, the contents of consciousness, readings, analogies of subject or style—in short,
the studies of external sources on the other hand. Here
is the double origin of the work. Here are therefore the
two types of research which criticism must adjust, not
confuse.

From my book Mme Ayda borrows the whole network of associations I grouped around the Maria phantom and the free composition, but the very existence of this network implies in Mallarmé as in everyone else the existence of a deep unconscious trunk from which fantasies and works branch out. But from M. Kurt Wais[31]—that is, from the other type of research—and perhaps from Dr. Mondor's biography, Mme Ayda borrows the idea that Harriet is an important source.[32] Moreover, the early poems she has been allowed to glance into show her the bad opinion that the Mallarmé of 1859 had of God.[33] The pleasure of reinterpreting the whole work in the light of these "findings" I can well understand— but we have to avoid the dangers of an ambiguous method.

Such an ambiguity appears in the very definition of the symbol. Well-informed by his own study of myths, M. Cellier adopts the correct meaning of the term in that matter. The poet, he says, does not use mythic symbols "out of delicacy," but because the feelings of his soul are "indefinable."[34] The indefinable is, for the psychoanalyst, the unconscious; for the theologian, mystery. The real symbol represents nothing which could be seen or said otherwise; it is a dynamic sign that points toward a new form of being. In the sphere of wholly conscious ideas and images, on the contrary, the word "symbol" rightly has the ordinary meaning that Mme Ayda makes use of: "One generally means by symbols, signs, concrete things or beings which have a conformity of meaning either with other concrete things or beings, or with abstract ideas."[35] Such a definition should be kept exclusively for allegories and metaphors, that is, for horizontal ways of relating a conscious content to another conscious content, while the symbol is a vertical relationship which combines dynamic attraction with meaning. A conscious symbol is always a sort of ciphered message,[36] which has to be translated into plain language in order to be understood. That is certainly how Mme Ayda understands Mallarmé's hermetic symbolism. In her mind, Mallarmé's ciphering is not conventional, since it tallies with events in the poet's life, but it is conscious and voluntary. To grasp it, one must find the code and then translate. "Burned breast of the antique amazon" means Harriet's diseased lungs. A psychoanalyst does not translate into plain language when he interprets, in spite of what is commonly believed. He does not say (except to gain time), "burned breast" means "breast of the dead mother." He interprets the symbol almost as a doctor does a symptom: one does not decipher a measle bump. In my view the image of the "burned breast," when it appeared in the poet's consciousness in the midst of other conscious present realities, was a manifestation of this internalized "mother," partly stabilizing, partly dangerous, who lived in the poet's unconscious its own autonomous life from the time of the death of Elizabeth, his mother. And this very manifestation was itself autonomous, involuntary, and, as it were, imposed on the conscious ego from this "outside" which the unconscious remained for him. A benevolent manifestation, nonetheless, in poetic creation, since the charge of energy it bears gets a new use from the therapist, Orpheus. But this is another story. I am simply pointing out the difference between deciphering and interpreting. Only the latter is suitable to psychocriticism, that is, the study of the "internal source."

I have said enough of this new methodological aspect of literary criticism. Circumstances have given me the occasion to make this brief survey of Mme Ayda's book, which is full of interest in many ways, and I must express my gratitude for the opportunity. M. Cellier's work seems no less fascinating from this point of view: the analysis of Mallarmé's youthful poems[37] will afford me, no doubt, more adequate opportunity to refer to his study.

CHARLES MAURON

1

Maria Mallarmé

INTRODUCTION

So MUCH has been learned about the life and work of
Stéphane Mallarmé that it might seem there is nothing
more to be said on the subject. In my opinion, this is
not the case, and I would like first to say briefly why I
think so. Criticism has borne on two points:

1. The literal meaning of the work. Since Mallarmé
is often obscure, there has been an effort to dissolve the
obscurities and hunt down the most probable interpretation of poems or difficult passages. This is the foundation work that such critics as Soula,[1] Thibaudet,[2] Mme
Emilie Noulet,[3] and I have done.[4] Not that these are
the only authors who have engaged in textual elucidation, nor that each of them has confined himself to this
type of investigation. But their efforts *have* been parallel; in fact, every true Mallarméan does very much the
same sort of research on his own.

There are at least three reasons why a reader may
avoid solving the problem posed in some obscure passage in Mallarmé. First, he cannot work up any interest
in it; second, he is perfectly happy to see in it a pure
play of verbal sonorities; third, distrustful of the role of
the intellect in poetry, he demands the right to enjoy
without understanding. I believe that in general those
who love Mallarmé adopt yet a fourth attitude: they
seek both to understand and to enjoy. Through a series

23

of tentative steps they arrive at interpretations of detail and eventually at a general picture of the whole. Since these interpretations do not always agree with one another, can we speak of objective results? I believe so. If, for instance, I compare what Mme Emilie Noulet makes of such and such a work and what I make of it—I refer to the literal sense, the word-by-word meaning of the text as grammatically analyzed—I can find few differences of opinion. Soula's and Thibaudet's analyses are older, and it would not be too difficult, I believe, to agree on what seems to be obsolete in their work. M. Chassé somewhere in his book[5] asks that before any general evaluation of Mallarmé's thought is made, there should be unanimous agreement on the literal interpretation of obscure passages. I believe that this request has lost its force. The proof lies in the fact that M. Chassé's own suggestions, several of which had already been made by Thibaudet, would, if accepted, change only petty details. In fact, agreement has, in my opinion, been reached on all the essentials. Since each of these critical works grew out of an individual effort, there is no one literal, objective interpretation which sanctions the agreement that has been achieved. There has been no Mallarméan council to establish the tables of the law. I am nonetheless persuaded that a fairly broad agreement does exist; it has emerged little by little from studies and from the exchange of ideas. In the final analysis, on the points that are still in question, the debate, as Mallarmé himself wrote, "remains grammatical." The points will be wrangled over for years to come. But the essential job has been done, and the reader who wants to will be able in coming generations to understand Mallarmé far more easily than we did.

2. Biographical information. On this score, as everyone knows, we owe almost everything to Dr. Mondor. He has assembled the documents; he has arranged and published most of them in a series of works: *L'Amitié de Verlaine et Mallarmé, Vie de Mallarmé, Mallarmé*

plus intime, and *Propos sur la poésie.* Frankly, I regret
—and others will join me in this—that the publication
of the known documents has not been completed and
that the little game of releasing now a letter, now the
variant of a line, now a poem of his youth, at intervals
of several years or more, should be so long drawn out.
But here too the basic facts are today in our hands. New
publications will send bibliophiles or collectors into a
dither; no doubt they will interest the general reader
because of the confirmation they give to this or that
hypothesis; but to the extent that Mallarmé's character
and life can be known, the broad outlines and most of
the details now seem to have been traced. Practically all
the material that criticism could ever draw on, either to
understand his work or to grasp his personality, is at our
disposal. Indeed, we have all made free use of it.

The documents published by Dr. Mondor have inevitably caused Mallarméans to change certain of their
interpretations in detail or in general. Dates have been
made definite, the biography of the poet has been filled
out, and the poems have fallen into place in the canon.
As a result, groupings or periods in his creativity have
come to be recognized, requiring or suggesting all sorts
of new interpretations. A good part of this work of adaptation is to be found in the edition of the *Oeuvres
complètes;*[6] it will soon be brought to accurate completion except, once again, for a few details.

This is the twofold achievement to date. What remains to be done? Almost all the analysis in depth. I
believe I can say this without arrogance or show of para-
dox. Mallarmé has been studied time and again, often
with superb results. But so many of these meditations
preceded the elucidation of texts and knowledge of the
biographical facts that they must be brought into question. In criticism, as in every other science, the vitality
of thought springs from a vibration between personal
intuition and external fact. The two poles are indispensable; the latter has only just now taken final shape. So

25

much has been said about Mallarmé that readers are entitled to feel somewhat weary. They will do well, however, to realize that all this work was, in a sense, preliminary. When Sainte-Beuve wrote of Port-Royal, he relied on clear texts and documents that had already been assembled, for the most part, by historians. Up to a recent date Mallarmé's texts were not clear; the documents had not been assembled. Whenever a poem of Mallarmé's has become literally intelligible to us, it has only reached the point where one of Baudelaire's poems started. And since Dr. Mondor's biography has put each poem in its proper place in the flux of Mallarmé's life and creativity, is it not obvious that interpretation in depth may now begin?

I raised the same question in an earlier essay when I objected to Thibaudet's book (not to Thibaudet himself, who was not really at fault)[7] for studying facets of Mallarmé's work as though it were a chiseled block, when all the evidence showed that the poems made up a series and had a successive meaning. The pieces inspired by Méry differ from those written at Tournon, for the obvious reason that the Mallarmé of forty was not the Mallarmé of twenty. In a man's work there are not only the constants of his spirit but the variants of his personal history. The one factor should no more be slighted than the other. Everything must be taken into account. Could this have been done in Mallarmé's case twenty years ago? The answer is no—however admirable and remarkable certain intuitions may have been—and I believe that the real task, which like the earlier is necessarily collective, is now beginning.

I will give a single proof. It relates to what is, in my view, the most important event in Mallarmé's life: the death of his sister.

MARIA

Maria died at thirteen, when Stéphane was fifteen. What is the significance usually ascribed to this event? Neither

Soula nor Thibaudet mentions it; Mme Emilie Noulet merely notes the fact in passing. Dr. Mondor, who has furnished us with all the details known on this subject as on so many others, does not use it as the basis of any psychological evaluation of Mallarmé. As a matter of fact, Maria's death does not even appear in the biographical chronology of the *Oeuvres complètes*.[8] By and large, everyone has agreed not to grant any importance to this "poor young phantom." This, in my opinion, is a grave misunderstanding of profoundly significant facts.

Mallarmé's work contains a single text that explicitly mentions Maria and her death. It is *Plainte d'automne*, at the opening of *Divagations*.

> Since Maria left me to inhabit another star—which, Orion, Altair, or you, green Venus?—I have always cherished solitude . . . , strangely, oddly, I have loved all that is summed up in this word: downfall [*chute*]. So, in the year, I prefer the last languid days of summer, which immediately precede autumn; in the daytime, I like to go for a walk when the sun is poised just before it vanishes, with rays of yellow copper on the gray walls, and red copper on the window-panes . . . a barrel organ played languishingly and melancholically under my window. It played in the great avenue of poplars, whose leaves appear dull to me even in spring ever since Maria passed there with candles, one last time. . . .

The reader will forgive the necessary excisions.

When he was about twenty,[9] Mallarmé spoke of the death of his sister as having occurred unexpectedly five years before; he saw it, at that time, as an event of some significance for his inner life. This is the fact. It is a rather surprising fact when we realize that Maria was but a child when she died. This is not to say that a brother cannot be affected for a considerable time by the death of a sister just reaching adolescence. But it does appear extraordinary, one must admit, for this

brother, already grown, already a great poet, to give
the death of this child sister as the source of his aesthetic tendencies. An hypothesis suggests itself: Mallarmé may have chosen this unhappy event, the most
recent in his life, as a theme for the expression of a literary sadness. Against this interpretation, I will cite a
second text, which is the letter written by Mallarmé to
Cazalis on July 1, 1862; Cazalis had just sent his friend
a picture of Ettie Yapp, his beloved. Mallarmé replied:
There is a touching word that illuminates your
whole letter; it is, "Accept, my dear Mallarmé, this
portrait of our sister." This is easy, since we are
brothers, and yet it is very sweet. Yes, she will rank
in all my dreams with the Chimènes, the Beatrices,
the Juliets, the Réginas, and what is better, in my
heart, alongside this poor young phantom who was
my sister for thirteen years and who was the only
person whom I adored, before I knew all of you:
she will be my ideal in life as my sister is in death.
The date of this letter is very close to that of the *Plainte
d'automne*. I consider the sentence quoted as crucial.
Indeed, the word "sister" might at first seem to be
merely a natural way of putting it; literary excitement
prevails as he names off the great *amoureuses;* and then
suddenly his true sister appears, from outside literature
("this poor young phantom, who was my sister for thirteen years") and in such circumstances that we cannot
doubt the sincerity of the feeling. The end of the sentence is extraordinary: Maria has become an ideal dead
girl whom Ettie represents in life. I intend to develop
the implications of this analogy between Ettie and
Maria. In fact, I shall have to tie the first thread of this
network at once. But first I must emphasize the fact
that any hypothesis of a purely literary melancholy in
Plainte d'automne is without foundation.

To repeat, around his twentieth year Mallarmé saw
in Maria's death an important event of his inner life. He

said so movingly and directly to his dearest friend, confiding, indeed, that this young phantom was the only creature he had loved till then. Without wishing to psychoanalyze, we may properly recall that when his mother died, Mallarmé had been speedily committed to the care of his grandparents, whom he loved only moderately, and soon had had to divide his life between studies at boarding school and bourgeois family Sundays, with the result that Maria, in the absence of the remarried father, remained the only vital link that attached Stéphane to his mother and her tenderness. Be that as it may, here now the child had become his "ideal in death."

Let us return to Ettie. She did not marry Cazalis, despite his years of courtship, but much later married Maspéro, the Egyptologist, the companion of Lefébure, who was, with Cazalis, Mallarmé's best friend. After his wife's death, Maspéro attended the evenings on the Rue de Rome. We are thus working in a very narrow circle of human relationships. Ettie had died in 1877, and it is in all probability for Maspéro, who was left alone in the world, that Mallarmé wrote the famous sonnet, *Pour votre chère morte*. It is, then, Ettie who says:

> Sur les bois oubliés quand passe l'hiver sombre
> Tu te plains, ô captif solitaire du seuil,
> Que ce sépulcre à deux qui fera notre orgueil
> Hélas! du manque seul des lourds bouquets s'encombre.

> [In woods forgotten when winter, somber, passes
> You lament, O solitary captive of the threshold,
> That this sepulcher for two which will be our pride
> Alas! with only the lack of heavy bouquets is encumbered.]

This poem is remarkable in the canon because it has an extraordinarily direct and simple gravity. It delineates the lonely man, who, unable to share the "sepulcher for two," awaits, at midnight before the last embers of his fire, the visit of the phantom which will seat itself in the now-empty armchair opposite him.

Qui veut souvent avoir la Visite ne doit
Par trop de fleurs charger la pierre que mon doigt
Soulève avec l'ennui d'une force défunte.
Ame au si clair foyer tremblante de m'asseoir,
Pour revivre il suffit qu'à tes lèvres j'emprunte
Le souffle de mon nom murmuré tout un soir.

[Who wishes often to receive the Visit must not
With too many flowers charge the stone that my
finger
Raises with the listlessness of a force defunct.
Soul trembling to sit before the hearth so bright,
To live again it suffices that from your lips I borrow
The breath of my name murmured a whole eve-
ning.]

Despite the fact that Mallarmé was writing for Maspéro, he was also writing for himself and his dear dead sister. Ettie was linked with Maria, and we remember —if only vaguely—that the décor of this room, where a lonely man awaits a phantom's visit, often appears in the life of Mallarmé. It is the same décor, in fact, in which he worked out, from 1862 to 1866 (between the ages of twenty and twenty-four), all that part of his work in which obsessions, despairs, and funereal concerns came thick and fast. Let us note further that if the décor of the sonnet *Pour votre chère morte* repeats the décor of the Tournon evenings, the feeling differs. There is no anxiety in the 1877 poem; Mallarmé was thinking sadly of Ettie, and since the connection Ettie–Maria was a conscious one, as the letter to Cazalis proves, the anxiety that goes with an unconscious conflict was no longer present. Mallarmé was also thinking of the dead Maria with the sadness of any normal person. We have strong reason, then, to think that even at thirty-five Mallarmé still remembered the young phantom with an emotion which often opened up in him sources of the most genuine poetry. Can we, however, change these strong probabilities into at least a quasi-certainty? I believe that we can.

The next text to be considered is that of the French exercise, a composition of his youth, which was published by Dr. Mondor in *Mallarmé plus intime* and was entitled *Ce que disaient les trois Cigognes*. That Mallarmé should have preserved this composition among his papers is in itself remarkable enough. The explanation is not far to seek. The manuscript in fact carries, Dr. Mondor tells us, this note scrawled in the adult hand of the poet: "Story—on any topic—in the fourth or fifth year of the lycée." Now what is this subject freely chosen? One winter's night, in the middle of a forest ("In forgotten woods when winter, somber, passes"), a man is alone in his house, by the fireside, and he dreams of his dead young daughter. In the cemetery nearby, she leaves her grave, comes to visit her father, sits near him before the fire, dances, sings, and vanishes in the morning. The style is hardly childish, and some of the chief Mallarméan themes crowd into the story, as Dr. Mondor puts it in a single discreet statement: ". . . This particular reading is especially for those whom the rose, the snow, the dawn, blue, lilies, winter griefs, dreamy songs, and an experimental vocabulary will set thinking."

It is natural to suppose that Mallarmé wrote *Ce que disaient les trois Cigognes* after Maria's death, but we have no absolute proof that he did. Mallarmé places this composition "in the fourth or fifth year." He entered the fifth in October, 1857, after Maria's death in August. But since Dr. Mondor writes, ". . . the date of the composition must not have been far from the date of the death of Maria Mallarmé, the schoolboy's sister," he evidently thinks there is a cause and effect relationship between the two events. The other hypothesis, that it was a coincidence, must not have deserved mention.

31

And how improbable such a coincidence would be!
At twenty, Mallarmé saw his sister's death as the most
important event of his inner life. At fifteen, he had described a survivor who was awaiting the visit of a dead
girl. At thirty-five, he described the same survivor at the
same fireside expecting the same visit. But at seventeen
did he not exclaim, in *Sa Fosse est fermée,*

> . . . n'était-ce pas assez pour ta faux déplorée,
> Dieu, d'avoir moissonné ma soeur, rose égarée . . .
> Hier! c'était ma soeur! aujourd'hui mon amie!

> [. . . was it not enough for your lamented scythe,
> God, to have reaped my sister, distracted rose . . .
> Yesterday! it was my sister! today my friend!]

All the evidence constrains us, then, to equate the
young dead girl of the story with Maria. As for the Mallarméan themes listed above, which will play such a
role in the melancholy poems of 1862–1866, the same is
true: they are not thrown together by chance; a central
emotion evokes and arranges them. The subject of the
story indicates quite clearly what this emotion is.

These convergences are significant in their own right.
Numerous details will remove all doubt as to their true
meaning. I will select only one. The finest lines of the
sonnet of 1877 are perhaps

> . . . la pierre que mon doigt
> Soulève avec l'ennui d'une force défunte.

> [. . . the stone that my finger
> Raises with the listlessness of a force defunct.]

Now the free composition of 1857 mentions "poor dead
souls . . . sewn in their pale shroud, without being able
to lift it with a finger. . . ." If the woods and the tomb
under the snow, the flowers, the hearth, and the wait
for the phantom did not supply enough convincing
analogues, the strange and feeble finger lifting the
shroud or the coffin stone would furnish us with unim-
peachable evidence of a continuity which must from

now on be given its due weight. The Mallarméan themes already evoked in the story of the fifteen-year-old student are interrelated; they are attached to the common center that a sorrowful event of the first importance creates in the poet's life and work. To give an explanation in depth of the one or the other, one must specify the role of this first emotional shock, then discover its echoes and symbols and follow the threads of the associations of ideas—in other words, study the complex network of emotions and expressions, of which his sister's death is, at least at first, the unique center. Whoever sets himself to this task gradually becomes convinced of the basic importance of Maria's death to Stéphane, and in the process arrives at a new way of seeing Mallarmé's work.

THE SHIMMER BELOW

The quasi-certainty that Maria's death played a crucial role in Mallarmé's life and work would be enough to prompt us to resort to psychoanalysis. Let us recall that Mallarmé lost his mother when he was five, the time of the normal Oedipal crisis. The two shocks were tied up with one another, the second reopening the first wound. One does not have to be a great psychologist to realize that a conjuncture of the sort can have profound and far-reaching emotional repercussions. A large number of neuroses originate in traumas experienced in infancy. We will return to that shortly. But there is another reason, purely literary, which by itself would have inclined us to a psychoanalytic study of Mallarmé. It is what I will call here, briefly, the "shimmer below." Simple acquaintance with Mallarmé's poems suggests the idea that there is a network of constant images, attracting and eliciting each other in such a way as to produce harmonies which are repeated from poem to poem. In *Mallarmé l'obscur* I studied several of these harmonies. One of them, for instance, groups in various configurations the elements of a musician-angel; another shows

33

extraordinary regularity in uniting images of hair, flames, sunset, triumph in love, and death. I recall this study purely to stress its experimental character. These lines of association are an incontestable fact and do not depend on any special theory. They suggest the idea of fixed obsessive points which determine the arabesque of the particular poem in a more or less ingenious or peculiar "obvious" [*lisible*] sense of the poem, from a sort of constant architecture, probably subconscious though revealing itself, for our analysis, below the obvious level.

In order to be perfectly clear, let us take one example. The figure of the musician-angel in *Sainte* stands out. The angel himself, his wing, the ancient instruments, the raised finger, the feminine presence, and the silence in which an exquisite harmony is created are present and, I dare say, normally grouped. But consider *Don du poème;* the wing has become the dawn's; "angelic" is applied to the lamp; the feminine presence is that of a mother rocking her daughter; the ancient instruments would resound in her voice if she spoke; as for the lifted finger, it could press the breast for the newly born poem. The parts of the musician-angel are still present, then, but scattered. A new arabesque connects the fixed points. If one is satisfied with the arabesque itself, which I have called the "obvious" content of the poem, *Sainte* and *Don du poème* have nothing in common. But the subconscious web remains identical in the two cases. The result, which I have just illustrated by a single example, and which does not stem (let us repeat) from any a priori hypothesis, leads us quite naturally to think of psychoanalysis. It may be recalled that psychoanalysis to a certain extent assimilates written work to dreams, and sees dreams as superimposing what it calls a manifest content on a latent content. The manifest content is the dream as it appears to us, as we tell it upon awakening; the latent content is the deeper meaning, the inner significance of the symbolic rebus which

34

first appeared. I shall not for the moment push that analogy any further, since all I intended to do was demonstrate that a comparative study of Mallarméan texts is bound to show the superimposing of two planes, two designs, and, presumably, two logics, since their surface pattern is found to change repeatedly while, by contrast, the inner design remains constant.

These were the conclusions I drew in *Mallarmé l'obscur* before Henri Mondor's first book came out. This publication confirmed them, in my opinion, though it also made them inadequate. For, if the death of his mother and sister was the critical event in the poet's inner life, there is a good chance that the web of these obsessive metaphors converges toward this emotional center. At a stroke the network changes into a complex, or rather, reveals a complex. In psychoanalytic terminology a complex is simply a network of emotional connections, as one may imagine it, with knots and threads, on the model of a nervous system.[10] We need not inquire here how psychic systems are formed, responding as they do both to their own natural order of development and to the accidents of a particular life. Each of us has his own, just as he has his nerves or veins. If one of the points of the network is affected, the shock fans out from center to center along the lines of least resistance. Hence the obvious fact that some minor matter, a word, a gesture, can be charged with a degree of emotion out of all proportion to its objective significance. The reason is that it stands for something else in the emotions: it is bound by often unrealized connections to memories, images, ideas powerfully invested with emotion, and these constitute (in current parlance) our sensitive spots.

Let us limit ourselves for the moment to this somewhat vague concept and return to Mallarmé. If the death of his sister was one of his sensitive spots, everything that by natural or accidental association became connected with this death was—as it formed a cluster—

necessarily to create around this sorrow-center a complex, inside of which the emotion (like an electric current along tangled lines) was to flow with the greatest ease. We are thus led to a type of analysis which would not be purely literary in the classic sense, nor yet properly psychoanalytic.

Between the critical method which Sainte-Beuve used for Racine and the one Marie Bonaparte[11] or Dr. Laforgue[12] applies to Poe or Baudelaire, there is room for a number of formulas. I do not think that we have yet hit on the best one. One hurdle is cleared, in any case, as soon as the critic admits, under the "obvious" sense of the poem, an unconscious meaning which should be unraveled. Through this doubling, this superimposition, the work acquires a new dimension: that of unconscious depth. One may probe more or less extensively into the meaning indicated by this dimension; one may plunge more or less deeply into the author's unconscious. Two points should be made on this subject. First, assuming that the author's works provide the material for a true psychoanalysis, only a real psychoanalyst would be able to conduct it satisfactorily. It is not certain, on the other hand, that the critical gain is in proportion to the depth which would be reached. Beyond a certain point the literary and the medical interest may well cease to have a common standard. Perhaps the lowest layers of the human psyche lose all distinction: basically, complexes are as similar from person to person as livers or spleens are; their accidental peculiarities do not concern art. From this point of view, psychoanalysis would contribute to critical method not so much through precise analyses as through new methods of considering the human soul and its means of expression. Future experience will decide. Once more I would like to take a particular example and show how, in itself, the notion of a double meaning—manifest content and latent content—can enrich our interpretation of a text.

Las de l'amer repos is one of Mallarmé's clearest

36

poems. The few difficulties it has—and they come from extreme suppleness of phrase—vanish if the reader concentrates. Bored with indolence and with a labor that has been cruelly sterile, fatigued by the long vigils at Tournon, Mallarmé dreams of being the serene Chinese artist who finds his ecstasy in painting a rarefied landscape upon an exquisite cup. The "obvious" sense strikes us at once. To see through to a latent meaning, however, we do not need the eye of a practicing psychoanalyst. The toil that Mallarmé complains of is haunted with the idea of death:

> . . . et plus las sept fois du pacte dur
> De creuser par veillée une fosse nouvelle
> Dans le terrain avare et froid de ma cervelle,
> Fossoyeur sans pitié pour la stérilité,
> —Que dire à cette Aurore, ô Rêves, visité
> Par les roses, quand, peur de ses roses livides,
> Le vaste cimetière unira les trous vides?—

> [. . . and seven times more weary of the hard pact
> Of hollowing out in vigils a new grave
> In the greedy, frigid earth of my brain,
> Gravedigger without pity for sterility,
> What say to that Dawn, O Dreams, visited
> As I am by roses, when, for fear of its deathly pale roses,
> The vast cemetery unites the empty graves?—]

Is it only a manner of speaking? a poetic image? We could believe it (although for Freud there was no "manner of speaking" without some deep cause) if the obsession with death were not to be found everywhere in Mallarmé's poems during this period. We will suppose, rather, and justly, that this cemetery is not unconnected with the one in his free composition, and hence with the cemetery in which young Maria actually lay. I purposely avoid specifying the relationships which might unite these different terms. In any case, it is not a question of a logical connection. During the vigils when Mallarmé wrote his poems, death haunted his unconscious. No doubt he was unaware of it, but the secret obsession manifests itself nonetheless in the multiplicity of funereal images which emerged spontaneously in his mind: his thought is sterile, his brain resembles a cemetery, he himself works in it like a gravedigger. How could he help being weary? What exhausted him was not so much the amount of work done as its funereal quality. Here he is, then, dreaming of an art from which sorrow would have disappeared. He wishes

> Imiter le Chinois au coeur limpide et fin
> De qui l'extase pure est de peindre la fin
> Sur ses tasses de neige à la lune ravie
> D'une bizarre fleur qui parfume sa vie . . .

> [To imitate the Chinaman of limpid heart and subtle
> Whose pure ecstasy it is to paint the end,
> On cups of snow stolen from the moon,
> Of a bizarre flower which perfumes his life . . .]

The idea of death seems to have vanished. However, snow—moon—flower are three key elements of the free composition. Snow and moon form part of the symbolic décor, but the flower plainly represents the young girl, whose death and resurrection are signified respectively by the white roses and the red rose. The association flower—death is, moreover, constant with Mallarmé in this period. Several verses earlier, in the same piece, cemetery roses pale as death had appeared. But in this second part of the poem every macabre nuance has disappeared, since what is involved in principle is a dream of escape out of anguish. The Chinese artist, nevertheless, does paint on the snowy cup the *end* of a flower, and this word would be highly incomprehensible if, in his unconscious, the flower did not stand for the dead Maria. Proof of the fact is given in the following lines:

. . . la fin
D'une bizarre fleur qui parfume sa vie
Transparente, la fleur qu'il a sentie, *enfant*,[13]
Au filigrane bleu de l'âme se greffant.

[. . . the end
Of a bizarre flower which perfumes his transparent
Life, the flower which he felt, as a *child*,
On the blue filigree of his soul grafting itself.]
This flower comes from childhood; it was grafted on
the soul of the poet when he was a child. The word
"graft" distinctly marks the living bond which was earlier established between brother and sister and which
persists in the unconscious of the survivor. Thus Mallarmé dreamed of escaping from his death-obsession,
but as always, and by a classic process, the dream of
escape still reflected the obsession, but in the form of an
achievement which has been stripped of anxiety. The
end of the poem confirms this hypothesis. It is certainly
not by chance that the Chinese artist further chooses to
paint a "young landscape." What does this landscape
contain? The moon again, whiteness, and cold. But
there is a new element to consider:
Une ligne d'azur mince et pâle serait
Un lac. . . .

[A line of thin, pale blueness would be
A lake. . . .]
We know from other poems that blue "obsessed" Mallarmé at this time. The fact that it symbolized the ideal
does not keep it from being associated with Maria—
quite the contrary. We will remember the sentence apropos of Ettie: "She will be my ideal in life, as my sister is
in death." But in the poem *Soupir*, addressed to the
"serene sister" (calm as the calm crescent), Mallarmé's
dream ascends to "the wandering heaven of your angelic
eye" as toward "the softened azure of October pale and

pure"; the whole landscape which follows plainly recalls the one in *Plainte d'automne,* and consequently the idea of Maria. Cold water, explicitly called "dead water," also appears. This series of converging signs establishes beyond question the association between the line of blue on the cup and Maria's stare. We will further notice that this azure is that of a lake; that there is another poem of Mallarmé's in which the association lake—eye is given, *Pitre châtié:*

Yeux, lacs avec ma simple ivresse de renaître

[Eyes, lakes with my simple frenzy for rebirth] and that in the final line of *Las de l'amer repos* the reeds are assimilated to eyelashes:

Non loin de trois grands cils d'émeraude, roseaux.[14]

[Not far from three huge emerald eyelashes, reeds.]

Once more, this second interpretation necessarily remained unconscious to the author; but the secret obsession with his dead sister kept on suggesting from the depths of the subconscious the choice of image, which was a compromise between the immediate reality (that is, the state of mind and the poem he was concerned with) and the secret obsession which thus found a way of revealing itself.

I have just used the word "compromise," and I should rather like to emphasize it. It would be wrong to suppose that the latent meaning of the poem (which we see vaguely under the "obvious" meaning) constitutes its *true* meaning. In a poem, no more than in a man, do I see one unique truth, but rather a hierarchy of truths, which are, moreover, bound together by correspondences. None of these tiers is of absolute importance, and if a scale had to be set up between the two contents of the poem which we have just distinguished, the manifest and the latent, I would certainly not make the former into a simple reflection of the latter. We will take up again later the problem of inspiration. However, we

40

must discard the idea that subconscious reality inspires the poem. It is tied to the poem by a thousand threads, it perhaps nourishes the poem, it surely seeks to win it by devious means; in any case, it raises suggestions which readily become obsessive. It proposes and whispers the words. But that is not inspiration, and, in the final analysis, the spirit of the poet is moved by other solicitations. Once we have made this reservation with a view to further investigation, we may say that the unconscious has some voice as to subject-matter in the creation of a poem. In order to distinguish this voice beneath the other one, psychoanalysis is obviously indicated.

Marie Bonaparte's *Edgar Allan Poe*

Death of mother and sister, manifest and latent meaning of the poems: here are two good reasons to give our research a Freudian orientation. A third reason is furnished us by the appearance of kinship that binds Mallarmé to Baudelaire and Poe. It is well known that these last two have been the object of psychoanalytic studies by Dr. Laforgue and Marie Bonaparte.[15] The work of Bonaparte on the American poet is a veritable monument; it is with her work that we shall be concerned here. We must of course add that Mallarmé translated Poe and extolled him long after he had thrown off the influence of Baudelaire. The reason was that he felt no threat to his originality from poems in a foreign tongue, but also that Mallarmé's unconscious and Poe's were probably more similar. Baudelaire loved his own living mother; the American poet remained fixated on a dead mother. Mallarmé's unconscious, too, was turned toward the dead.

I shall make one comment about Baudelaire. The reader will see later that in my opinion the beheading of John the Baptist in the *Cantique* (the second part of *Hérodiade*) represents a castration symbol. Mallarmé's St. John thus pays for getting a glimpse of the princess in the nude.[16] As I have just shown, there is a certain analogy between this beheading and the one in *Pauvre Enfant pâle,* a prose poem in *Divagations.* Now *Plainte d'automne,* another prose poem on the dead Maria (and first version of *Hérodiade*) and *Pauvre Enfant pâle* (first version of the *Cantique*) were published for the first time together, with a common dedication: to Charles Baudelaire. From this dedication and from the date of publication, the annotator in *Oeuvres complètes* believes he is able to deduce that they were the first prose poems by Mallarmé. Mallarmé, then, not only admired Baudelaire as a stylist; he sensed in him a brother under the skin, suffering from a secret malady which was at least related to his own.

Mallarmé always reread Baudelaire, but he made a special study of Poe. From his twentieth year on, he busied himself with a translation of Poe's poems; took it up at the same time as Lefébure (who bowed out to him); and applied himself to the task more or less continuously until around 1872, when he began to publish them. Now it is precisely between 1862 and 1872 that the poet's work and life register a time of anxiety, the time when he most resembles Poe. In the spring of 1866 he wrote to Cazalis: "Three months gone by, relentless over *Hérodiade;* my lamp knows it! . . . I have written the musical overture and I can say that it will be of an extraordinary power. . . . I will have created what I dream is a poem worthy of Poe and which his do not surpass."[17]

A remark I have already made applies here too: Poe certainly does not have the rank in English literature that Baudelaire and Mallarmé assign him, and which they have in their own literature. No doubt the enthusiasm of the two French poets is due mainly to their unconscious kinship. On this plane, the strongest ties united Poe and Mallarmé. It is no surprise, then, that Marie Bonaparte's analysis gives us precious information in detail, beyond the general thesis she took from Freud.

She does not make a comparison between the two poets. But she gives the text of certain works of Poe (in Mallarmé's translation) with their psychoanalytic interpretation, and the reader of Mallarmé can easily profit from this.

For example, let us take another look at the poem of the "Chinaman of limpid heart and subtle." The free composition of 1857, *Apparition,* and *Hérodiade,* as we have said, suggested an association between the "calm horn" of the moon and the unconscious memory of the young dead sister.[18] Here is what we find in *Ulalume* (a poem of Poe's that Mallarmé must have particularly liked, since he inserted his translation of it into the very limited selection of *Vers et proses*) apropos of Astarte with the double crescent:

> Et maintenant, comme la nuit viellissait et que le cadran des étoiles indiquait le matin, à la fin de notre sentier un liquide et nébuleux éclat vint à naître, hors duquel un miraculeux croissant se leva avec une double corne—le croissant diamanté d'Astarte distinct avec sa double corne.
>
> Et je dis: "Elle est plus tiède que Diane, elle roule à travers un éther de soupirs: elle jubile dans une région de soupirs[19]—elle a vu que les larmes ne sont pas sèches sur ces joues où le ver ne meurt jamais et elle est venue passé les étoiles du Lion pour nous designer le sentier vers les cieux—vers la léthéenne paix des cieux—jusque-là venue en dépit du Lion, pour resplendir sur nous de ses yeux brillants—jusque-là venue à travers l'antre du Lion, avec l'amour dans ses yeux lumineux."
>
> Mais Psyché, élevant son doigt, dit: "Tristement, de cette étoile je me défie,—de sa pâleur, étrangement, je me défie. . . ."

[And now, as the night was senescent
And star-dials pointed to morn—
As the star-dials hinted of morn—

43

At the end of our path a liquescent
    And nebulous lustre was born,
Out of which a miraculous crescent
    Arose with a duplicate horn—
Astarte's bediamonded crescent
    Distinct with its duplicate horn.

And I said: "She is warmer than Dian;
    She rolls through an ether of sighs—
    She revels in a region of sighs.
She has seen that the tears are not dry on
    These cheeks, where the worm never dies,
And has come past the stars of the Lion
    To point us the path to the skies—
    To the Lethean peace of the skies—
Come up, in despite of the Lion,
    To shine on us with her bright eyes—
Come up through the lair of the Lion,
    With love in her luminous eyes."

But Psyche, uplifting her finger,
    Said: "Sadly this star I mistrust—
    Her pallor I strangely mistrust. . . ."]
    The poet in vain reassures Psyche, for here is where
the crescent leads:
        . . . et nous allâmes à la fin de l'allée, où nous
    fûmes arrêtés par la porte d'une tombe; par la
    porte, avec sa légende, d'une tombe, et je dis:
    "Qu'y a-t-il d'écrit, douce soeur, sur la porte, avec
    une légende, de cette tombe?" Elle répliqua: "Ula-
    lume! Ulalume! C'est le caveau de ta morte Ula-
    lume!"

[And we passed to the end of the vista,
    But were stopped by the door of a tomb—
    By the door of a legended tomb;
And I said: "What is written, sweet sister,

On the door of this legended tomb?"
She replied: "Ulalume—Ulalume—
'Tis the vault of thy lost Ulalume!"]
Not so great a poet as Mallarmé but a greater neurotic,
Poe expresses his obsession more crudely, but there is an
obvious analogy with Mallarmé's poem, where the cemetery appears only as a symbol, at the beginning of the
piece: the macabre is "evaded" in *Las de l'amer Repos;*
it is achieved in *Ulalume.*

Further back, in the same verses of Mallarmé, we
were startled by another detail: the end of this flower
   . . . qu'il a sentie, *enfant.*
Au filigrane bleu de l'âme se greffant.

> [. . . which he felt, as a *child,*
> On the blue filigree of his soul grafting itself.]

The more direct expression of a child's love is again
furnished by Poe in *Annabel Lee:*
   . . . Mais pour notre amour, il était plus fort de
tout un monde que l'amour de ceux plus âgés que
nous;—de plusieurs de tout un monde plus sage
que nous,—et ni les anges là-haut dans les cieux,
ni les démons sous la mer ne peuvent jamais dis-
joindre mon âme de l'âme de la très belle Annabel
Lee.

> [. . . But our love it was stronger by far than the
>   love
>   Of those who were older than we—
>   Of many far wiser than we—
> And neither the angels in Heaven above,
>   Nor the demons down under the sea,
> Can ever dissever my soul from the soul
>   Of the beautiful Annabel Lee.]

Marie Bonaparte establishes beyond question that Annabel Lee, who, like Elizabeth, Poe's consumptive
mother, died from exposure, is only Elizabeth's image

as Poe recalled it from childhood. We will show just as readily that the flower "grafted" on the soul of young Stéphane is the symbol of a beloved sister.

I have provided these two examples merely to illustrate briefly an undeniable parallelism. The conclusion is obvious: repeat for the author of *Hérodiade* the analysis already attempted for other authors. I am not unaware of the fears that such a proposal can (quite rightly) excite. I shall, however, set aside without examination the objections in principle. For one thing, this is not the place to sift them; for another, any hypothesis must, in my view, be judged by its results. Two practical objections do deserve attention: (1) Is the author qualified for this analysis? (2) Is there any need to push literary study as far as psychoanalysis?

I shall have something to say later on the first question. As to the second, I can well understand why it should be raised. One does not need Freud's authority to say that his sister's death caused Mallarmé deep sorrow and that his work reflects this grief. Literary analysis stops where personal grief begins; psychoanalysis includes also the grief of repressed erotic impulses, self-criticism, and guilt, since it deals not with sorrow but with neurotic anxiety. Do we find all this in Mallarmé? Unfortunately, I believe we do.

Let us consider, first, Mallarmé's life. One chapter in this book is devoted to an essay in which Dr. Jean Fretet gives a precise medical diagnosis of Mallarmé, who is said to have had a schizoid temperament, which served as a basis for melancholy impulses from 1862–1869 but not thereafter. Subscribing to a somewhat different thesis (better founded, we think, on reality), we attribute the depressive crises primarily to a mother fixation which came from the double emotional wound and which resulted in an obsession that was at the same time forbidden and constantly revived by the fantasy that accompanies literary creation. This anxiety varies rather curiously in a seasonal rhythm; circumstances of life

46

and thought also influence it. As a result, there are both periodicity and fluctuation. The basic obsession is nonetheless chronic. Combined with a contemplative and poetic vocation, which is as fundamental and as real as anything can be in a spirit like Mallarmé's, it explains most of the symptoms of retirement into himself that Dr. Fretet gathers under the term "schizoid." That the physical make-up of Mallarmé must, in spite of everything, be so labeled is a possibility. The reader will judge, once the discussion is completed.

The facts Dr. Fretet uses are patent enough. Mallarmé did suffer terrible crises of anxiety between his twentieth and thirtieth birthdays. Merely on this score the intervention of psychoanalysis seems justifiable. Can we say as much for repressed eroticism and for the guilt feeling which is associated with it? The reader will take some convincing on this point: to this end, there is an accumulation of small proofs that will emerge as the hypothesis is tested; but this experiment cannot take place without a sort of preliminary and provisional consent to the theory. I will recall only the theme of *Hérodiade*. If the princess so violently cherishes the "horror of being virgin," if she greets with abnormal reactions the slightest amorous suggestion made by the Nurse, it is obvious that she is struggling against an inner longing which is confessed in the last lines. The sinful curiosity of St. John, and the punishment that follows, belong to the most classic expression of the Oedipus complex. Like neurotic anxiety in real life, the literary expression of sexual guilt, inhibition, and obsession with death justify the use of psychoanalytic procedures.

In adopting the grand lines of the Freudian thesis we must of necessity go back from the sister to the mother. The mother's death, when Stéphane was five and was in the full normal Oedipal crisis, facilitated this already quite natural transfer, since the little sister, in the home of the grandparents, remained the only link with the earlier life and its maternal tenderness. However, the reader

47

of Mallarmé, who is more concerned with the poems than with psychoanalysis, may recoil at the prospect of taking this step. For Maria is the avowed subject of one piece, at least, of *Divagations,* and the relations already established by the letters to Cazalis and the free composition give the "poor young phantom" an incontestable place in Mallarmé's work. The mother, on the other hand, figures nowhere. Is it not too daring to make her the center of the work?

The answer is that an unconscious center could not, by definition, show on the surface. We are led to it by chains of association and by cross-references. Although I could touch on several very sensitive places in Mallarmé's work where the mother is all but present, I should like—limiting myself this time again to a single example—to cite a prose poem of Mallarmé which is almost contemporary with *Plainte d'automne* and the *Pauvre Enfant pâle:* I mean the excellent *Démon de l'analogie.* Its "inexplicable gloom" is familiar:

La Pénultième est morte, elle est morte, bien morte, la désespérée Pénultième.

[The Penultima is dead, she is dead, quite dead, the hopeless Penultima.]

The absurdity of the leitmotif which thus haunted Mallarmé's soul is among those that Freud brilliantly explicates in the *Psychopathology of Everyday Life.* For the Viennese master, every action, although apparently meaningless, has an unconscious significance. What can be the meaning of the "accursed fragment" singing on Mallarmé's lips? His insistence on a death is striking. But let us translate Penultima—this "remains . . . of a linguistic toil"—by its common equivalent: "next to last." Who is the next to last one dead? The last is Maria; the next to last, his mother. Thus a famous enigma would be solved.

As a reader, I would deem this solution hypothetical in the extreme were it not for a certain number of significant associations. The absurd phrase in question is bound up with the sounds of ancient instruments and with a grazing of wings. When Mallarmé found himself again in front of the window of an antique shop (which, let it be said in passing, plays here the role assumed elsewhere by the window and its panes), his finger makes the gesture of the angel in *Sainte;* he thinks he hears "the voice itself (the first, which undoubtedly had been the unique one)" ("The voice recalling viola and harpsichord" of the young mother in *Don du poème*), and he sees, hung on the wall, "old instruments" (the maternal, womb-shaped mandora of *Une dentelle s'abolit*) "and, on the ground . . . the shadow-hidden wings of ancient birds," the wings of downfall (*chute*), those of Psyche in Poe's *Ulalume*, those of the dawn in *Don du poème* and of the precipitate angel in *Fenêtres*. Thus all the details converge toward the triple idea of dead past, maternity, downfall. The reader will decide whether so much testimony leaves much doubt as to the identity of Penultima.

SEARCH FOR A METHOD

A true analysis must be made by a practicing psychoanalyst. Dr. Fretet has good reason to distrust the parlor practitioners. But is it a question of a true analysis? It is doubtful. A sick person under treatment confides his most intimate thoughts to his doctor, sometimes over the course of several years; he brings a large mass of raw materials, associations, and dreams. On the other hand, the analysis, by transference, permits a sort of lived-out drama, of which the psychiatrist and the patient compose the real characters (not to mention the imaginary ones). The study of a literary work does not permit anything similar. The materials are restricted in number; far from being crude, they are doubly elaborated by a critical intelligence and an exacting aesthetic sense. Not only does the author not tell everything, but he modifies what he is saying in order to secure special effects. Finally, this author is dead, and it is, curiously enough, his work which has come to life and which maintains personal relations with the reader.

The consequences of these facts emerge clearly in all analyses of literary and plastic art and even of musical art which have been attempted with such talent by a great number of physicians, from Freud to Charles Baudouin. The consequences are equally noticeable in the analysis of myths, legends from folklore, and religious rites. The impossibility of working from the life constrains the analyst to be satisfied with interpreting literary or other material in the light of concepts and results achieved by what is properly medical experience. In sum, a given poem is treated as if it were a dream, sent by letter, with some biographical references added. The limited character of this study, the unavoidable application of a general symbolism, and the fact also (it must be said) that the human unconscious is of an extraordinary monotony—all this gives to aesthetic psychoanalysis what is often a rather oversimple appearance, as the reader well knows.

I do not wish to touch on the question of values here —the harmony between the beauty of poems and their unconscious symbolism. Dalbiez,[20] Baudouin, and Odier[21] have written now-classic volumes on these delicate relationships between psychic functions and spiritual, moral, or aesthetic values. For the moment I do not wish to deal with such an important question. I do not blame psychoanalysis for elucidating a poem in its own way, that is, in depth, giving this interpretation to us as the underlying meaning and pretending at times that it is the only one or the most important one, the one that all the others must be simply reflections of.

I admit, and peculiarly in the case of Mallarmé, as the result of an experimental study of mine, that this lower-level meaning exists, that it forms the unconscious substructure of the poems, that we gain by exploring it, and that the illumination of psychoanalysis will be extremely

50

valuable to us in that attempt. But I can see little disadvantage today in a layman's fixing at least the main lines of such research before the intervention of the practicing physician. The general ideas of psychiatry spread little by little like those of physical medicine. Their use by the nonspecialist, if discreet, can be advantageous. To probe the unconscious of Mallarmé, after all, would be nothing more than an indiscretion and lack of piety if the end in view were not the beauty of the work, which to my mind all true knowledge has a way of enriching. But this descent into depths in which one is in danger of losing his way, the nonspecialist may perhaps be able to make more spontaneously; daily practice has not inured him to visits below. The reduction—even if obviously a correct one—of a great poet to his entrails is somewhat shocking to the average reader. Psychoanalysts are now aware of this. The average reader, for his part, has had to recognize the true worth of a science in which he has been invited to share. A common ground now exists. It is to that point precisely that literary criticism can and must now descend, without losing sight of its own goals, which are not medical but aesthetic.

With this shift of perspective goes a change of method. Even if he uses the results of modern psychology, the literary critic does not seek a diagnosis; thus he does not use the work as material to be put aside once the truth has been grasped. Doctors always try to go beyond the symptom; but when the symptom has turned into a work of art, it alone matters; from this one goes out, to it one returns.

I have therefore endeavored, in what follows, to enlarge classic literary criticism so that it will include psychoanalysis, keeping the literary point of view always central. My earlier studies have helped me here. From the underlying network of obsessive metaphors (as described in *Mallarmé l'obscur*) to the idea of a complex, the transition is easy. It appears almost inevitable, as proven by the examples given above, as soon as certain biographical details are juxtaposed and a certain number of mutually illuminating texts are noted. Though at first sight it looks fragmented, Mallarmé's work offers extraordinary unity when one achieves the right perspective. Pieces quite remote from one another turn out to have the same meaning and may be compared to the different stages of an etching.

When Mallarmé, in the Biography of the 1898 edition [of his works], qualified many of his poems as "studies with a view to doing better, as one tries out his pen-points," he spoke more truly than is commonly believed. For my part, I always let myself be guided by the notion that the key to an expression or a work is to be found in other expressions or work. I have listened to resonances, followed associations, and sought out persistent groupings, the metaphorical systems. It involves, I dare say, using psychoanalysis superficially, sketchily. Yet the network which is thus traced connects quite naturally with the deeper network of classic complexes.

I wish, then, that the reader would take what follows not as a true psychoanalysis, which would be presumptuous on the part of a nonpractitioner, but as an expression of the common critical method. Its advantage appears to be that it establishes, quite solidly, hitherto unperceived relationships, and thus gives to Mallarmé's life and work a unity that has not previously been recognized.

2

Poetic Alienation

IN 1946 DR. JEAN FRETET published a work, *L'Aliénation poétique*,[1] which serious criticism must take into account from now on. The title is surprising. Does it simply mean a return to Lombroso's thesis, which rather childishly ascribed genius to insanity? Dr. Fretet in his introduction denies any such idea. He also distinguishes his approach from those to be found in certain crude psychoanalyses. "The error committed by Lombroso (that genius equals insanity), the abuse of trust on the part of many psychoanalysts, have discredited many armchair practitioners" (p. 9). We are thus warned from the start that Fretet's is a thesis which is far subtler and, from the professional standpoint, more firmly anchored. *L'Aliénation poétique* includes a general statement plus clinical studies of Rimbaud, Mallarmé, and Proust. It is specifically the study of Mallarmé which concerns us here, but this study is comprehensible only in the light of several general considerations.

Dr. Fretet's basic idea is not easy to grasp, not from any lack of literary "straightforwardness" or excess of medical barbarisms (the book is, on the contrary, quite engaging), but because his basic idea is to some extent involved with a personal view. Dr. Fretet does not care for excessive rationalization. "Excessive rationalization has a very debatable sovereignty; its model, paranoia, is a madness of the emotional life" (p. 11). This obscure

53

statement, since it assimilates logic to madness and to a madness of the feelings and thus tends to upset our classifications, clearly indicates at any rate the author's disrespect for ready-made ideas. He likes neither reason nor thinkers; neither classicism nor (let us add) the Jesuits, whose influence—nefarious and destructive of poetry, he thinks—he studies in French literary history. To him Nietzsche's example reveals, insofar as mental health is concerned (for to Fretet mental health is the enemy of mystic morality as well as of the Romantic malaise—in short, the enemy of all inspiration) a pure and simple case of the will to power. The so-called classic equilibrium, in brief, is Rome.

To the sane man, whose ego when integrated responds only to its own voice, its own assertion, Dr. Fretet opposes the alienated individual. The word "alienated" is meant to be taken in all its etymological force: one alienates something, one is alienated for others' advantage. The alienated individual hears the voice of an "other," suffers from an obsession, obeys it. Now the poet comes under this general definition. The value of his alienation is not at issue, for the moment; the fact is that the poet forgets his reasonable self in order to listen to a strange voice. What voice? The voice, says Dr. Fretet, of the sick body. Once Boileau and his Reason had been silenced, all our romantic writers, from Rousseau to Proust—like Racine before them—dared to give expression to their suffering body, that is, the spirit, the "Other." They have spelled out in literature their natural physique, with its miserable defects. However, they have not made their confession without some shame. The soul of the poet develops a moral censorship which tends either to inhibit him or to drive him mad. Racine, Rimbaud, Mallarmé may be taken as examples of inhibition; Nerval, Lautréamont, of insanity. Another solution is suicide. Thus Dr. Fretet does not confuse the poet with simply any insane man. The poet gives up his ego for the benefit of the illness; letting

54

the illness speak, he achieves perception and testifies to the experience. Consciously mad, willingly insane, he takes upon himself, like Christ, all the sins of the sick body and estranges himself for the advantage of this "Other." Condemned for such behavior, he becomes the victim of his own reproach. Thus, oscillating sharply above and below the middle point of normal and simple health, he presents the image of a divine invalid, more attractive but more disquieting than the ordinary man, poised in logic and will to power. Poetry is a redemption from sickness. But it implies sickness as a prerequisite. The writer's work, his style itself, will bear witness to the fact. This is what Dr. Fretet tries to prove by thorough and minute clinical examination.

Let us see what he makes of Mallarmé. Dr. Fretet is not a psychoanalyst. Thus he does not delve into an author's psychic history, particularly the events of his childhood—the traumas, the emotional shocks, the conflicts—whose echoes, reverberating in the artist's mature work, will largely explain it. Following an older medical and psychiatric tradition, he classifies the case according to the hereditary background as well as the accidental deviation.

In the diagnosis he performs on Mallarmé, these two elements are sharply distinguished; the background is schizoid, the attack consists of fits of depression. The reader must not be disturbed by these technical terms, which sum up facts that are perfectly familiar. "The schizoid state," writes Dr. Fretet, "is marked by the absence of spontaneity; depression tends to deny existence. When these two combine, they prevent individual affirmation. Only a pure, abstract intelligence remains, and it is deprived of the emotions which enliven and individualize our existence" (p. 115). Such a resumé sounds brutal because of its very briefness, but if we go back to the symptoms on which he bases his diagnosis, he will soon see a portrait of Mallarmé that is unde-

55

niably authentic. I will group them somewhat otherwise than Dr. Fretet did, in order to enable the reader to see the whole picture at a glance. Leaving aside for the moment the attacks of depression, we will concentrate on the schizoid state, or more simply, the temperament, of Mallarmé.

Affective Symptoms of the Schizoid State

(1) Femininity. Love of antique furniture, bibelots, trinkets—life at the fireside in a carefully arranged interior—love of mirrors—affectations, mannerisms, mimicry—erotic life calm, without passion for the object and almost confined to love of self: "As for me, poetry takes the place of love because it loves itself";[2] however, sexual ambiguity is tied up with introversion and narcissism, which leads us to the second series of emotional symptoms.

(2) Affective narcissism. Looking in the mirror; lack of interest in his professional career or social life or contemporary historical events; withdrawal into himself; absence of élan. In brief, the bonds with the external world are to a large extent cut. Dr. Fretet says, "The schizoid has no need to communicate. Still less, to be effusive" (p. 88). Thus, there are no outbursts, no confessions. Thus retirement into self brings about a sterility which spells of melancholy will aggravate.

Intellectual Symptoms of the Schizoid State

(1) Lack of assertiveness (corresponding to the femininity of the affective schizoid state). Thought subtle, devoid of naturalness, ambivalent, ironic, concealing and revealing, affirming and denying.

(2) Mental narcissism. Thought, cut off from reality, gazes at itself in the mirror: "My Thought has thought itself." It achieves thus, in extreme purity and concentration, the feeling of identity between ego and nonego. The result is an acute sense of correspondences, of

metaphors, of reflections back and forth between exterior and interior worlds, but at the same time a neglect of the boundaries between thought and reality—hence, a belief in magical expression and in the omnipotence of ideas, as well as a penchant for the occult.

These are the major features. For detail, the reader may refer to Dr. Fretet's work. However, the accuracy of the portrait is by now recognizable. But how should this group of signs be interpreted? It may readily be conceded that the artist expresses in his work his physical features—indeed, this much seems perfectly obvious. Let us go even further and admit that any temperament at all is a deviation from the normal, and therefore, if it is marked enough, it constitutes a beginning of insanity. Mallarmé was as susceptible to the cold as a cat; we know it, we smile at it, perhaps we even love him all the more for it if we are cold-natured ourselves. But in the last resort all this amounts to very little. Objections and misunderstandings begin when the very characteristics of any contemplative life are presented as symptoms of abnormality, even if a mild case of it.

Lack of spontaneity, of contact with the external world, withdrawal into oneself? What shall we say of a person affected with such symptoms? He may be sick, but also he may be living a life which in all ages has been deemed superior. If this distinction is illusory, the consequence is that Socrates and Beethoven cease to be superior men. But if the distinction holds, vital deficiency must not be confused with spiritual superiority under the learned term "schizoid state."

Actually our comment on this general tendency to withdraw into the self applies to almost all the symptoms Dr. Fretet lists. At each step we must answer the same question. What of contemplation in the mirror? One may ask if all perception is not narcissistic by definition, and in particular if all thought which goes deep is not bound to "think itself." Descartes, Poincaré, Claude Bernard are scientists, but first and fundamen-

57

tally they reflect on scientific method. St. John of the Cross meditates on the mystical way; Mallarmé, on the poetic. This can hardly take place without isolation from the exterior world. What of the confusion of ego and non-ego, of thought and reality, mystic play of correspondences? If this were schizoid illusion, all human thought might be said to be more or less grounded on that illusion. Men who are still called "superior" have more or less definitely believed that the borderline between the I and the not-I does not have the sharpness that our egoism would give it, and that external is not separated from internal reality as crudely as the intellect supposes. When the Hindu mystic says "*That* is you," when the moralist demands that I love another as myself, when the scientist verifies an astonishing connection between mathematical thought and real phenomena, are they then victims of a schizoid illusion, or are they seekers after spiritual truth? The work and its value must, in the final analysis, determine our answer.

Now the work of Stéphane Mallarmé is beautiful; therefore, it is good. Any explanation of its worth in terms of sickness or of its beauty by symptoms leads to terrible confusion. Finding the sick man congenial and health a bit odious, as Dr. Fretet does, is no answer. He apparently wishes (at the price of contradicting himself) to mix the delights of poetry and diagnosis in a most irregular fashion. The relationship between psychosis and art is undeniable. The artist often resembles a sick person. In any case, his thought strongly resembles that of sick people, of children, of primitives. But the greater the apparent similarity, the more clearly the distinction must be drawn, lest the very idea of the superior individual be lost. Finally, what of the belief in the omnipotence of ideas, in verbal magic? No doubt infantile beliefs do exist in this area. However, I can no more charge Plato with infantilism than I can at one and the same time admire and mock the incantation that all beauty involves.

Dr. Fretet goes so far as to detect some lack of spontaneity even in irony and humor. We forgive this defect in Montaigne. The diagnosis of the taste for antique furniture is also enlightening: "Mallarmé acquired these old things one by one and arranged them with loving care. Odd taste in France, where the first and certain clue to a man's mental health is the unsightliness of his home, which is left free for the exercise of his wife's taste and for the vandalism of his children" (p. 77). The taste for knicknacks, for dress, and many a symptom of femininity in Mallarmé most certainly deserve our attention. I doubt that we must interpret them as the sign of a lack of vitality. Spiritual life, harmonizing contradictions, does not stress the distinction of sex any more than it does the distinction between ego and non-ego. Though opposed to perversion, it sometimes resembles perversion. It may even be nourished by a real perversion. Art supposes a mixture of male and female qualities, of activity and passivity. Though art transcends these opposites, the spiritual person or vital artist in life often resembles someone ambiguous or neuter.

Obviously I cannot treat such a question in a few meager lines. My purpose here as elsewhere is to show how prudently one must interpret the symptoms of abnormality in an artist. It would be more in keeping with the sum total of our experience to draw a conclusion at this point, to admit that a poet is made for his poems, and that a secret harmony orients all his psychic functions to this end. That is not, perhaps, true of his first efforts, but it becomes truer and truer as the artist develops within a man and uses him even without his knowledge to serve the artist's ends. The abnormal as a symptom of sickness would therefore be distinguished from the abnormal as the sign of a superior mutation. It is precisely this distinction which the medical term "schizoid" confuses.

Next let us consider depression. "There were three attacks of true depression in Mallarmé's life. They were not cases of emptiness of soul nor of ennui, but depression in the medical sense—illness. The first attack lasted three months; the second, eight months; the last, two and a half years" (p. 97). Nothing could be more explicit. A little earlier Dr. Fretet speaks of "periodicity" and of "cyclothymic disequilibrium," an alternation of depression and euphoria, of abated and accelerated activity. The diagnosis is, naturally, based on Dr. Mondor's minutely documented biography. Reference to Mondor shows that Dr. Fretet has simplified, forced, omitted, and at times even falsified the facts a little in order to have them follow the pattern he wishes. The reader must not exaggerate the harshness of this criticism. A scientific hypothesis, grouping and interpreting a cluster of given phenomena, is always more or less arbitrary and false. If experience provides the points, it is the scholar's eye that runs the curve through them, and there is no such thing as an unprejudiced eye. I do not, then, question the bases for Dr. Fretet's diagnosis, but I think another hypothesis would take fuller account of the facts.

To sum up my point of view, I believe Mallarmé lived from adolescence to the age of thirty under the pressure of almost constant anxiety and obsession; the cause of this obsession should not be sought, then, in attacks of mental illness but in some unvarying psychic element. I also believe that the source of this permanent injury was the death of his mother and sister. However, the anxiety, though constantly present, did fluctuate, and I would like to show that the fluctuations were of three sorts:

1. There were accidental variations, related to the events of external life—loves, joys, fatigues, chagrins— which slackened or revived the profound grief.

2. Mallarmé underwent a seasonal rhythm. In general, he was more depressed in winter, livelier and happier in summer.

3. As his spiritual life unfolded, his anxiety, without changing its nature, changed in its expression and form.

60

The poet's conscious mind, which was naturally quite ignorant of its wounds and unconscious fixations, gave his obsession first a poetic and then more and more a metaphysical interpretation. Nevertheless, the illness became progressively more acute. When the metaphysical crisis reached its peak (at Besançon, Avignon), Mallarmé almost went insane. He voluntarily gave up a type of speculation which had become too dangerous, and returned to everyday existence by a series of compromises between his unconscious obsession, his art, his thought, his pleasures, and social exigencies.

This, then, is the curve I would offer in place of the oversimplified one Dr. Fretet traces. I will, however, start with Dr. Fretet's curve, precisely because it is the simpler of the two. I apologize for the critical form which my exposition must thus take.

Dr. Fretet's curve presents certain lows and highs; let us examine them one by one.

THE FIRST PERIOD OF DEPRESSION (three months in the spring of 1862)

Mallarmé was twenty. This period coincided with the birth of his love for Marie Gerhard (the Mme Mallarmé-to-be), and preceded by several months his departure for London in the company of the young lady (early November, 1862). Dr. Fretet situates this first attack of depression between the end of February and the beginning of May. Now it was on March 15 that Mallarmé published two poems in *Papillon: Sonneur* and *Guignon*. These poems, which were certainly composed before the beginning of the crisis, are nonetheless marked with black pessimism; they prove that the idea of suicide came some time earlier. Again, it was in the course of the three-month period to which Dr. Fretet ascribes this first depression that Mallarmé wrote a historical drama (March 19), formed two deep friendships (with Lefébure and Cazalis), and engaged in the flirtation with Marie. This last fact is not even referred to by Dr.

Fretet, since the hypothesis of a mental ailment with its own evolution quite obviously has nothing to do with a love affair. If we are, on the contrary, led to adopt the psychoanalytic point of view, the beginning of an amour assumes much greater significance, since there certainly was some sort of psychic effort on Mallarmé's part to create a relationship between his new love and his attachment to the dead. The emotional disturbance of this period, assuming that it did exist, would thus find a natural explanation. Dr. Fretet therefore changes the facts when he writes of the happy period which (according to him) succeeded the crisis: "In August, he tried out his eloquence and aggressiveness in a sort of manifesto which would appear in September. *Meanwhile he fell in love with Marie*"[3] (p. 98). The letter to Cazalis in which Mallarmé avowed that he was "taken in the snare laid in a tuft of grass *du Tendre*"[4] is dated April 4, 1862, and his "intense suit"[5] had already lasted six weeks. The birth of Mallarmé's first great love thus exactly coincides with what Dr. Fretet calls an attack of depression.

"HIGH" PERIOD (May, 1862–November, 1864)

Let us go on with the quotation begun above:

Meanwhile he fell in love with Marie. Intoxication with tender feelings, joy in carrying out plans, departure for London without a sou but with her (November, 1862), vexations, recklessness, separation, then reunion of the lovers, whose marriage was made difficult by poverty. In April, 1863, came a trip to Sens and the death of his father. If adversity had been enough to induce melancholy, Mallarmé would have been a depressive, nothing less. He was active and enterprising . . . making a living, pursuing his studies. . . . Finally he married . . . was appointed . . . to Tournon, set up house there. . . . All that was lacking was a little daughter. She was born. . . . At this moment of peace and happiness the spiritual illness—grief, anxiety, and torpor—which had appeared in the spring of 1862, abruptly reappeared (p. 98).

See how lightly the stay in London is treated: the carrying-off of Marie with him, the lovers' ecstasies and quarrels, the work, and the marriage. The texts of this period reveal, on the contrary, that Mallarmé at this time passed through his major crisis, the previous ones having unfolded on a quite different plane. Mallarmé settled on marriage only after a difficult inner struggle and great suffering. Since the girl evidently expected marriage, why did Stéphane hold back so long? Why were there so many tears between them? separations? reconciliations? thoughts of suicide? Money was not the reason, as Mallarmé expressly stated: "You imagine that I am poor; but I am not . . . the truth is: I am receiving 3,600–4,000 francs a year in London. I have a 1,200-franc apartment. How many married clerks of forty have no more! In March, on the 19th, I will come into 20,000."[6]

The crisis had causes that were far deeper:

At this moment I detest Marie, I hate her . . . Why? Why? Why? My poor head is affected . . . Don't pay any more attention to my letters: one day they turn Marie into a white dove, the next they will call her all sorts of things . . . I hate Marie, and when I look at her picture, I go down on my knees.[7]

I am alone, Marie left yesterday for Brussels. It's all over. I feel sure I will never see her again. Yet she was my sister and my wife . . . yesterday, she was right here within these walls; today she is only—a word. The absent are only a name: there are moments when it is doubtful whether they really exist. The dead have an advantage over them in that they have a tomb one can see and pray upon . . .[8]

Ambivalent feelings, a mixture of love and hate, the evocation of sister and death—this is the drama that Dr. Fretet passes over in silence. Several times during this period the idea of suicide occurred to Mallarmé. Dr. Mondor describes him wandering around in London. His literary production was as feeble as his work. *Château de l'espérance,* which he composed at this time, reveals a hopeless obsession. In short, the various signs of depression and of flight from reality are as strong in this as in every other period.

The first year at Tournon is, again, counted by Dr. Fretet as happy. But from the moment of his arrival Mallarmé considered himself as "exiled in this black village." To finish *L'Azur,* in January, 1864, he had first "to beat down his distressing impotence." The theme of *L'Azur* informs us of his mental state: the afflicting obsession continued. He sent Lefébure his poem, *A une Putain.* Faced with this "well of sorrow," the friend sensed the part which unconscious causes played in Mallarmé's poetry. "It is probable that the causes go far back in your life and that they have found a corollary in the spleen which creates your strength as a poet and your unhappiness as a man."[9] There could be no better summary of the thesis I wish to defend here.

THE SECOND PERIOD OF DEPRESSION (November, 1864–mid-June, 1865)

As we have just seen, the onset of this "depression" coincided with the birth of Geneviève. Winter came at the same moment, and Mallarmé for the first time tried to express his obsession through the leading female character of *Hérodiade.* The end of the "depression" coincided with the possibility of other conditions of work: the child being older and temperatures warmer, *Hérodiade* was abandoned in favor of the *Faune.* This switch would undoubtedly strike Dr. Fretet as being the result of restored health. The reader will probably not be able to understand until he has finished this book the real reasons which lead me to reject this attitude. If Mallarmé was composing *Hérodiade* because he was sick, he was surely writing bad poetry. We can put it the other way, too, and say that he was ill because he was writing *Hérodiade*. But these over-simple formulas conceal what is in fact a complex reality. Let us look at it more closely.

In October, Mallarmé began *Hérodiade;* he sensed that he was about to begin a time-consuming major work; perhaps he took up his rough drafts again. He began work, as is usual in the month of October, with the restfulness of summer behind, and before him a vision of long, studious evenings. "I want . . . to succeed," he wrote Cazalis in October; "I am inventing a language. . . ." All at once a set of material circumstances opposed and even blocked this enthusiasm. First, the fatigue of teaching; Dr. Fretet is unjust when he declares that Mallarmé took the rowdiness of his class in stride; actually, he was always complaining of it. On November 19, Geneviève was born. At a stroke he lost both the silence of the house and a part of his rest. ". . . I have not yet resumed work; with her cries this bad baby has banished Hérodiade, of hair cold as gold, heavy-robed and sterile."[10]

These letters in which Mallarmé speaks of the newborn child testify to the reality, without evasion. From the first he was a perfect, a tender father, who trifled with his daughter and was amused with her; he was also an artist who could ill bear the presence of this intruder. Naturally, we may recall here the ambivalence revealed in London in his attitude toward Marie. His motives were obscure, and I am not certain that the birth of Geneviève did not reopen in its turn a deep wound; it is odd, in any case, that in the letter announcing this event to his grandmother, Mallarmé wrote: "One thing that has been very sweet is that she chose to be born on my poor mother's birthday, St. Elizabeth's day."[11] But enough of these tentative suggestions. It is certain that Geneviève represented life, as Marie represented it, and that the mere presence of life aroused a certain hostility in him because he wanted to dream and write.

Between the active and the contemplative life, a compromise must be found, but it is not found easily or suddenly. The circumstances were admittedly difficult for Mallarmé. Three months later, when he put aside his deepest discouragement, he clearly indicated its causes:

> Unfortunately, I do not enjoy all this enchantment that hovers about a cradle. . . . I am too much the poet and too taken with Poetry itself to savor, when I cannot work, an inner happiness which seems to me to take the place of the other happiness, the great happiness, the one the Muse gives. . . . However, I have been at work for a week. I have begun in earnest on my tragedy, *Hérodiade;* but how sad not to be exclusively the man of letters! At each moment, my finest energies or rarest inspirations, which I cannot retrieve, are interrupted by the hideous task of being a pedagogue, and when I return, with papers behind and simpletons at my coattail, I am so worn out that I can do nothing but rest.[12]

This letter dates from March, 1865, in the very middle of the melancholy attack presumed by Dr. Fretet. It shows, first, that Mallarmé did, in fact, work during this particular winter; second, that his fatigue and depression are to be explained at least in part by quite valid external causes. They may be insufficient in themselves. But there are also valid inner causes to evaluate before we accept the hypothesis of a morbid attack, since Mallarmé himself confessed to them and since they are related to the literary quest for which indeed he lived: "If only I had chosen an easy work; but it is just like me, sterile and crepuscular, to have taken an appalling subject whose emotions, when they are lively, are carried even to the point of atrocity, and if they drift, have a strange mystery about them. And my verse, it makes me ill at times and wounds like steel!"[13]

It would be wrong, in my view, to interpret these words as a literary exaggeration. Mallarmé spoke the exact truth. He spoke with courage, it must be conceded, when his paternal feelings were involved; why should he not tell the truth about his work? It is clear, therefore—and study of the poem will confirm this hypothesis—that the subject of *Hérodiade,* far from representing a simple pretext for beautiful verse, was the painful reflection of a personal anxiety. External difficulties, inner conflict, the invention of a language—these sum up the facts of the period. Is it really necessary to tack on a morbid depression? The change of atmosphere between the winter and the following summer—that is, between *Hérodiade* and the *Faune*—we will see repeated almost every year. I will give, further on, a table of winter depressions and summer enthusiasms. But the cold plays such a considerable role in Mallarmé's work that no one ignores the constant nexus which is established (by detours that are often unconscious) between winter and, in short, the tomb. Toiling at *Hérodiade* in these painful external circumstances during this winter of 1864–1865, Mallarmé felt (for the first time, I believe, and incessantly), and wished to feel, sought furiously to feel in order to express it, the cold interior of this mirror, which was also a tomb, since a phantom arose from it. These relationships between world and thought, in which Dr. Fretet would see a schizoid illusion, were truly experienced by the poet. Illusion or truth, he experienced it and founded upon his feeling of it the art he sought to realize.

For my part I feel convinced that the secret harmony between actual winter and the mirror of *Hérodiade* was a necessity if it was to help Mallarmé in his own searches. He suffered no less from the cold of night than he did from the anxiety that accompanied his dream. When summer came, he left the frozen poem for the *Faune,* its sunlight and abandon. Must one interpret this as marking the end of a crisis? The difference in activity between the two periods is not at all what Dr. Fretet suggests. During the summer the poet in three

67

months wrote the first version of the *Faune*, true, but during the winter months he had written the overture to *Hérodiade*, pushed his style to an unheard-of point, and recognized an impasse there, since he put it aside in March to begin the dialogue; he himself said he was working furiously. And he was rather pleased with the way things were going. Besides, during the same winter, he wrote *Une Négresse*, *Brise marine*, and an article on Glatigny. He perfected *Tristesse d'été*. Even when Mallarmé was in a good period—one that Dr. Fretet would recognize as free of attacks of depression—he did not always do so much in six months. Far from it.

The only remaining basis for a medical diagnosis is a series of despairing passages of November-December, 1864. But my own interpretation of them is that a renewed hatred of life (even while he was with people he continued to love—a fact that made the conflict distressing), a rousing of inner phantoms due to his poetic labor, the fatigue of daily duties, his work late at night, his lack of sleep, and the cold, these objective conditions combined to throw him into a physical and mental depression.

SECOND "HIGH" PERIOD (mid-June, 1865–August, 1866)

A "happy year," says Dr. Fretet. "There are continuous impressions of well-being and of power, and they witness to fecundity" (p. 102). There were certainly happy times, some rich in meaning, others adventitious. The *Faune*, as offered to Coquelin, did not have the success he hoped; however, Mallarmé had a feeling of success; in fact, he had discovered one of the essential paths of his sublimation, the one which had to do with a personal compromise between art and eroticism. Moreover, his reputation grew. I cannot enter into a digression on Mallarmé's feelings about glory. It would be necessary to go into all the nuances, to take account of his highest aspirations, as well as of certain components, what psychoanalysis calls the "spectacular" complex, a certain feminine and discreetly dramatic taste, whose shy theatricality does not deceive anyone. Mallarmé loved glory in his own way, but he certainly loved it. Experience proves that every success (outer or inner) is an excellent cure for a tendency to depression.

Christmas, 1865, Mallarmé spent at Paris, and attended a party gotten up by Leconte de Lisle "almost in his honor." He was asked to contribute verses for the May issue of *Parnasse Contemporain* (founded in February, 1866). Let us add that he now lived in his new apartment at Tournon, more comfortable and more sunshiny quarters, from which he could look out on the Rhône: the path of "aquatic reveries" which would lead him to Valvins is marked out. Vève had grown. External circumstances had improved. However, Dr. Fretet's phrase quoted above—"There are continuous impressions of well-being and of power"—is hardly believable, since it overlooks an essential fact: that the metaphysical crisis, in which Mallarmé's mental health all but gave way, unquestionably began in this very winter (1865–1866). On that point we have the testimony of the famous letter to Cazalis (March, 1866), in which Mallarmé declared that he had "faced two abysses . . ." which drove him to despair. "One is Nothingness," the exploration of which would bring Mallarmé to the *Folie d'Elbehnon;* the other was the supposed chest ailment for which he would consult Dr. Béchet at Avignon in August. Now these two discoveries were the result of three winter months spent on *Hérodiade;* Mallarmé came through "drained . . . worn to a frazzle, unhappy and sterile."[14]

In the following months he thought of his poetry only as a function of a more abstract line of reasoning. He escaped to the "glaciers of Aesthetics." In fact, he abandoned the room where he had dreamed of Hérodiade, and the mirror of his obsession, to descend the mental steps of *Igitur* toward suicide, which he considered the supreme intellectual affirmation. Everything Dr. Fretet deems insane in the following period actually began in the middle of what he calls a year of "well-being and power."

THIRD PERIOD OF DEPRESSION (August, 1866, to 1869)

There is no question that we assay here the most somber years of Mallarmé's life. On the evidence, however, the crisis does not seem to me to have the causes, the simple character, or the time limits that Dr. Fretet assigns.

Several of the causes of this depression were external: the harshness of the winter at Besançon, the persistent fear of a chest infection, the administrative worry (transfer from Tournon to Besançon was a demotion), the house-moving in October, 1867, and almost at once a pulmonary congestion. At the same time it must be admitted that he underwent a moral and mental crisis. However, as we have seen, it began, not in August, 1866, but in March, after the winter's work on *Hérodiade,* when Mallarmé announced that he had discovered nothingness. From then on he was thinking beyond poetry, as a metaphysician. All the Besançon and Avignon letters attest to that. In April, 1868, he wrote to Coppée: "As for me, I have for two years committed the sin of visualizing the Dream in its ideal nakedness, while I ought to have been heaping up between it and me a mystery of music and forgetfulness. And now that I have arrived at the dreadful vision of a pure work, I have almost lost my mind and any sense of the most familiar words."[15]

We are in the trough of the depression; its beginning date is explicitly provided: spring, 1866. On May 3, 1868, Mallarmé wrote to Lefébure: "Decidedly, I am descending from the absolute . . . but this two-year involvement (you remember? since our stay at Cannes) will leave a mark on me that I shall consider a consecration."[16] Mallarmé was at Cannes in late March and early April, 1866.

All our evidence agrees, then: what one might call the "crisis of the absolute" started in March, not in August, 1866, insofar as such a crisis can have any sort of beginning in a mind of his type. The quotations given above establish the nature of the drama; it was an effort to pass beyond aesthetic expression. Beyond the poem Mallarmé wished to attain an ideal purity, the icy peak of his own contemplation of world and self.

> Là-haut où la froidure
> Eternelle n'endure
> Que vous le surpassiez
>   Tous ô glaciers[17]

> [There above where eternal
> Coldness does not permit
> You to surpass it
>   O glaciers all]

Such unquestionably was the way the crisis appeared to Mallarmé's conscious mind. The hypothesis that it was simply an attack of depression does not mesh with the dates and does not at all explain this appearance. If I use the term "appearance" in referring to this spiritual drama, it is because I see a latent content under the manifest content. Mallarmé's conscious mind saw the truth; a metaphysical debate did take place. But I believe that another debate paralleled it in the depths. There are three reasons that lead me to believe this. First of all, as Mallarmé himself said, the crisis of the absolute arose from the work on *Hérodiade*. *Hérodiade* is the poem of an obsession; the anguished phantom, yearned for and dreaded at one and the same time, which appeared in the mirror all through the "dear agony," has nothing in common with rational philosophic thought. Consciously, Mallarmé could not realize that he was devoting his nights to the evocation and poetic expression of a dead woman. But we have strong reasons for believing this to be so. It is not surprising, then—it is even quite normal—that this exhausting search of his should have ended in the discovery of nothingness. "Nothingness" should be understood, not as superficially conceived in the logical intellect, but as deeply and sorrowfully felt, like a wound one might die from, though it cannot be localized or given a specific name. It is one thing to "think," in the popular sense of the term; it is quite another to live out one's thought. Mallarmé lived his out. Thus the metaphysical sickness prolonged the poetic sickness, nothingness succeeded the phantom; but in the final analysis it was still the same dead loved one, the same absence. This is why his "pure thought" was, quite naturally, charged with the anxiety which his verses had been lately expressing— and that is my second reason. For rational thought is not in itself distressing. But Mallarmé's philosophic quest became progressively more agonizing each day. He may have changed his mode of expression, but not his obsession. This obsession found too easy an answer in the idea of suicide. We will see by study of the poems that his unconscious often suggested to Mallarmé one specific remedy for his obsession: to rejoin the dead. Now (and this is my third reason) his metaphysical meditation led Mallarmé to the same conclusion, as *Igitur* proves. Thus he eventually renounced the absolute not only to escape madness, but also to escape suicide.

Here, I think, we have reasons enough to suppose that this flight toward the glaciers corresponded unconsciously, and by a strange symmetry, to a descent into the tomb such as the *Folie d'Elbehnon* describes. If we admit this hypothesis, then the other theory of a morbid and rather accidental attack of depression becomes useless. Furthermore, the end of the crisis must be dated from the moment that Mallarmé gave up the absolute —that is, in May, 1868. "Decidedly, I am descending from the absolute . . . ," he wrote at this date. "I am coming back down into my now-two-years-abandoned self: after all, poems merely tinted with the absolute are quite beautiful. . . ."[18]

Dr. Fretet prolongs Mallarmé's depression into the following year. He thus neglects the mood of convalescence which marked the summer of 1868. In the same letter, Mallarmé asked Lefébure for the address of the shop where Cazalis bought his hammock: ". . . I would like to hang one just like it between the laurels in my yard, and sleep in the shadowy adulation of their leaves. . . ."[19] He did not wish simply to sleep, he dreamed of composing; he had already begun to write the *Sonnet en YX,* in which Dr. Fretet sees a sign of near-lunacy:

> Four months, May to August, were scarcely enough for the working out of the monstrous sonnet of rhymes in YX, which was the expression of a painful need to fail, a spiritual exercise like the macerations and mutilations which depressives inflict on themselves through a desire to be purified. Furthermore these several verses, impenetrable in their obscurity and lacking in beauty, are the only ones (p. 105).

Further on I will indicate the significance of this sonnet, and show how it pictures the room in *Igitur,* that is, the one in which Mallarmé himself meditated—but in the absence of its owner ("For the Master has gone to draw tears from the Styx"). *Igitur* descended the stairs which led to nothingness. Once the thought had reached its goal and denied its own self, the room stayed empty. The themes of the sonnet are found again in other places: in *Igitur,* in *Triptyque;* and I no longer have any doubt as to their true interpretation. But I do not wish to anticipate. Let us limit ourselves to noting here that the *Sonnet en YX,* "tinted with the absolute," sets out to tell the story of a crisis. But the point is that the sick man has put the crisis behind him.

Igitur recounted the crisis at greater length but with a development of the same themes. Mallarmé expressly said he wrote *Igitur* to throw off his illness, to do away with his obsession. "It is a tale by which I want to defeat that old monster Impotence, which, by the way, is its subject . . . If it [the tale] is completed I am cured; *Similia Similibus*" (November, 1869). According to Dr. Fretet, Mallarmé wrote *Igitur* after his depression ended (March, 1869). But it is obvious that *Igitur* and the *Sonnet en YX* are in the same vein, that they express the same thought and tell the same story. Mallarmé was exorcising his own madness. He worked on *Igitur* at Lecques in the summer of 1869,[20] but there were signs of recovery as early as the summer of 1868 (the summer of the hammock and the *Sonnet en YX*). Lefébure wrote in July: "You wrote me such a charming letter that I have been too stupefied to answer it."[21] This same month, Mallarmé sent Cazalis a letter in which the phrase Dr. Mondor cites does not have at all a sad tone: "We are having one of those extraordinary heat waves when, even behind shutters and within the protective shade of the walls, the mind is indistinct like an aquarium which vague silver fins slide through."[22] In the same letter, he conjured up the outings at Fontainebleau, spoke tenderly of Cazalis' and Ettie's love, and rejoiced to think of the coming holidays. He welcomed Cazalis and tasted at Bandol "the brutal nuptials of sea-bathing." Where is the melancholy in this? As a matter of fact, we must wait until the winter months of 1869 to find a new depression. In its turn it will yield to the warmth of spring.

It is time to close this detailed examination. In the following years, 1869–1874, Dr. Fretet sees a phase of "underexcitement." Mallarmé kept busy. Actually, once he had come down out of his dream he was bound to come up against an exacting reality-situation. The couple was short of money. In January, 1870, Mme Mallarmé fell sick; by the end of the same year she was expecting another child. This series of shocks was to put the poet through his London experience again: in both instances there was antagonism between the self-centeredness of his inner life and the sharp exigencies of everyday life. Freud would refer to it as a conflict between the pleasure principle and the reality principle. As in London, Mallarmé accepted reality. He groped for new expedients; he even thought of higher diplomas; then at Avignon he set up his course of private tutoring in English. Transferred to Paris, he wrote for the *National Observer* and set about translating Poe. The poems of 1873—*Toast funèbre, Quand l'ombre menaça* —reveal a calm Mallarmé. All in all, I do not see anything from 1869 to 1874 which has a morbid character. The metaphysical crisis slips by. We are in the period of compromises and sublimations, beyond anxiety. Study of it must be reserved for later—it would add nothing to our evaluation of Dr. Fretet's thesis.

At the beginning of this critique I suggested a more complex curve, which would represent the play of diverse elements. The constant factor is, in my view, anxiety and obsession—with dead mother and dead sister. I have not used most of the arguments that are suggested by the work itself, since in this chapter I wanted to stress the constancy of the neurotic element as against the morbid variations, the attacks of depression, diagnosed by Dr. Fretet. All that was necessary in that connection was to show that the obsession operated outside the periods of depression both in his life and in his work. All along, moreover, this hypothesis gained strength from the fact that it was related to the content of that work, to the anxiety of *Hérodiade,* and to the metaphysical thought which indeed made the poetic quest of these first years much longer. While the attacks of depression would appear and disappear like any illness, independently of the events of the writer's emotional and poetic life, the deep obsession, as suggested by circumstances, letters, and poems—that is, by the whole documentation—must have, on the contrary, modified his life and been modified by it. The preceding analysis shows this

75

modulated continuity, and not the harsh intrusion, on three occasions, of an alien morbid factor into an existence that was otherwise determined.

Insofar as Mallarmé was ill, the illness was a part of himself, expressed itself in his work, and shaped his thought. I can easily see something of this sort; I nowhere see illness interrupt a specific work which would have developed without its intervention. I would emphasize this point. Illness does not come from without to destroy the poetry; it is in the poetry, constitutes one of its elements, and to some extent explains it (to what extent, we shall find out later). Furthermore, the illness evolves; the same obsession is expressed in different modes; it orients the poetic, then the metaphysical, quest. Just when it is about to win out it withdraws, and Mallarmé escapes by a series of adjustments to the poem and to life. Thus the expression "constant factor," which I used earlier, is not absolutely accurate, since his obsession has its own evolution; but I believe that no matter what forms it assumes it derives from a single source, so that one may at least speak of continuity, with the idea that this continuity is at the opposite extreme from the "morbid attack" theory supported by Dr. Fretet.

I spoke of two other variables. In the course of the preceding analysis, the reader will have noted the play of external events and their interaction with the deep obsession, on the one hand, and with the spiritual events in Mallarmé's life on the other. This interdependence will stand out more clearly in the chapters that follow.

The third element is cyclic. It has nothing in common with the cyclothymia conjured up by Dr. Fretet; it refers simply to the alternation of the seasons, to which Mallarmé was particularly sensitive. Each winter brought on a depression, which apparently reached its lowest point—no doubt because of the cumulative effect —between February and May. What Dr. Fretet calls the "first depressive attack" struck in the spring of 1862. In winter, 1863, came the London crisis; in winter-spring, 1864, he wrote despairing pieces (*L'Azur, Fleurs, A une Putain,* and so on). In February, 1865: "To be a worn-out old man at twenty-three . . ." (letter to Cazalis). In March, 1866, he discovered nothingness and the hole in his chest. In March, 1867, he announced his escape from a terrible crisis—it was the Besançon winter. In February, 1868, he hesitated to read Cazalis' book: "It seemed to me that you laid it in a sepulcher." In February, 1869, he was obliged to dictate his letters and did only the minimum.

What is the evidence that points the other way? In summer, 1862, there was his love affair with Marie and his departure for London with her. In the summer of 1863, he was married in August and moved to Tournon. In the summer of 1864, Mallarmé escaped to Avignon, Paris, London, friends, and the literary life. From June to September, 1865, he wrote *L'Après-midi d'un faune.* Summer, 1866, seems to be an exception: Mallarmé felt physically ill and went to consult Dr. Bechet at Avignon; his metaphysical crisis had begun, actually, during the spring. The summer of 1867 was also quite bad after the Besançon winter, which was a very hard one physically and mentally. On the other hand, in the summer of 1868, in the warmth of Avignon, Mallarmé, as we have seen, could idle in a hammock and, now that he had come back down from the glaciers, begin the recital of his spiritual adventure, a recital which was to free him of it; he went to Bandol. In 1869 he wrote *Igitur* at Lecques.

This enumeration appears significant in itself, but I would like to stress the fact that before the metaphysical crisis Mallarmé's obsession coincided with winter; it was winter when he wrote *Hérodiade,* but he very consciously dedicated his summer to *L'Après-midi d'un faune.* The happy sublimation of this latter poem, the compromise which it represents between poetry and eroticism, was a safeguard against that lure of death which, however, the work on *Hérodiade* necessarily

77

broke down. But after the metaphysical crisis, Mallarmé could write, that summer, the *Sonnet en YX* and *Igitur*. It is because they are the report of a completed spiritual adventure, which was henceforth without danger for the poet.

To return to our starting point in this chapter, I shall say a word about Dr. Fretet's general thesis and its application to Mallarmé. May one speak of poetic alienation in this case? Do we hear in Mallarmé's work the voice of the "other"—that is, of the sick body? Mallarmé's temperament is certainly expressed in his work. But if we redefine "schizoid" to leave out certain traits which are common to all contemplative life (and which it is therefore an exaggeration to call morbid), we find that Mallarmé had but few quirks. It would be more interesting to analyze them than merely to label them under a general term. In any event, to use the term "alienation" is distinctly to exaggerate. And since, in addition, the depressive attacks do not seem to be verified, the general idea that Mallarmé's work owes its merit to the expression of a sick body falls almost completely flat.

Mallarmé certainly wanted "something other" than everyday life; he said so in fitting terms in the *Conférence à Oxford*. In this sense we might take up Dr. Fretet's expression and say that the poet wished to alienate himself. However, there are two "other things" that may be opposed to everyday life and its reasonable equilibrium. The first is death; the second, creation. Progress toward the one comes through relaxation; toward the other, through effort: from the standpoint of energy, they are opposites. Death is not merely an external event. We bear it inside us in the form of our past. Since what we call love is precisely the capacity another thing has to fascinate us, if we love our dead past abnormally, it lives again despite its death, and

78

haunts us. This obsession entails fantasies and a lack of adaptation to real circumstances: it is neurosis.

Certainly life reacts. For active men, in favorable circumstances, conflict often ends in a compromise that gives a share of satisfaction both to the deep obsession and to the exigencies of normal life. Let us note that this so-called normal life is composed of love or at least of interest in present events and objects. The average sane person is above all wrapped up in the present. The cured neurotic conciliates, in what is often called sublimation, living interests with dead interests. But the artist presents a special case, one that the psychologist rarely examines. The artist creates. To put it another way, he is a man capable of being delighted with a future object, vaguely glimpsed or sensed. About this point of fascination (invisible to others) the subject of the work turns, and a new thing is created. Mallarmé calls it "giving words the initiative," which is an exact description of the poetic experience, though it is obvious that words are stirred up and put together only under the influence of an organizing center which, besides, is more or less unconscious and which forms, once the work is complete, what we commonly call its soul.

Not until the final chapter shall I enter into a discussion of the problems raised in this connection. I would simply like to stress this point: if an artist too carries his dead past along with him and is obsessed with it for some reason, the compromise which will cure him will tend to reconcile that obsession less with so-called active life than with the very specific spiritual and technical demands of the work which he is here to create. Just as the normal man wishes to live, so the writer wishes to write. His work will reflect the death he carries within him. The phantoms of his past will haunt, not his present acts, but his future creation. From this point of view, if we insist on the term "alienation," we could say that the neurotic poet is doubly alienated: to the benefit of death, and to the benefit of creation. In this duality he would find his true health, which is not that of the average man, to whom creation remains alien. Is the artist therefore necessarily neurotic? I think not. To cite only one example, Johann Sebastian Bach strikes me as typical of the artist whose work reflects nothing of death. But for reasons we are beginning only with great difficulty to sense and which are connected with man's emotional development, it is possible that artists are peculiarly subject to neurosis. The anxiety Mallarmé suffered from was unquestionably there; it is one of the elements of his work; it is not the essential part of it. Thus, even in replacing Dr. Fretet's psychiatric theory with a psychoanalytic explanation, we will have examined only one side of the question, only one of the two alienations of the poet. The second is the more important.[23]

3

Before Hérodiade

Ce que disaient les trois Cigognes, the free composition
which I have already cited,[1] was written by Mallarmé
at fifteen. It is a psychological document of the first order. Mallarmé's spirit is mirrored in it at a time when
he had not yet faced his love difficulties. Mallarmé lost
his sister when he was fifteen; at twenty, after at least
a year of casual flirtations, he fell in love with Marie
Gerhard. Thus, love followed death in his adolescence.
At some point near the death of Maria, the strange
dream of resurrection was wedged in.

Mallarmé's life is unique in the degree to which it
unfolds like a dialogue or a struggle between inner
dream and external reality. The love of a flesh-and-blood
woman is of course a part of this external reality, just
as the trial of life itself is. At fifteen, Mallarmé the
schoolboy knew neither. He did, however, dream intensely, so that the free composition has the extraordinary advantage of presenting this inner fantasy in its
pure state, before he had any encounter with reality.
Of the two voices of the dialogue, which are later en-
twined, we hear only the first; reflected in it is a spirit
which is far enough from childhood for the dream to
have taken shape, but still far enough from adulthood
for it to have remained uncorrected by life. Having
said this, I should like to raise several points, reinforc-

ing my remarks as best I can, with quotations for the reader who does not have the text at hand.

On an earlier page I gave a summary of this free composition. Nick Parrit, the woodcutter father of the young girl, is alone with a cat by the fire in his hut, one snowy night. The angel, who has winged from the church portal, tolls the resurrection (for one night) of young Deborah, who comes to dance before the fire, only to vanish at dawn after a number of vicissitudes. This theme, naturally, offers nothing original (Mallarmé had only to draw on the elements of a good religious education). The fact that a boy of fifteen chose it *is* unusual. Our students in the fourth year of the *lycée* rarely compose fairy stories. The recent death of Maria suggests an explanation.[2] But something more is needed —an imaginative and dreamy nature. When we look at the story more closely, what is striking and even a bit frightening is the absoluteness of the dream: things outside the dream simply do not exist as far as the author is concerned. The angel flies from the church portal; but of the building itself, of the surrounding village, not a single word is given. We do not know whether there is furniture, utensil, any token whatsoever of day-to-day existence in Nick Parrit's hut. We do not know what the old man is seated on. He has a fire, a pipe, and a rose.

Since the subject of the story is fantastic, the contact with reality is bound to be feeble. It is actually reduced to the minimum. Men, their work, their life—completely absent. A single human being remains, in a meditative withdrawal. During the entire story, he will make almost no sign, evidently content to be the one for whom the spell is cast, the one who not merely looks but receives, for he is the wretched one to whom the supernatural is freely offered.

The heroes of adolescents ordinarily triumph by ruse or force, tour sea and land, discover, contrive, and conquer. Stéphane's hero at fifteen already suggests the choice which will determine the poet's way of life: he awaits the "visit" and the dream by the fireside. What is left has no reality except as a prop, and deserves no further mention. And so, along with a temperament which, to start with, is that of a cold-natured person, an attitude, a natural tendency, emerges—schizoid or contemplative, as one likes. At this stage, especially, it is hard to decide which. The refusal to live that is implied in such a text, as I have suggested, might well worry an educational psychologist. But Nick Parrit's cabin might just as well recall the famous poem of the Japanese Buddhist monk:

> I have left everything behind, I have departed, and for five springs and five autumns I have begun to create for myself a dream retreat among clouds that float the luminous summits of Mount Ohara. . . . Now, I am old. . . . Sixty. I have built a small hut—last leaf of the stripped bough. I have set up this tiny temporary hut as a voyager makes himself a shelter for a night or as an old silkworm weaves a last cocoon.

The hut, ever smaller and more devoid of furnishings, is a true symbol of contemplative life. The true question, in the final analysis, is this: is the dream that is pursued in the hut sterile or not? vivifying or mortal? From this point of view the 1857 composition has definite promise. For if boys of fifteen ordinarily have but few dreams, those who do dream can rarely boast of such style:

> Aussitôt les cloches tintèrent à l'église du village voisin, et le séraphin extatique qui était sculpté sur le portail descendit silencieusement à terre. Il tailla un long voile dans la neige constellée à jour par les pas des bouvreuils, et le jeta sur sa robe azurée, si bien qu'il paraissait vêtu d'un linceul blanc semé d'étoiles bleues. Il cacha sa tête pensive

dans ses bras, et, les cheveux dénoués sur ses ailes frissonnantes à peine, s'étendit dans la nuit, et plana. . . .

Et quand le chat eut frotté ses moustaches le long des jambes de Nick Parrit, le vieillard prit ses deux pattes blanches, ornées de manchettes, en ses mains, si bien que Puss, laissant sous son habit noir passer la queue qu'il portait en rapière, gravement campé et comiquement gauche dans ses canons de dentelles, avait l'air d'un mousquetaire ivre qui aurait oublié son feutre parmi les liserons de la tonnelle.

[Then the bells struck in the church of the neighboring village, and the ecstatic seraphim who was sculpted on the portal descended silently to earth. He cut a long veil in the snow pierced by star-shaped finches' tracks, and cast it upon his blue robe, so that he appeared to be clad in a white shroud sown with blue stars. He hid his pensive head in his arms, and, hair loosened over barely shuddering wings, stretched himself into the night, and soared. . . .

And when the cat had rubbed its whiskers along Nick Parrit's legs, the old man took in his hands its two white paws, ornamented with bands, so that Puss, allowing his tail (which he bore like a rapier) to pass under his black coat, gravely encamped and comically awkward in his lace flounces, had the appearance of a tipsy musketeer who had forgotten his hat among the convolvulus of the bower.]

There are dreams and dreams. The beauty of this one, its expression in the vernacular, the budding mastery of spirit moving effortlessly from one to the other—all this reassures us against any threat of morbidity. But we should at least consider the possibility. I find a suggestion of it in this suppression of the real—a suppression too absolute for a child—as well as in the obvious obsession with a tomb.

Young Stéphane identifies himself, as I have said, with Nick Parrit. This identification with the father forms a part of the Oedipus complex. But antagonism toward the father is also expressed: "They say that God the Father is quite old: he made a mistake, no doubt, and cut her down with the stroke that was intended for me. . . . Finally, when God the Son succeeds him, he will not throw upon the child the earth which was to cover the ancestor!" The word "ancestor" seems to indicate further a witticism directed against Stéphane's grandfather, his real teacher, rather than against his absent, sick father. No doubt there is also something startling in the latent eroticism which is revealed in the statement, "Deborah laid her head in the hands of the old man, not saying a single word, but their thoughts billed amicably at one another, like two doves separated for a day."

I do not doubt that a thorough analysis of the free composition will uncover classic instances of sexual symbolism: the stripping of the rose is one. On the surface, though, everything is discreetness itself. No incestuous thought, I am sure, entered the conscious mind of the adolescent youth. But his dream ramifies from the Oedipal situation and thus springs from the ancient trunk of sexual instinct. Curiously, the song of the girl who has thus been restored to her father by the angel's trumpet makes use of eighteenth-century coquetries:

> Quand, frappant mon tambour basque,
> L'épaule nue, ivre et fantasque,
> Sur mon front penché j'arrondis
> En pur croissant mes bras suaves,
> Ou fixe avec des poses graves
> Mes yeux bleus au bleu paradis,
> Tel vieil abbé, diseur de messes—

S'il écartait mes chastes tresses
Blondes comme n'est pas le miel—
Sémerait sur mon col sans voiles
Plus de baisers qu'il n'est d'étoiles
Qu'il n'est d'étoiles dans le ciel!

[When, striking my tambourine,
Shoulder bare, tipsy and fantastic,
I curve my soft arms
Into a pure crescent on my bended brow,
Or fix with grave posture
My blue eyes on the heavenly blue,
Some likely old *abbé*, speaker of Masses
—If he scattered my chaste tresses
More blond than honey—
Would sow upon my neck unveiled
More kisses than there are stars,
Than there are stars in the sky!]

This same "saltarello" had already been sung by the annunciatory angel, "contrary to the belief of the ignorant that angels sing only hymns." The erotic vein which, from *Placet futile* and the *Faune,* will continue through the *Rondels* to Méry Laurent, begins here. It will never be entirely disentangled from the funereal. We will find again in *Hérodiade* this gesture of the girl in refusing to let her tresses be touched by too rash a hand; she in turn will hesitate between the "white night[3] of ice and cruel snow" and sensual love to come. It is already in this fringe that Nick Parrit (that is, Stéphane) dreams, and in this fringe also that Deborah Parrit (that is, Maria) appears and dances. As a new incarnation of the same phantom, Hérodiade too will appear in this narrow belt between winter and summer, tomb and fire. But before coming to *Hérodiade,* we shall have to consider the conscious love difficulties. We have not yet reached this point.

The theme unfolds in a fluid atmosphere, without anxiety or guilt feeling. I wish the reader to take note of this fact, for we are now about to touch on the work itself: as early as the first poems, we shall find Maria, but the atmosphere will be changed. A sadness will appear that will not cease growing until the crisis of metaphysical anguish in 1867–1868. The reason is that the exigencies of reality in all its forms—experiencing real love, making a living, creating literature—little by little inflame a yet latent conflict: then, a feeling of guilty impotence will overwhelm the poet. At fifteen, the conflict between reality and dream did not exist, or as yet presented only a childish form.

The transition is provided by the poem entitled *Apparition*:[4]

J'errais donc, l'oeil rivé sur le pavé vieilli
Quand avec du soleil aux cheveux, dans la rue
Et dans le soir, tu m'es en riant apparue.

[I wandered then, eye riveted on the worn pavement
When with sun in hair, in the street
And in the evening you appeared to me, laughing.]

Dr. Mondor supposes that the girl so described is Ettie Yapp. Indeed the hypothesis seems probable. We have already quoted the letter in which Mallarmé treated Ettie and his sister Maria together: "She will be my ideal in life as my sister is in death." In the same letter, Mallarmé promised Cazalis, who was distracted with love for the girl, some verses on Ettie: ". . . I promise you they will be exquisite . . . storms of lyricism would be unworthy of this chaste apparition you love. . . ." We find in this sentence the title of the poem that Stéphane would not complete until a year later, but for which he evidently kept his original feeling. The word "chaste" is typical.

In the same letter, Ettie was described as a "white and auroral" ray of light. Ettie Yapp was then in London; Mallarmé met her there six months later, in December, 1862, when his own love affair with Marie had entered a critical stage. "Ettie was, as always," he wrote Cazalis, "exquisitely simple; she did the honors in a way to enrapture you with each of her questions . . . all that, and further, the gentle pride and deep goodness of her somber blue glance, gave her the air of a seraphim who had turned into a Quaker and still remembered heaven. Quaker is a bit strong: it would be true if Quakers trembled with the shudder of the stars."[5]

This brotherly enthusiasm would make us no more than smile if the words "emparadiser" [enrapture you], "séraphine" [seraphim], "frisson d'étoiles" [shudder of stars], did not catch the eye. Joined to "chaste, auroral, white," they put us vaguely back into the atmosphere of the free composition. We have already shown that the sonnet *Pour votre chère morte* proves the Ettie-Maria association. A number of clues, moreover, indicate to us that Mallarmé's affection for Ettie, circumspect as it was, never lost its depth.

The rupture between Cazalis and the girl occurred in 1864; four years later, at Avignon, Mallarmé still pretended to believe it impossible: "Do not your souls know, by means of the Dream, how to make a joy out of a bitter thing?" Ettie remained the "delightful child" of Fontainebleau. When the break-up was confirmed, Mallarmé felt the shock even more dolefully than Cazalis: ". . . as for me (and I speak of myself because you are one of the only persons my interests allow me to identify myself with), I *suffer* when I think of you . . . this story which is just a little my own. . . ."[6]

This brings us back to *Apparition*. If Mallarmé wrote the poem for Ettie and Cazalis, he clearly had in mind his own affair with Marie. Behind the two young women who were alive, the dead one may also be seen in profile. Let us recall that in June, 1863, when the poem was finished, Mallarmé had regained his own composure: after a tragic crisis he resolved to marry Marie. In July, 1862,

88

when Cazalis asked him for some verses upon his beloved, Mallarmé still treated his flirtation with Marie as a vacation trifle: ". . . I have set mirror traps for the lark . . . and the bird is content to twitter from a distance, invisible. That amuses me."[7]

Between these two dates, July, 1862, and June, 1863, the storm passed. One may then suppose that Mallarmé wrote *Apparition*, retaining his initial feeling of 1862, but a feeling enriched with an experience of his own—enriched *for him* with a budding anguish. Love of the real young woman (whether named Ettie or Marie) was even now like unfaithfulness to the dead one. There was some disgrace in abandoning the dream in favor of life; there was some guilt in being alive. The first four lines symbolize, in images that are now familiar to the reader (moon, seraphim, violas, death, sobs, flowers), the sadness of the ideal dead one who has been betrayed.

> La lune s'attristait. Des séraphins en pleurs
> Rêvant, l'archet aux doigts, dans le calme des fleurs
> Vaporeuses, tiraient de mourantes violes
> De blancs sanglots glissant sur l'azur des corolles
> —C'était le jour béni de ton premier baiser.
> Ma songerie aimant à me martyriser . . .

> [The moon saddened. Seraphim in tears
> Dreaming, bow in hand, in the calm of the
> Vaporish flowers, drew from expiring violins
> White sobs gliding on the blue of corollas
> —It was the blessed day of your first kiss.
> My dreaming, in love with my self-martyring . . .]

Here the voluptuous self-punishment begins:

> S'enivrait savamment du parfum de tristesse
> Que même sans regret et sans déboire laisse
> La cueillaison d'un Rêve au coeur qui l'a cueilli.

> [Intoxicated itself subtly with the perfume of sadness

89

Which even without regret and without vexation is
   left
By the gathering of a Dream in the heart that
   picked it.]
The first tentative step toward dispelling the dream and
grasping reality at once awakens a slight anxiety and
provokes a retreat. However, the youthful reality appears and triumphs:
   . . . tu m'es en riant apparue

[. . . you appeared to me, laughing]
But in what way? By confusing herself with a phantom
yet more distant, the mother behind the sister:
   Et j'ai cru voir la fée au chapeau de clarté
   Qui jadis sur mes beaux sommeils d'enfant gâté
   Passait, laissant toujours de ses mains mal fermées
   Neiger de blancs bouquets d'étoiles parfumées.

[And I believed I saw the fairy with the cap of light
Who through my lovely spoiled-child dreams
Used to pass, always letting from her ill-closed
   hands
Snow down white bouquets of perfumed stars.]
   There is nothing abnormal in grafting new, adult
loves onto older, childhood attachments. In fact, this
seems to be the rule in emotional development. The
network of our feelings expands, somewhat like the
branches of a tree. But the trunk is formed of our childhood affections. There is no difficulty, we repeat, as long
as the adult feelings—though attached to the past—
adapt to present reality. But when one of these branches
is arrested in its growth, trouble sets in. Part of ourself,
remaining infantile, loses contact with reality when we
grow up. This part of us, infantile, fettered, is from then
on unable to achieve satisfactions freely and normally;
it begins to have dreams in its prison. What such dreams
have in common with art, we shall try to discover in
Mallarmé's connection later in this work.

I would like to dwell a moment here on the life of Mallarmé. What is called in psychoanalysis a fixation on the sister and the mother evidently arrested or diverted a normal emotional development in him. A brutal blow cut the branch, and in the 1857 free composition we are almost spectators (so to speak) as the dream grows out of the wound. The wound closes, but the way is blocked for the imprisoned sap. Thereafter it will be much more difficult for it to feed a living affection than to sustain a feeble and resigned dream. Nick Parrit, following his daughter's death, was "buried . . . in [a] desolate solitude." The retreat from life which secludes a man with his own phantoms could not be better defined. Infallibly, in such a case, the phantoms are idealized by the intense love which focuses on them for lack of another outlet. They become, as Mallarmé wrote, "our ideal in death." Real objects of love can expect to receive a share of the normal affection due them only insofar as they recall this ideal and participate in it. But further: these ghosts which we love because they were part of our childhood are sexually taboo. The obsessed spirit can love only what recalls them, but as soon as it loves it feels vaguely guilty. Anxiety seizes the spirit: if, on the one hand, it buries itself in the past, it feels that death is inevitable; if, on the other hand, it turns towards real life, it feels unfaithful and unable to love the reality, or, if it does so, feels a sense of having fallen.

It is understandable that such an illness would make an engagement arduous and a fiancée's role difficult. A rival that one is unaware of occupies his heart in her stead: she must resemble that rival in order to be loved —but at what risk! In Stéphane's case, a fresh complication sprang perhaps from the identification (noted above) between Maria and Ettie, Ettie becoming in life the ideal angel that Maria was in death. The fact that Ettie loved Cazalis made her at once attractive and untouchable, which satisfied the ambivalence of the taboo. And Marie? In June, 1862, she was only a flirtation. At the beginning of November she left with Mallarmé for London. Marie certainly loved Stéphane, who was not without sensuality. But there was more to it than that. When Mallarmé accepted the idea of marriage, after considerable turmoil, he wrote to Cazalis, using this remarkable sentence: "She has a look all her own which at once pierced my heart and which could not be withdrawn without giving me a mortal wound." In *Frisson d'hiver* he was specific: "You love that sort of thing, and this is why I can live near you. Haven't you wished, my sister with the look of yesteryear, that in one of my poems these words should appear: *the grace of faded things?*" Here is the point where the grafting occurs: Marie is united with Maria by her look, and by the fact that the one is dead and the other cherishes the past. True tenderness, stemming from this identification, grew and became confirmed: nothing was ever to break it. But of the depth of this feeling Stéphane and Marie were still unaware in London. Faced with a bewildered young woman, Mallarmé was seemingly unable to make a simple decision.

I do not wish to digress (any more than I did in the preceding chapter) about this episode. Furthermore, most of the documents which treat of it are still unpublished. However, in order to convey to the reader an idea of Mallarmé's emotional development at this period, perhaps a page can profitably be devoted to gathering a number of quotations from texts scattered in Dr. Mondor's work.[8]

April 4, 1862, letter to Cazalis: ". . . You know that I am a blunderer and that I have fallen into the trap I laid in a tuft of grass *'du Tendre'*[9] . . . From our combined melancholies perhaps we can make one happiness. . . . It may be a piece of folly I am committing. No, no. I shall be less alone during vacation."

July 1, 1862, letter to Cazalis: "These days, it's true, I have set mirror traps for the lark in the field of gallantry and the bird is content to twitter from a distance, invisible. . . ."

June–July, 1862, to Marie Gerhard: he declares his love.

July 7, 1862, letter to Cazalis: ". . . If only I could be caught in my trap, and, since she's sure to love me, have an affair with her!"

August 23, 1862, letter to des Essarts: ". . . I am savoring my intoxication. I am sure that my sweet Marie adores me and lives only for me."

September 25, 1862, letter to Cazalis, while Marie is away: "I would love to fly away there with my sweet sister, Marie! . . . I know an angel. Named Marie. . . . Oh! my poor Marie, I love her so much. I really miss her, and I am so sorry for her!"

September, 1862, there was talk of marriage. "In Fontainebleau forest, one summer day, in the full transport of sunlight, freedom and love, he spoke to Marie of their coming marriage in London."[10]

November 8 or 10, 1862, arrival in London with Marie.

November 14, 1862, letter to Cazalis: "I read, I write, she embroiders, knits. . . ."

December 4, 1862, Marie told Stéphane she must leave. Letter to Cazalis: ". . . she dreads embroiling me with my family. Then she said: 'I am in the way here.' She has more courage than I do. . . . She is sick and has the fever. . . . For me to lose Marie would be to lose half my life, the better half. . . ."

December 30, 1862, letter to Cazalis: Mallarmé spoke particularly of Ettie and of his evening with the Yapps.

January 10, 1863, departure of Marie. Letter to Cazalis: "Oh! I felt then, for the first time, . . . I, poor child abandoned by everything that was my life and my ideal, how vast was this word *alone*."

January 14, 1863, letter to Cazalis: "I'm going to write her and she's coming back. . . . We are going to be married."

January, 1863, Marie's letter to Cazalis: ". . . I shall never again return to London. . . . He must see how much I have already sacrificed for him, and see also that I can do nothing more for him, otherwise I only stand to lose everything."

January 30, 1863, Mallarmé resolved to get married, letter to Cazalis: ". . . I shall not be everlastingly unhappy, and that's what frightens me, because *Marie* will be. . . . 'It's all over as far as I'm concerned,' she says, 'but I can't cry, I feel that I can only endure quietly —will God give me the strength?' Can I consent to that? . . . Cast her away like an old bouquet? . . . It would be dishonest, criminal, not to marry her. . . . More than that: even if I didn't love her I still ought to do it. . . . I must, I will do it. . . ."

February 3, 1863, letter to Cazalis: "Marie refuses. . . . At this moment I hate Marie, I despise her. . . . Why? Why? Why? My poor head aches terribly. . . . I hate Marie, and when I see her picture, I go down on my knees. . . ."

February 10, 1863, letter to Cazalis: "Marie arrived this morning. . . . What ecstasy to see her! this is all I know. . . ."

March 4, 1863, Marie left again.

March 5, 1863, letter to Cazalis: "I am alone, Marie left yesterday for Brussels. It's all over . . . Nevertheless she was my sister and my wife."

March 18, 1863, Mallarmé went to Sens, perhaps to receive the money at his coming of age, and at almost the same date, hurried to Brussels and Marie, whom he had resolved to marry.

April 12, 1863, death of Mallarmé's father.

April 27, 1863, letter to Cazalis: "Besides, is there such a thing as happiness in this world? And should it really be sought anywhere but in dreams? It is the false goal of life; the true goal is Duty. Duty, which is named art, struggle, or what you will . . . I am not hiding from myself the fact that there will be times when I

94

will have to put up a terrible fight—and face great disenchantments that will later become tortures. I am not concealing anything from myself. Only I wish to look with a clear eye, and invoke oh so gently this will power I have known only by name . . . I am marrying Marie . . . I am not acting for myself, but only for her."

In a letter to Cazalis, Mallarmé combatted the hostility of des Essarts. He spoke of Marie's physical and moral virtues; found that she was not "aeolian or seraphic"; displayed a sure tenderness toward her; and expressed appreciation for her exemplary innocence. It is a rather superficial discussion; more profound is the sentence: "She has a look all her own which at once pierced my heart, and which could not be withdrawn without giving me a mortal wound."

June 3, 1863, letter to Cazalis indicating that even after the decision to marry and after an apparently very happy visit with Marie, Mallarmé did not like the life he was entering. "Here below there's a smell of cooking." This letter contains *Fenêtres* and *Château de l'espérance*.

August 10, 1863, marriage in London.

Mallarmé, during this sojourn in London before his marriage, seems to have written only two poems: *Château de l'espérance* and *Fenêtres*. A letter to Cazalis (June 3, 1863) presented the first one: "I am sending you another poem, *L'Assaut*, which is as vague and frail as a dream. Of tresses which suggested to my mind the idea of a flag. My heart, seized with military ardor, bounds across frightful landscapes and lays siege to the stronghold of hope in order to plant this banner of fine gold on it. But the madman, after this short spell of insanity, sees Hope, which is only a sort of veiled and sterile phantom."[11]

In the period in question, the tresses can be only Marie's. The psychoanalytic meaning of the poem is therefore clear. The castle, haunted by a single phantom, symbolizes the past, dead and finished. For the first time, Mallarmé speaks of it without recognizing it and expresses only the anxiety of the conscious mind faced with the impenetrable unconscious. However, he feels it necessary to make reality triumph—the love which the banner of fine gold stands for. Such is the hope that the apparition ruins, at the end of the poem. No doubt the cat is from Baudelaire, but possibly also from Mallarmé's free composition, for we shall find it again, in *Plainte d'automne*, directly associated with Maria's name. We shall have to speak again of the copper and the "marshes of blood" apropos also of the piece on Baudelaire in *Symphonie littéraire*. In a general way, *Château de l'espérance* is the poem of Mallarmé which most nearly resembles the nightmares of Poe. *Fenêtres* seems to be of quite a different kind.

I would like the reader to put these three images side by side: Nick Parrit in his hut—the somewhat anxious lover of *Apparition*—the dying individual in *Fenêtres*. He will thus be able to measure the ravages achieved in a short time by the conflict between dream and reality. Nothing disturbed Mallarmé's adolescent thought before love intruded; the first contact with reality agitated him; the hour of decision started a panic.

Je fuis et je m'accroche à toutes les croisées
D'où l'on tourne l'épaule à la vie. . . .[12]

[I flee, and I cling to all the windows
From which one turns his back on life. . . .]

We will soon see flight change meanings. The terror of the "sad hospital" now hurls Mallarmé toward the blue of the windows; the vengeful blue will cast him back toward the hospital. It is, in all its purity, the dilemma of the anxious who nowhere find a solution. Who hasn't experienced this, at least in dreams? Who has not waked up, terrified by the assurance that no evasion is possible? Mallarmé was in that situation when, by accepting marriage, he settled the features of his later life. "Here below there's a smell of cooking," "Here below is in control." There was nothing to do but await death while looking out the window.

I wish to stress one very important detail in Mallarmé's work. When the dream was a happy or at least a calm one, it was on this side of the glass, in the room —that is, in life. When it was an impossible one, it was shown beyond, behind the glass, still visible but forbidden. Deborah Parrit danced in her father's hut; Maspéro waited for the visit of Ettie before his fire; memories of Paphos and the Amazon of antiquity with burned breast lingered in the room, leaving the cold to skulk outside with its "scythe-like silences";[13] the sage Chinaman brought into his life the "young landscape" which he painted on his cup.[14] Behind the panes, by contrast, appeared what could never be attained: the blue, the Ideal, the Glory of setting suns, the icy constellations. We shall see later that the window—the boundary between this side and the other side—represents nothing else than the stone of the sepulcher which has grown transparent. Thus *Fenêtres* launches a symbolism to which we shall often be returning. We cannot as yet give proofs. Let us be satisfied with approximations. The window stands for the evasion of life; that much is certain. What sort of evasion? The poem indicates three.

1. Evasion in the direction of sunset.

. . . et quand le soir saigne parmi les tuiles,
Son oeil, à l'horizon de lumière gorgé,
Voit des galères d'or, belles comme des cygnes,
Sur un fleuve de pourpre et de parfums dormir
En berçant l'éclair fauve et riche de leurs lignes
Dans un grand nonchaloir chargé de souvenir!

[. . . and when evening bleeds among the tiles,
Its eye, on the horizon gorged with light,
Sees hulks of gold, beautiful as swans,

97

Sleeping on a flood of purple and perfume
Rocking the tawny rich light of their lines
In a huge nonchalance charged with memory!]
It is the triumphal dream of the instinctual life: glory,
power, love of women—temporal plenitude. Mallarmé
renounced it in advance. All that splendor was in the
past: the sun set, the galleys were antique, nonchalance
was charged with memory. Our poet was already assuming the attitude of Igitur, heir of generations whose glory
was to be snuffed out in him. The hour of physical decadence had sounded. Numerous texts, in the work and
in the letters, confirm this interpretation. Such an outlook, in a man of twenty who was by no means moribund, could be justified for only two reasons: a depressive obsession with death; and the feeling (more
objective, in a sense) that spiritual life begins where
instinctual life leaves off.

2. Evasion through poetry.

Je me mire et me vois ange! et je meurs et j'aime
—Que la vitre soit l'art, soit la mysticité—
A renaître. . . .

[I look at myself and see an angel! and I die, and
love
—Let the looking-glass be art, be mysteriousness—
To be reborn. . . .]

Here is the great resurrection theme. In an earlier version the poem read "I dream" instead of "I die."
"Dream" and "death" are equivalent terms. In characteristic fashion, "window" is rendered here as "mirror."
In Mallarmé's symbolism, the mirror can be placed
neither entirely in the room nor out of it. It constitutes
an intermediate reality between this side and the other
side, the borderline between life and death. The man
who looks at himself in it is a living person turned
toward death, toward the past. Hérodiade will search
for memories in her looking-glass. This intermediate
reality is, we have said, that of narcissistic dream. Mal-

larmé saw himself dying and being reborn in it, blending himself with the figure of the angel which is now so familiar to us. For this rebirth takes place

   Au ciel antérieur où fleurit la Beauté!

[In the earlier sky where Beauty is flowering!]
in which we again find the association seraphim—past—flowers.

3. The leap through the window.

The preceding evasion can satisfy only in dream life the desire for mystic union with the dead woman. Why settle for a dream? Why not leap into the beyond? The solution of suicide is affirmed in *Igitur*, when the crisis of anxiety has attained its maximum intensity.

   Est-il moyen, ô Moi qui connais l'amertume,
   D'enfoncer le crystal par le monstre insulté
   Et de m'enfuir, avec mes deux ailes sans plume
   —Au risque de tomber pendant l'éternité?

[Can I, O I who know bitterness,
Smash the crystal insulted by the monster
And flee, with my two unfeathered wings
—At the risk of falling for all eternity?]

The last two verses establish the intense guilt feeling which accompanied this wish. The fall became absolute.

   Let us summarize the psychological situation that is expressed in this poem. All real success in life is denied in advance, is out of reach, is forbidden in fact. Suicide would realize a guilty wish immediately punished. There remains the dream in the mirror, between real life and the tomb.

   Et nous sommes encor tout mêlés l'un à l'autre
   Elle à demi vivante et moi mort à demi.
                    Victor Hugo, "Booz endormi"

[And we are still all mingled, the one with the
      other,
She half-living and I half-dead.]

Stéphane married Marie in London on August 10, 1863. On September 17 in France he received a certificate of aptitude for the teaching of English. He assumed his duties at Tournon at the beginning of December, after he had returned to London with Marie for a brief visit in November. That is, he passed the autumn near Paris, at Passy with his grandparents or at Sens with his stepmother.

Six years before, young Maria had been buried in the cemetery at Passy. In the company of his young wife, Stéphane was once more in the place that was "charged with memory": there are numerous facts to show that his unconscious assimilated her to his dead sister. It is not too daring to suppose that the dreams of September and October, which were inevitably tender and serious, lie at the root of the poems *Soupir* and *Plainte d'automne*. The first dates from April, 1864; the second was published in July of the same year. The closest autumn is that of 1863, precisely when the memory of Maria, as *Plainte d'automne* shows, must have become confused with the picture of Marie as it appears in *Soupir*. We at once notice that in the poem Marie is called "sister":

Mon âme vers ton front où rêve, ô calme soeur,
Un automne jonché de taches de rousseur,
Et vers le ciel errant de ton oeil angélique
Monte. . . .

[My soul toward your forehead in which dreams,
    O calm sister,
An autumn strewn with russet,
And toward the sky wandering from your angelic
    eye
Mounts. . . .]

However, as soon as they settled at Tournon in December, the struggle between dream and reality started again. It no longer assumed the form it had taken in the winter preceding. The decision for a life shared with

Marie had been made; this particular crisis had been surmounted: Mallarmé would not come back to it. The arrangements he made for a modest and faithful life dispelled any idea of temporal success. There remained, then, art or suicide. Mallarmé was to make during the course of that winter a major effort to achieve the first solution: in February he wrote *Las de l'amer repos,* in which he declared:

. . . plus las sept fois du pacte dur
De creuser par veillée une fosse nouvelle

[. . . seven times wearier of the hard pact
Of hollowing out a new grave at each vigil.]

Despite this toil, in December and January he composed only *Azur* and *Angoisse,* and this contact with the dream appears to have been as painful as the contact with life in the previous winter. The atmosphere of *Azur* is one of a guilt pursued by a justice, so certain of its vengeance that it can be ironical. However fascinating it may be, the ideal is an enemy. Let us lift out of this poem the following significant words: "ironie" [irony], "accable" [crush], "maudit" [accursed], "remords atterrant" [overwhelming remorse], "mépris navrant" [harrowing scorn], "idéal cruel" [cruel ideal], "nous faire peur avec sa victoire méchante" [terrify us with its evil victory], "l'Azur . . . traverse ta native agonie ainsi qu'un glaive sûr" [Blue . . . traverses your native death throes like a sure blade], "Où fuir?" [whither to flee?]." The beyond is revealed as more hostile than the near—hostile by virtue of the single fact that it is out of reach beyond the window panes, but surely also because it awakens, as soon as one tries to draw near it, a feeling of interdiction, of taboo, hence of guilt. It is understandable that exactly in this period Mallarmé should be thrown back (at least in fantasy) on a combination of carnal love and nothingness, which had the advantage of being at the same time a flight

101

from strain and a symbolic realization of the unconscious desire for union in death. This attempt gives birth to *Angoisse* (February, 1864):

Je fuis, pâle, défait, hanté par mon linceul,
Ayant peur de mourir lorsque je couche seul.

[I flee, pale, undone, haunted by my own shroud,
Fearing to die when I sleep alone.]

For, although dreading to die, he asked "deep dreamless sleep" from her who "knows more of nothingness than the dead."

Thus one sees Mallarmé, anguished, seeking an answer in the three directions that *Fenêtres* indicated: sensuality, art, suicide. Death barred the three paths; for love conducted to a funeral bed, and the dream to a phantom. The soul fell back, then, on "bitter repose" and "ennui," a situation equally untenable. Actually, art was the only possible solution because of its progressive character—each success acquired, each poem completed, could give Mallarmé a little of that self-confidence which alone would keep him from foundering. Happily, spring seemed to bring several successes of the sort: *Fleurs, Soupir, Pitre châtié*, perhaps *Tristesse d'été*. But first a word about *Frisson d'hiver*.

The first prose poems, all famous, coming at the beginning of *Divagations—Phénomène futur, Pipe, Frisson d'hiver, Plainte d'automne,* and *Pauvre Enfant pâle,* finally *Démon de l'analogie*—were all composed around 1864, and I believe they can be assigned to the winter and spring in question. Summer was to be devoted to vacation trips, and, starting with October, Mallarmé began on *Hérodiade,* which the birth of Geneviève in November interrupted, but which was again taken up in December. Clearly, the chances of error are not great. From the psychoanalytic point of view, the general meaning of *Plainte d'automne* and *Pénultième* has been given; *Pauvre Enfant pâle,* I have said, must be compared to the *Cantique de Saint-Jean:* we shall consider it along with *Hérodiade*. *Pipe* no doubt reflects a strange overlay of the happy visit to London in November, 1863, on the terrible winter of 1862–1863. But *Frisson d'hiver* surely gives the atmosphere of the young ménage at Tournon, before Geneviève's birth. The title of the poem does not prove that it was finished at the beginning of 1864; on the contrary, the Bengali birds which figure in it were brought back from Avignon at the end of the summer.[15] In any case, the child had not yet been born: we have then a perfect right to seek the inspiration of the poem in the earlier verses. These petty details will undoubtedly weary the reader, but in a study of psychic evolution the date of an emotional nuance must be nailed down.

Fundamentally, *Frisson d'hiver* leads us back to Nick Parrit's hut. It is furnished, and the visitor is a real woman. This marks the strides made between sixteen and twenty-two. But everything happens as if the interior of the room had been so saturated with a dream that both furniture and woman had been imbued with it, and had receded from it—they the real objects and he the living person—in this intermediate fringe that separates present from past. The Saxony clock which "is slow" once came by "stagecoach"; the mirror is peopled with phantoms, nude ones (a detail which vaguely disturbs the real woman: "Bad boy, you often say wicked things"); the chest is very "old," its wood "gloomy"; the curtains are "deadened," the engravings "ancient," the Bengalis seem to have "faded" with time.

However, "peculiar shadows hang from the worn-out panes"—cobwebs, perhaps, but a bit disquieting and funereal. Again and again they appear, then tremble, "shiver at the top of great windows." We already know the window symbol. The point is that the atmosphere grows chill in spite of the tenderness of the speaker and the fire reddening the gloomy wood (in the free composition, transition from white rose to red rose signifies the change from death to life). The young woman who is called the "sister with the look of yesteryear" no doubt has a passion for the "grace of tarnished things." She wear a faded robe and leafs through an old German almanac in which "the kings it gives notice of, are all dead." But all that does not satisfy her completely, for here is the conclusion of the poem:

> . . . la tête appuyée parmi tes genoux charitables
> dans ta robe pâlie, ô calme enfant, je te parlerai
> pendant des heures; il n'y a plus de champs et les
> rues sont vides, je te parlerai de nos meubles . . .
> Tu es distraite?
> (Ces toiles d'araignées grelottent au haut de
> grandes croisées.)

> [. . . head leaning on your charitable knees in
> your faded robe, O calm child, I will speak to you
> for hours; there are no more fields, and the streets
> are empty, I will tell you of our furniture . . . You
> are disturbed?
> (These cobwebs shiver at the top of great windows.)]

This "shiver" after the marriage is the equivalent of the bouquet of sadness of the "first kiss," before. Dream and reality refuse to mix. Each shudders when the other draws near. In November, Geneviève would arrive; Marie would turn into "the young woman suckling her baby"; Stéphane would assist the new life to unfold in an atmosphere of love. But the dream would then take a sharply divergent path: *Hérodiade* would no longer have anything in common with Marie Gerhard. In this early part of 1864, on the contrary, for the last time, Mallarmé tried to assimilate life to the dream, the living woman to the dead one. For it was exactly at this point that *Plainte d'automne* came and, as we have seen, it speaks expressly of Maria; and *Soupir,* which describes Marie as Maria; *Pénultième,* going back to the dead mother; and *Symphonie littéraire,* in which, under the aegis of Baudelaire, Mallarmé once more repeats his own story.

I have said enough about *Plainte d'automne* and *Pénultième* in the first pages of this book.[16] My purpose there was to give the first proofs of the thesis to be developed thereafter. *Plainte d'automne* assumed a crucial importance at that point because its subject was obviously Maria. Going at such speed we would have loaded down the exposition by presenting the reader immediately with the bulk of the necessary interrelationships. We can now slacken pace a little and consider at what point *Plainte d'automne* and *Soupir* join.

The first of these pieces has Maria as its subject, and it is not clear to whom the second is addressed if not to Marie. In *Soupir* we find dream—calm sister—autumn—sky—angelic eye—blue—melancholy—white jet of water—October pale and pure—dead water—dying of leaves—the yellow sun trailing a long ray. *Plainte d'automne* presents corresponding terms: desperately dream—autumn—twilight of memory—white dead creature—agonizing poetry—leaves of poplars, downfall, decadence—when the sun lingers, before vanishing, with rays of yellow copper. It is in the same scenery of autumn at sunset, the same seraphic atmosphere. With one important difference: the dead Maria is absent from the first landscape, whose feeling is therefore more painful than melancholy. Marie appears in the second poem, whose attenuated sadness is thus diffused around her. The dead woman serves as a background for the living one. October has its wan purity, it is the leaves that are dying, and it is the cold water which is dead. Reflecting pools play naturally enough the role elsewhere assigned to the mirror; they signify, as in *Frisson d'hiver* and later in *Hérodiade*, the presence of the narcissistic fantasy turned toward a dead past. In *Frisson d'hiver*, Mallarmé called Marie "my sister with the look of yesteryear" and "calm child"; here he calls her "calm sister." The will to identify present with past seems obvious.[17]

The same symbolic keys will release the meaning of *Symphonie littéraire* and, particularly, the part which concerns Baudelaire. Let us recall that this piece, published in 1865, must have been completed in April, 1864, according to a Lefébure letter. It is thus contemporary with *Fleurs* and *Soupir,* and within several weeks of the first prose poems. We are not surprised to see the "dismal reflecting pools" appear in it.

. . . Dans le granit noir de leurs bords, enchassant les pierres précieuses de l'Inde, dort une eau morte et métallique, avec de lourdes fontaines en cuivre où tombe tristement un rayon bizarre et plein de la grâce des choses fanées.

[. . . In the black granite of their rims, enchasing the precious stones of India, sleeps a dead, metallic water, with heavy copper fountains upon which sadly falls a ray bizarre and full of the grace of faded things.]

These last four words figured, it will be remembered, in the sentence about the "sister with the look of yesteryear" in *Frisson d'hiver.* The dead water is that of *Soupir,* the precious stones augur *Hérodiade,* and the rim of the basins in black granite appears funereal enough to keep us from having to insist on the fact. The copper fountain recalls the "copper chateau" where black Hope lived, as the yellow copper rays recall the sunset in *Plainte d'automne* or *Soupir.*

Nulles fleurs, à terre, alentour,—seulement, de loin en loin, quelques plumes d'aile d'âmes déchues.

[No flowers, on the ground, round about—only, at long intervals, some wing feathers of fallen souls.]

The variant in *Divagations,* curiously, puts "bouquets" back in place near these true tombs. The fallen wing[18] introduces a symbol of guilt which is now familiar to us:

perhaps it shows, as the comparison with the wings of ancient birds in *Pénultième* seems to suggest, that the unconscious memory of his dead sister was here passed by and that a deeper and more melancholy plunge directly reached the Oedipal zone. But here the autumn and the sunset of *Soupir* supervene:

> Le ciel . . . verse la pâleur bleue des beaux jours d'octobre, et bientôt, l'eau, le granit ébénéen et les pierres précieuses flamboient comme aux soirs les carreaux des villes: c'est le couchant.

> [The sky . . . pours out the pale blue of fine October days, and soon, water, ebony granite and precious stones blaze as the windows of towns do at night: it is sunset.]

As to *Fenêtres*, we noted the association of sunset with the idea of the victory of time (the past) and particularly the triumph of love; this link is made explicit in the pieces to Méry. But in *Plainte d'automne* or *Soupir*, we could question whether the purpling of the sky and foliage have an erotic significance. The fire in the free composition and in *Frisson d'hiver*, the red rose of Deborah, the copper of *Château de l'espérance* awakened, in fact, such an idea. But we were entitled to see in autumn, which was associated with the memory of Maria and the face of Marie, only a kind of splendor, gloomy but absolutely pure, a decadence without guilt feelings. *Symphonie littéraire*, on the contrary, confirms the abiding presence of a guilt feeling in triumph. Here is the statement that establishes this connection; it follows directly upon the preceding quotation:

> . . . C'est le couchant. O prodige, une singulière rougeur, autour de laquelle se répand une odeur enivrante de chevelures secouées, tombe en cascade du ciel obscurci! Est-ce une avalanche de roses mauvaises ayant le péché pour parfum?— Est-ce du fard?—Est-ce du sang?—Etrange coucher du soleil! Ou ce torrent n'est-il qu'un

fleuve de larmes empourprées par le feu de ben-
gale du saltimbanque Satan qui se meut par der-
rière? Ecoutez comme cela tombe avec un bruit
lascif de baisers . . . Enfin, des ténèbres d'encre
ont tout envahi où l'on n'entend voleter que le
crime, le remords et la Mort.

[. . . It is sunset. O prodigy, a singular redness,
around which an intoxicating odor of shaken hair
pours, cascades, from the darkened sky! Is it an
avalanche of evil roses with sin for perfume?—Is
it rouge?—Is it blood?—Strange sunset! Or is this
torrent only a flood of tears purpled in the Bengal
light of the mountebank Satan, who moves from
behind? Hear how it falls with a wanton sound of
kisses . . . At last, inky shadows have overrun the
place where only crime, remorse, and Death can be
heard to flutter.]

No doubt the reader will point out that the scenery of
this text tends to exhibit Baudelaire and not Mallarmé.
We could accept this as fact if the cluster of symbols
were not precisely the one Mallarmé used for the expression of his own anxiety. Here, as always, the painter
traces his own portrait as much as his model's. He de-
picts what he understands of Baudelaire, but what he
grasps is his own, also. The images of *Symphonie littéraire* are valuable because they lead us, without transition or reason, from the dead water into a tomb that is
half-basin, half-mirror, to a night of remorse and crime,
as we pass from the fallen feather to October pale and
pure, sunset, avalanche of roses, and scattered hair.

In the free composition of 1857 we found tomb, floating hair, and flowers projected in a ruddiness that spoke
of fire and resurrection. The basin–mirror had not yet
appeared, nor the feeling of crime. Stated in another
way, the narcissistic consciousness was not as yet
haunted by an impression of decadence and guilt. This
latter feeling we have seen emerge in *Apparition;* take

shape in *Fenêtres,* after the London crisis; reappear in the winter of 1863–1864 with *Azur, Angoisse, Las de l'amer repos, Fleurs, Frisson d'hiver, Soupir, Plainte d'automne, Pénultième,* and finally *Symphonie littéraire.* Whence could it issue if not from a veto placed a priori upon everything that is purple in real life, upon all temporal success, considered as both infidelity to the dead and as only too clear, too anxiety-provoking, a realization of the Oedipal wish? The dream was fascinating but taboo; when life came too near the dream, it grew criminal; when it slipped too far away, it lost all interest.

The time has come to ask the reader's indulgence for the meanderings of this chapter. I believe that our conclusion justifies them, to a certain extent. A soul gripped with anxiety has only the desire to flee; in this respect it is simple, if you will, as living creatures are simple because each of their acts is an expression of their whole being. But this desire to flee pushes the soul toward all exits at once: that of life, of dream, and of suicide, which Mallarmé was always skirting by allusion, without ever daring to close with it.

I have assumed in the reader a knowledge of Mallarmé's life and his work. It was not for me to redo the critical work which had already been done. I wished to show how a single anxiety—guiding Mallarmé successively (if almost instantaneously) toward the real and toward the dream, fixing his attitude in the two cases, rejecting one for the other, denying him both—finally drove him to live and write in a certain style which was to be his own, and explained his development. In doing so, I do not pretend to have drafted more than a diagram; reality was to prove, as always, more complex. But this diagram has already become quite difficult to follow because it mingles outer and inner and goes from an event or a series of events (like the courtship of Stéphane and Marie) to this or that poem or series of poems. Hitherto, I think the two series had much too often been considered as independent. They tend to be so, to an extent, although the poems to Méry Laurent once more weave together very closely the threads of literary creation and those of real life; but it is near the source that this mutual dependence is strongest. Between the London crisis, the constant remoteness from life, on the one hand, and the obvious melancholy of the first works on the other, a connection seems likely. When Dr. Fretet speaks of morbid depression, he explains a certain number of depressed moments, but in no wise the texts and their networks of symbols. The obsession with the vanished dead and the double Oedipal wound, on the contrary, furnish a simple explanation both for the troubles of the living man and the obsessive metaphors of the author.

The period we have just considered is thus the one with the greatest number of reciprocal resonances. In the period from *Hérodiade* to *Igitur*, on the contrary, events play only a feeble role. The drama passes onto the plane of the interior life; but the same forces direct it. If our hypothesis is accurate, it should still be able to elucidate. We shall see how well.

4

Anxiety This Midnight

MY AIM in the first part of this book was to clear the ground and give the reader, through the use of concrete example, the general directions he would need. So in chapter 1 our thesis emerged from the comparison of certain basic texts. In chapter 2, which was devoted to the work of Dr. Fretet, I criticized his diagnosis as far too simple for our taste in that it failed to give a detailed enough psychological explanation for Mallarmé's behavior, or for his work. In chapter 3, finally, I tried to test my own hypothesis in the light of the facts of the crucial period between Mallarmé's fifteenth and twenty-second year, when the poet's spiritual and temporal destiny were settled.

After this analysis, it would seem natural to use a chronological order for the rest of the book. But as soon as we try it we run into difficulties. Of course, Mallarmé's development can be schematized. Thus, we would establish the period 1862–1868 as one of anxiety. Ideas of absolute thought and death became more and more closely associated. His metaphysical crisis sprang from his work on *Hérodiade* and threatened to become very serious after his Besançon stay. A second period would begin in the summer of 1868 with the composition of his *Sonnet en YX* and would go on through *Igitur* and *Toast funèbre* to the relatively happy Paris

111

years and then to the Méry Laurent affair. A third period would show a renewal of anxiety and the return of old themes: the *Cantique de Saint-Jean* completes *Hérodiade*, and *Coup de dés* reproduces (as I will show) the themes of *Igitur* and the *Sonnet en YX*.

Such a development of my thesis would be perfectly clear in principle. In practice it would involve many repetitions, and it would lack clarity from the psychological point of view. For if Mallarmé developed (and I am sure it is most important to show the evolution of both his life and his dreams), he did so in the course of a life-long struggle with one particular problem, which grew out of the events of his childhood and the peculiarity of his own nature. This problem, as posed to the whole personality, admitted of a number of solutions, and these could be expressed in several different attitudes, each of which had its own logic. First, the deepening anxiety, which would lead to suicide if sublimation failed. Next, resignation to what I should call boredom behind a windowpane, the acceptance of prison. This state of mind, too, admitted of nuances and a development. Finally, there was a livelier, sunnier attitude. Mallarmé often assumed this more erotic view because it corresponded to one of his basic tendencies.

These three attitudes recur throughout his life; they break the chronology. Moreover, there is another difficulty in making a close analysis of texts: Mallarmé would work on or publish at one date poems that reflected a previous state of mind. Hence a chronological study of his works does not really coincide either with his creative development or with any clear psychological order. Considering all these things (and partly to avoid innumerable repetitions), I have abandoned historical sequence, except to show the development of this or that attitude. The attitudes themselves will be the subject of the following chapters. I have defined three; they will make up chapters 4, 5, and 6.

Anxiety is, then, the subject we will broach first. Preliminary data have been furnished by the 1857–1864 texts. *Hérodiade* and the metaphysical crisis fill the winters from 1864–1868. This will be the first theme, and we will consider it only from the point of view we are using in this study. A second group includes *Sonnet en YX, Igitur,* the *Triptyque,* and *Coup de dés.* In order to avoid more useless repetition and to achieve the maximum effectiveness, I have chosen *Coup de dés* as the basis of my second analysis of anxiety (p. 128); *Igitur* and the others I shall study simultaneously in the perspective of the great poem of 1897.

"Hérodiade"

Ambivalence is the rule in Oedipal love or love that reflects a hidden Oedipal situation. Love leads on; taboo frightens away. This is easy enough to understand. But there is a point I must make even more emphatically. When the object of the fixation is already dead, no adaptation can be made; when the dead one lies inside in the dark unconscious, as in an interior tomb, there is a constant restaging of the Oedipal drama, whose protagonists are the conscious and the unconscious. The nocturnal unconscious becomes confused with the mother because it contains her; consciousness is equated with the son. I believe it is useful at least in the case of Mallarmé's own repression to take the stone that covers the tomb as representing the censor or superego. An unconscious drive—here, Mallarmé's obsession—strains to heave aside this obstacle so as to resurrect the past. But the conscious mind, which is fascinated with the doors of the sepulcher and seeks to pierce them with a glance, sees something there which is both a phantom and its own image. Meanwhile it is seized by the horror that accompanies the violation of a taboo. To repeat, there are two characters, and each carries its own contradiction within. Mother and unconscious represent the living death; son and consciousness, forbidden love that must be punished.

113

Such is the drama of *Hérodiade*. It can certainly be given symbolic meanings at different levels. Psychoanalysts will go back to Oedipal incest and the expression of infantile sexual curiosity. Nakedness surprised is a theme too well known to be emphasized. St. John the Baptist sees Hérodiade nude, and this infantile crime is punished with castration, which the beheading symbolizes, just as corporal union was symbolized by St. John's stare. When Mallarmé at the height of his metaphysical crisis wrote, "As for me . . . I have sinned by looking at the dream in its ideal nakedness, when I should have been heaping up between it and me a mystery of music and forgetfulness. And now that I have achieved the vision of a pure work I have almost lost my mind . . . ,"[1] he was merely transposing onto a spiritual plane the drama that Hérodiade and St. John the Baptist reflect in a more carnal (though veiled) manner. We shall study this transposition in *Igitur* and *Coup de dés*. Here I wish to point out that Oedipal factors—forbidden knowledge and punishment—are regularly present. The incipient madness of 1868 exactly corresponds, then, to the beheading of St. John the Baptist.[2]

But we are now only concerned with Hérodiade. Her name appears for the first time, as is well known, in the poem entitled *Fleurs:*

Et, pareille à la chair de la femme, la rose
Cruelle, Hérodiade en fleur du jardin clair,
Celle qu'un sang farouche et radieux arrose!

[And, like the flesh of woman, the cruel
Rose, Hérodiade blooming in the bright garden,
She whom a fierce and shining blood sprinkles!]

In the free composition the red rose represented the living sister. Her father had mysteriously preserved it on the chimney through the winter (and, as we shall see, had been preserved by it). The dead visitor, on the contrary, bore white roses, with which she mingled a

purple flower as she performed her dance before the
fire:

> . . . Seule demeura sur son front la couronne de
> roses blanches qu'ont les jeunes filles dans le cer-
> cueil. . . . Et quand elle commenca sa danse
> enivrée, elle cueillit quelques roses de cette cou-
> ronne, les effeuilla et, y mêlant les pistils de la
> royale rose rouge avec laquelle elle avait conservé
> son père, les jeta en l'air. . . .[3]

> [. . . Only the crown of white roses that young
> girls wear in death remained on her forehead. . . .
> And when she began her exultant dance, she gath-
> ered several roses from this crown, stripped them
> of petals, and, mingling with them the pistils of the
> royal red rose with which she had preserved her
> father, threw them in the air. . . .]

If the reader will refer to *Fleurs*, he will have no difficulty in discovering the associations of ideas that bind
this poem to Mallarmé's sister and mother: the blue of
past days, snow, stars, infancy, virginity, death. Thus
we have from the very beginning an easily decipherable
chain of images.

Let us come back to the cruel, purple Hérodiade.
Mallarmé is known to have first conceived of his heroine
in this light, which was certainly banal enough. ". . .
Did you ever happen to see Hérodiade's purpled mag-
nificence reappear in the obscure mirror which is ex-
tended by the surface of your black and twisted oak
table?" asked Lefébure in a letter of February 23, 1867.
This purple Hérodiade would have obviously been the
more traditional one. The reader can readily divine what
inner force drove Mallarmé to recoil from the purple
and choose a pale Hérodiade, whose "useless flesh" was
like the

> Nuit blanche de glaçons et de neige cruelle!

> [White night of ice and cruel snow!]

115

The guilt feeling which was awakened by experiences of love and by his first poetic efforts drove Deborah Parrit back out of the hut into the winter night and the tomb. There a sharper and more anxiety-stricken consciousness went to find her and love her.

The text of *Ouverture ancienne* being unfamiliar to many readers, I could not think of analyzing it here without reproducing it, and this detour would make my exposition too ponderous. I will therefore limit myself to a discussion of *Scène* and the *Cantique*,[4] which are so well known as not to have to be dealt with in detail. It will be sufficient to throw some light on them from the point of view we are using.

Let us notice that, from the first verses on, the young princess is identified with a dead woman:

. . . un baiser me tûrait
Si la beauté n'était la mort . . .

[. . . a kiss would kill me
If beauty were not death . . .]

Just a poetic figure, it may be said. This is doubtful, though, in view of what we find further on:

Prophétise que si le tiède azur d'été,
Vers lui nativement la femme se dévoile,
Me voit dans ma pudeur grelottante d'étoile,
Je meurs!

[Prophesy that if the summer's warm blue,
To which a woman naturally unveils,
Sees me, a chaste, shivering star,
I will die!]

This death is a punishment which supposes a previous taboo. It recalls the second death of Eurydice: we will come back to this point later.[5] Let us pause now over this idea of untouchable purity: if, as analysis of *Igitur* proves, the ideas of absolute thought and death were confused in Mallarmé's mind in 1868, in 1865 these two ideas of absolute beauty and death were already bound up in the poet's mind:

Si la beauté n'était la mort . . .

[If beauty were not death . . .]

To go on with the poem. The episode of the lions should be compared with what happens in *Soupir*. The basin, the fountain, the dream, are there. The "pale lilies" correspond to "October pale and pure." Stranger, and more richly instructive, is the way the autumn leaves of *Soupir* change into the lions of *Hérodiade*. At this point we make contact with the network of "temporal grandeur and decadence": autumn, sunset, dying torch, coiled hair, faded nobility, ragged flags, and so on. This is a set of images that is irresistibly awakened in Mallarmé by the consciousness of a fall. Because this idea of a fall, of punishment by death, goes hand in hand with every notion he has of erotic success, metaphors of the sort turn up in almost all of Mallarmé's erotic poems. But the network is even more inclusive, for it extends to every idea of temporal glory; and when eroticism entirely disappears, as in *Igitur* or *Triptyque*, the same impression of fallen loftiness is given, though it emerges in a less highly colored and more abstract form: the noble ancestors of Igitur (who are so much like those in Villiers de l'Isle Adam) have their correlatives in Sonnet I of *Triptyque*:

Tout Orgueil fume-t-il du soir,
Torche dans un branle étouffée

[Does all Pride smoke out evening,
Torch with a shake extinguished]

or

La chambre ancienne de l'hoir
De maint riche mais chu trophée

[The ancient room of the heir
Of many a rich but fallen trophy]

117

The general symbolism is of an extinguished fire. In *Divagations* we may take two new examples of it, in *La Gloire* and *La Chevelure vol d'une flamme.* I could cite twenty. We have already seen how *Plainte d'automne* exploited this symbol to combine Maria's death, the falling of leaves, and antique decadence. The moribund character in *Fenêtres* saw galleys in the gold of this same sunset. It is always the idea of past triumph. In *Soupir,* which we shall compare in more specific detail with *Hérodiade,* we see

> . . . sur l'eau morte où la fauve agonie
> Des feuilles erre au vent et creuse un froid sillon,
> Se traîner le soleil jaune d'un long rayon.

> [. . . on dead water where the tawny agony
> Of leaves wanders in the wind and hollows out a
>   cold furrow,
> The yellow sun drag a long ray.]

Now Hérodiade enters

> Sous la lourde prison de pierres et de fer
> Où de [ses] vieux lions traînent les siècles fauves.

> [Down into the heavy prison of stone and iron
> In which old lions drag the tawny centuries.]

Here are the same terms: tawny—drag. Here is the same impression: that a death is at hand. It may seem odd that lions replace autumn or setting suns, but the idea of grandeur and decadence forms an adequate link between these metaphors. The "old lions" signify: "all [male] power is forbidden, punished, and utterly unthinkable, for the dream alone is destined to reign from now on." The fire is extinguished in the verses

> Les lions, de ma robe, écartent l'indolence
> Et regardent mes pieds qui calmeraient la mer.

> [The lions dispel the indolence of my robe
> And look at my feet, which would calm the sea.]

Thus a chain of associations and poems connects the

beasts of *Hérodiade* to the death of Maria. It is extremely doubtful that Mallarmé was aware of the fact, but this need not bother us. In my opinion, at least, these lions can only gain by being placed in a network where the same sadness prevails.

Let us continue our investigation of symbols. Deborah Parrit, lifted from her tomb for a night, danced before a real fire; she dreamed little if at all, and she did not feel in the least guilty. Hérodiade dreams near chastened lions. It is because sin prowls around. The nurse is its external expression, but a rather naïve and faded version of it. No more artless proof could be given of Freud's theory of infantile sexuality than is to be found in this character of the nurse, who plays the role of temptress with such obstinacy. This same nurse recites the *Ouverture ancienne*, as if to give notice that a drama from childhood is to be staged for us.

As to Hérodiade, she is ambivalence itself; though attracted by love, as the last verses of *Scène* testify, she drives it away as if it were some sacrilege that must soon be punished.

Ce baiser, ces parfums offerts et, le dirai-je?
O mon coeur, cette main encore sacrilège,
Car tu voulais, je crois, me toucher, sont un jour
Qui ne finira pas sans malheur sur la tour . . .
O jour qu'Hérodiade avec effroi regarde!

[This kiss, these proffered perfumes and, shall I
        say it?
O my heart, this yet sacrilegious hand,
For I think you wished to touch me, make a day
Which will not cease without disaster on the
        tower . . .
O day that Hérodiade views with terror!]

Scène takes place in the morning, as *Ouverture* indicates. The day which is dawning is—as we said a moment ago—the equivalent of consciousness, of adult love, of St. John's glance. Hérodiade fears it; at each

119

new contact with reality she will recoil a bit further toward night and coldness. This is the development in *Scène.*

We started with the autumnal reverie, the one in *Soupir.* The water of the reflecting pool, though cold, was still fluid. As soon as the perfumes are offered (a second contact with reality, the first being the nurse's kiss) the pool becomes a mirror:

Eau froide par l'ennui dans ton cadre gelée . . .

[Cold water frozen by ennui, in your frame . . .] Guilt is acknowledged in the appearance of the nakedness which had been present in the Venetian looking glass of *Frisson d'hiver.* But the nurse wishes to touch a tress[6] and speaks of a mortal. To these only too specific remarks Hérodiade responds with a fantasy of escape. Where does she hide? At first, properly speaking, she descends underground:

Oui, c'est pour moi, pour moi, que je fleuris, déserte!
Vous le savez, jardins d'améthyste, enfouis
Sans fin dans de savants abîmes éblouis,
Ors ignorés, gardant votre antique lumière
Sous le sombre sommeil d'une terre première . . .

[Yes, it is for me, for me, that I flower, all alone!
You know it, amethyst gardens, buried
Endlessly in intricate, fascinating abysses,
Unknown gold, hiding your ancient light
Under the somber drowsiness of a pristine world . . .]

Hidden treasures always symbolize the maternal breast. But it may be presumed that here the somber subterranean sleep is that of death. What follows confirms this hypothesis: Hérodiade flees the "warm blue of summer" (which would see her nude) for the iciest and most terrible of beds.

. . . J'aime l'horreur d'être vierge et je veux
Vivre parmi l'effroi que me font mes cheveux
Pour, le soir, retirée en ma couche, reptile
Inviolé . . .

[. . . I love the horror of being virgin and I wish
To live amidst the terror which my hair gives me
That, by night, withdrawn into my bed, reptile
Inviolate . . .]
We are evidently approaching the image of a virgin
frozen in her tomb. Once more, I do not claim that
Mallarmé consciously realized the truth. But his uncon-
scious suggested the words to him, and suddenly we
pass from the cold virgin to the night of snow, the snow
which sparkled on Deborah Parrit's tomb:
La terre est en blanc comme une mariée et les con-
stellations limpides diamantent un ciel lacté.

Deux gémissements sinistres traversent cette
froide rêverie de la neige et du clair de lune . . .
seuls, les hauts cyprès dans l'effarement du vent
nocturne effeuillent les floraisons pensives de la
neige, pieusement et amicalement . . . "Hic jacet
Deborah Parrit . . . ," lut-il sur une pierre dont
un rayon de lune avait fondu la neige d'une façon
étrange . . .

[Earth is all white like a bride, and limpid constellations frost a milky sky.

Two sinister moans cross this icy reverie of snow
and moonlight . . . alone, the tall cypresses in the
distraction of the night wind strip the pensive
efflorescence of the snow, piously, amicably . . .
"Hic jacet Deborah Parrit . . . ," he read on a
stone from which a ray of moonlight had melted
the snow bizarrely . . .]
Here is what Hérodiade retreats to. Quite obviously
Mallarmé is portraying for us here his own flight from

life. Hérodiade represents, if you will, his infantile libido. In fright, she, also, ebbs toward her source:

> Arrête dans ton crime
> Qui refroidit mon sang vers sa source, et réprime
> Ce geste, impiété fameuse . . .

> [Restrain your crime
> Which chills my blood back toward its source, and stay
> This gesture, notorious impiety . . .]

Not even original autism is missing from this train of symbols. In the sleep of rediscovered death, Hérodiade sees herself at the center of a reality which now only reflects her:

> Et tout, autour de moi, vit dans l'idolâtrie
> D'un miroir qui reflète en son calme dormant
> Hérodiade au clair regard de diamant . . .
> O charme dernier, oui! je le sens, je suis seule.

> [And everything about me lives in the idolatry
> Of a mirror which reflects in its dreamy calm
> Hérodiade with the lucid diamond look . . .
> O supreme charm, yes! I feel it, I am alone.]

But things cannot stop there; it would mean the acceptance of suicide. The end of *Scène* succinctly gives us three symbols of potential evasion: the sealed chamber (the one, in fact, where Mallarmé has his fantasies); its opposite, a flight (". . . do you not know a land . . .") which parallels, feature for feature, the one in *Brise marine* ("I shall go"—"I would go there"); finally, carnal love itself:

> . . . Vous mentez, ô fleur nue
> De mes lèvres!

> [. . . You lie, o bare flower
> Of my lips!]

Fear of this last solution is precisely the one which had

provoked the retreat. Once it had tried all the possible exits, anxiety returned to its starting-point. Let us notice, however, that these last three symbols are barely suggested: their explanation is given in other works. The true subject of *Hérodiade* is the movement of retreat, whose stages we have noted. It starts in *Soupir* and returns through *Frisson d'hiver* to the free composition of 1857. And since the dead girl is bound by a natural tie to the dead mother, we have the entire chain, leading from the "enraptured nights" of Tournon to the Oedipal night of the unconscious.

Between *Scène* and the *Cantique de Saint-Jean,* a sin has been committed. The day and filial consciousness have dared to peer at night and the maternal unconscious. Historically, this event, or rather the thought which stands for it, corresponds to the critical period of 1867–1868: ". . . My thought has thought itself . . . I have committed the sin of becoming aware of the ideal nakedness of my dream. . . ." Actually, the event did not take place. If a real grafting had brought conscious and unconscious together, Mallarmé would not have come so near madness and suicide. He saw his own illness in such a way that he could not recognize it for what it was. He identified supreme knowledge with suicide but did not know he unconsciously meant, "I strain above everything to know a dead woman." And as that was impossible, he gave up supreme knowledge. We shall see how, in *Igitur* and *Coup de dés.* Logically speaking, *Igitur* belongs between *Scène* and *Cantique,* for the suicide of Igitur, who descends to the tomb of his ancestors and clearly recognizes death, exactly corresponds to the glance that St. John stole at Hérodiade's nakedness. And, in fact, Mallarmé had to live on and write the episode of *Igitur* in order that, a long time afterward (the interval being filled with various sublimations), when he was under the evidently renewed ascendancy of his old obsession, he might again attack the problem of *Hérodiade* and compose *Cantique* after *Igitur,* even after the punishment of Igitur. What did the unveiled Hérodiade become in Mallarmé's mind? No doubt she returned, like Eurydice, to nothingness:

. . . un baiser me tûrait
Si la beauté n'était la mort . . .

[. . . a kiss would kill me
If beauty were not death . . .]

Apparently this is the punishment as far as the unconscious is concerned: relapse. As for consciousness, the parallel punishment is castration, or decapitation— the flight of the severed spirit, madness. Icarus, Prometheus, and Kronos are blood brothers to St. John the Baptist. The punishment is the eternal parabola of what rises and falls, instead of hyperbole, which would have sanctioned flight to the infinite. And this is why the head of the decapitated saint continues to trace a parabola, descending like the sun in identical purple—for, naturally, we find in this higher fall the sunset and autumn. I should weigh down my thesis here if I were to follow this higher transposition too closely, but I did want to indicate the analogy between the sun that "redescends —Incandescent" at the beginning of *Cantique,* and the lions dragging their tawny centuries at the start of *Scène;* there is a correspondence, and the connection passes through *Plainte d'automne* and the death of Maria.

I have already said that *Plainte d'automne* had, significantly, been published at the same time as *Pauvre Enfant pâle,* under the same dedication to Charles Baudelaire. *Pauvre Enfant pâle* conjures up a young street singer Mallarmé probably saw in London. Allusions to the emotional situation of Mallarmé himself are obvious. The subject is the loneliness of a child, who wears himself out by singing too loudly and who must earn a hard living. He achieves the inevitable fate of the criminal, who pays for his mistake by decapitation: ". . . Your head is continually erect and wishes to quit you, as if it knew in advance. . . ."[7] The analogy between this head leaving the body to take flight, and the parabola of *Cantique*, is obvious. Furthermore, we read in the prose poem: "You probably came into the world with that bent, and from now on you will be fasting . . . ,"[8] which corresponds to the strophe:

Qu'elle de jeûnes ivre
S'opiniâtre à suivre
En quelque bond hagard
    Son pur regard

[Let it, intoxicated with fasting,
Follow obstinately
In some wild leap
    Its pure stare]

Finally, in both cases, a fatal, punished crime is involved. *Pauvre Enfant pâle* is not very different from *Aumône* and the vaguely anarchistic revolt of Mallarmé's first years. *Cantique*, on the other hand, was written at the end of Mallarmé's life, when his mind was soaked in symbols and was as remote as it could possibly have been from social reality. The crime had for a long time been entirely interior, but the correspondences between the two texts are no less striking, just as they are in the case of the double identification between Maria and the poor London singer on the one hand, and Hérodiade and the Mallarmé–St. John the Baptist of 1895, on the other.

I should like to say one word more for the reader who is shocked by the crudeness of the term "castration." We cannot avoid it in explicating the classic myths. I have spoken of the god Kronos. The scythe that Time holds is no doubt the one that brings death. But let us not forget that Kronos gelded his father Ouranos and in turn was castrated by his own son Zeus. Being put to death, being castrated, being dethroned, are synonymous in the infantile unconscious, where an implacable law of talion is the rule.[9] It is certainly the scythe of Kronos that we find in *Cantique*. It is also the one with which the "fatal law" threatens the old Dream, "desire and sickness of my bones." Yet the loftiest spiritual interpretations are not thereby excluded, either as regards the myth or the poem.

Along with the scythe, there is the blood. Its appearance is rare in Mallarmé's work; let us note, however, that we have already met it in *Château de l'espérance*, when the issue was precisely the assault on the unconscious:

> Mon coeur à son passé renonce
> Et, déroulant ta tresse en flots
>
> Marche à l'assaut, monte,—ou roule ivre
> Par des marais de sang,— . . .
>
> [My heart renounces its past
> And, unrolling your hair in waves,
>
> Marches to the attack, mounts—or rolls intoxicated
> In marshes of blood— . . .]

It is, as we have said, a nightmare à la Poe, and its marshes have analogues in the "warm marshes of Auber" in *Ulalume*. Blood reappears in *Symphonie littéraire*, between the sunset and the night of crime, remorse and death:

> . . . O prodige, une singulière rougeur, autour de laquelle se répand une odeur enivrante de chevelures secouées, tombe en cascade du ciel obscurci! Est-ce une avalanche de roses mauvaises ayant le péché pour parfum?—Est-ce du fard?—Est-ce du sang?—Etrange coucher de soleil! Ou ce torrent n'est-il qu'un fleuve de larmes empourprées par le feu de bengale du saltimbanque Satan qui se meut par derrière? . . .

[. . . O prodigy, a singular redness, around which an intoxicating odor of shaken hair pours, cascades, from the darkened sky! Is it an avalanche of evil roses with sin for perfume?—Is it rouge?— Is it blood?—Strange sunset! Or is this torrent only a flood of tears purpled in the Bengal light of the mountebank Satan, who moves from behind? . . .]

Thus, the same association between the ideas of Sin and blood is everywhere renewed. The connection between the setting sun and death is explicitly given in the sonnet *Victorieusement fui le suicide beau*. Poe worked might and main to elicit the macabre; Mallarmé scarcely touches it. Suffice it then to point it out. The higher level of meaning of *Cantique* is of course to be found elsewhere: in the idea that the parabola, even if it is a flight that falls back to earth, remains a flight which the glance tangential to its trajectory can pursue to infinity:

Là-haut où la froidure
Eternelle n'endure
Que vous le surpassiez
  Tous ô glaciers

[Above, where eternal
Bitter cold does not permit
You to surpass it,
  O all glaciers]

And these higher glaciers are exactly symmetrical with the

Nuit blanche de glaçons et de neige cruelle!

[White night of ice and cruel snow!]

into which Hérodiade retreated. The princess of the unconscious has gone back down to the Lower Depths; the glance of the conscious saint mounts toward Principle. Thus the drama concludes. It ends magnificently, but it does so by a separation and a flight toward two frigidities.

"COUP DE DÉS"

Coup de dés was written thirty years after *Scène d'Hérodiade*, but at the same time as *Cantique de Saint-Jean*. As we will show, a very close connection ties it to *Igitur*, to the *Sonnet en YX*, and to *Triptyque*. This same vein, now apparent, now hidden, but continuous, crops out between 1862 and 1870 and then more or less disappears, only to reappear in Mallarmé's last years. We indicated in the preliminary note[10] the reasons which led us to take *Coup de dés*, after *Hérodiade*, as the center of our study, grouping other works around it.

The title of the poem, as is well known, forms the dorsal bone of its structure. The work of art is organized around this intellectual proposition: A CAST OF DICE NEVER WILL ABOLISH CHANCE. What would this mean to a mathematician? This, I presume: that, extraordinary as it may be, a fluctuation is still a part of chance. In the language of probability, "miraculous" means "extremely rare"; but the rare is still possible. Everyone knows what Borel[11] has called the "miracle of typewriting monkeys."[12] One may, if he desires, compare Mallarmé with Borel. Both meditated upon the strong improbability that there is such a thing as philosophic order, and both apparently class order, or what appears to be order, as a sort of quite improbable disorder.[13] Suppose that someone marked on a blackboard all the possible closed curves: he would undoubtedly find many a grotesque figure among them, but also, at least once and even an infinity of times, he would find the perfect circle. What we call a regular law would thus be only a particular case in the sum of the imaginable irregularities. This fascinating thought leads the mind straight to atheism, since it envelops all the small orders we worship in an immense disorder and makes all our gods into extraordinary accidents of chaos.

I have drawn this conclusion to show that it is not at all foreign to Mallarmé's intellectual pessimism. Mallarmé may very well have thought this himself, thus attaching this general meaning to the chief idea of his poem. I shall grant it, however, only a very limited importance. Unquestionably Mallarmé struggled with this idea of triumphant chaos, and, to the extent that his intelligence deemed it irrefutable, he perhaps found it one of those "funereal ceilings" against which his "certain wing" (*aile indubitable*) beat. In passing, it should be said that this ceiling is easily broken through: if intelligence sees order as only one of the possible disorders, this simply means that order outrides our intelligence, which perceives on its plane only the projection of it, like the famous Platonic shadow on the wall of the cave. If the cave of intelligence is shown, in the final analysis (as the most modern scientific knowledge seems to prove), to be the true realm of possibilities and their combinations, all the shadows on the wall, ordered or disordered, will be chance shadows. Thus the point of view, not the reality of things, is impeachable. If Mallarmé had furnished the human treasury of spirit with no more profound thought than this one, it would not be reasonable to spend much time on *Coup de dés*. Happily, something quite different is involved.

I propose the following thesis. In 1868, at Avignon, Mallarmé reached the lowest point of a depressive crisis which had been weighing on him for several years, especially during the winter he worked on *Hérodiade*. The causes of this depression are, in my opinion, psychoanalytic. When Mallarmé returned to himself and to poems "merely tinted with the absolute," he resolved the crisis by writing *Igitur*. The characteristic of this text is to make a very close association between the ideas of absolute thought and of death. At the end of the story, association becomes fusion, and the two ideas are realized in a unique event, the metaphysical suicide of the hero. However, as I have suggested, Mallarmé personally avoided suicide and at the same time renounced both death and the absolute. He lived and worked on; a son, his second child, was born in 1871. The poems of the following period, especially *Toast funèbre* and the sonnet *Quand l'ombre menaça*, show us a Mallarmé fully armed against the fascination of death. Pushing back into the tomb "all that injures," he lodged human happiness in "the burning glory of the craft," the flowering of earthly talent. The love affair with Méry Laurent, various friendships, and literary success reinforced to a certain extent this attachment to life. But opposite these credits must be registered these painful debits: the death of his son in 1879, the break-up with Méry, and the fact that his work was always being put off and completed only in scraps, with great difficulty. Mallarmé was once more to fall into a depression which, if less anguished and far more secret than the first,[14] is detectable because of one essential fact: that the themes of the first depressive period reappeared in his poetry. Thus Mallarmé, in his very last years, took up *Hérodiade* again, wrote or corrected the *Cantique de Saint-Jean,* and published *Triptyque,* which, we shall see, is a new version of *Sonnet en YX* and *Igitur*. And thus the sea and the shipwrecks of *Brise marine* reappear in *Au seul souci de voyager,* *A la nue accablante tu,* and finally *Coup de dés.* Passing through the same emotional and mental state (with, however, the experience which had accrued from life and from his poetic virtuosity), Mallarmé naturally hit on the same thoughts again. *Coup de dés,* then, represents in the second depressive crisis what *Igitur* did in the first. We find in it the affirmation that absolute thought and death are necessarily fused. But there is this difference: in *Igitur* the metaphysical suicide of the hero effectually realized this fusion in a unique act; in *Coup de dés*, the act fails because of impotent hesitation (as in the life of the poet), and the affirmation is now given only in a conditional form: if the act *had* taken place, it would have consummated the union of thought and death.

I have made a resumé of my thesis in order to enable the reader to grasp it in its entirety. I shall now develop it briefly. The depressive crisis which lasted from 1862 to 1869 has been brought in here as a reminder. The only real point of interest to us is the association between the ideas of absolute thought and death which is the result of that crisis. *Igitur*, in fact, has no other subject. Sending the reader back to the text for further inquiry, I shall cite only a few passages. Here is one, in which is to be found the notion of shipwreck that *Coup de dés* will illustrate:

. . . le mal que je souffre est affreux, de vivre . . . il faut que je meure, et comme cette fiole contient le néant par ma race différé jusqu'à moi (ce vieux calmant qu'elle n'a pas pris, les ancêtres immémoriaux l'ayant gardé seul du naufrage), je ne veux pas connaître le Néant, avant d'avoir rendu aux miens ce pourquoi ils m'ont engendré . . .

[. . . frightful, the agony I suffer—merely living . . . I must die, and as this phial contains the nothingness which my race has postponed until I should arrive (this old sedative that my immemorial ancestors did not take, having salvaged it alone from the shipwreck), I do not want to know Nothingness, before giving them back what they engendered me for . . .]

Here is the throw of dice:

Je profère la parole, pour la replonger dans son inanité. Il jette les dés, le coup s'accomplit, douze, le temps (minuit)—qui créa se retrouve la matiére, les blocs, les dés—

[I pronounce the word in order to plunge it back into its inanity. He flings the dice, the toss is achieved, twelve, the time (midnight)—what was even now creative turns back into matter, blocks, dice—]

The chapter entitled *Le Coup de dés* begins with the following sentences:

Bref dans un acte où le hasard est en jeu, c'est toujours le hasard qui accomplit sa propre Idée en s'affirmant ou en se niant. Devant son existence la negation ou l'affirmation viennent échouer.

[In brief, in an act in which chance is at play, it is always chance which accomplishes its own Idea by affirming or denying itself. Against its being, negation or affirmation runs aground.]

These three texts would suffice—if it were necessary—to establish the connection between the 1869 story and the 1898 poem. It is no longer disputable that the act by which Igitur realizes his absolute thought is suicide. Generations of ancestors, wave on wave, shipwreck on shipwreck, have repeatedly deferred this act, left life as a legacy, permitted time and chance to unfold in all their manifestations. Their last heir, henceforth in complete and conscious lucidity, is to end the cycle by an ultimate act. He leaves the room where time is dying, descends to the tombs, carries with him the phial containing "the drop of nothingness which the sea lacks," and, before the ashes of his ancestors, closes the book, extinguishes the lamp, drinks of the phial, and rolls the dice. When they stop, according to the wonderful image given in the second quotation above, time ceases and nothing more remains, then, but space and inert matter—the cube. Meanwhile Igitur lies stretched out, on the tomb of his ancestors. What could be more romantically explicit?

As for the philosophic meaning which is ascribed to this deed by Mallarmé, it must be sought in the sentences on chance which have already been quoted. Probably following Hegel, Mallarmé conceives of reality and its process as the unfolding of the consequences of an idea. The word "chance" in this context no longer has simply the abstract meaning we have just given it. Its principle is the unfolding, in time, of a game—the game of life and death. Once chance is given this meaning, it logically develops consequences: events themselves. Thus generations of ancestors have followed one another. They have formed moments in chance, and have submitted to its law, as a fatality, without understanding it very well. The last in the family line, who is the hero of the tale, comes upon the scene. He is named Igitur, that is, *therefore*, and his name signifies that he is going to conclude, to conduct the sequence of generations to its logical end, as the last proposition of a theorem ends a series of arguments, consummates it, and validates it. For in this final hero, the Idea which has been developing until he comes along finally achieves an awareness of itself. He does not submit to the law; he recognizes it and knows that he is its last term. Now what is the destined end of "chance"? Nothingness. As mathematicians say, the sum of fluctuations is necessarily zero. So the idea, which has unfolded from generation to generation and and has finally achieved awareness of itself and of its law in the person of this last heir, recognizes itself as something whose sum is nothing and whose essence is nothingness. Approval of himself, of his law, of his ancestral development, and of his end thus amounts to an approval of nothingness. This *yes*, spoken at one and the same time to the sum of earlier fluctuations (that is, to the life of his ancestors) and to the nullity of this sum (that is, to the death of their heir), forms the logical essence of Igitur's suicide. The Idea in him thinks itself nothingness, THEREFORE (Igitur) *becomes* nothingness, and ceases to be.

I shall not pause to criticize this thesis. It assimilates

133

the flow of real things to a deductive development—in itself a distorted thought: we again find the shadow on the wall of the cave. But it is clear that the pessimism of the conclusion is surreptitiously introduced into the premises from the moment life and love are presented as a game of chance. This is to affirm a priori the final triumph of nothingness in indifference. Anyone is perfectly free to adopt such an attitude, and I do not dream of contesting this right; I maintain only that what is involved is an attitude, chosen for irrational reasons and not on the basis of proof. We shall therefore have to examine the irrational motives that prompted and probably forced Mallarmé to gamble (intellectually, at least, for in practice he made the opposite bet) on nothingness and pessimism. For the moment, let us pursue our thesis as we have summarized it above.

We have established the first point. At the period of *Igitur*, Mallarmé's mind associated, to the point of fusing them, the ideas of absolute thought and death. I do not know if I have clearly enough indicated that Mallarmé means by absolute thought "awareness of self." Absolute thought is thought that thinks itself. Mallarmé says this expressly in a famous letter (May 14, 1867): ". . . my Thought has thought itself and has achieved a pure Conception." The reflexive verb is significant. The content of the thought has disappeared as unimportant. What counts is that it has seen itself in the mirror. Narcissism and nothingness here form a combination which are known equally to mystics and psychiatrists. This point of extreme consciousness and worthless rational thought is precisely where the irrational enters the game and bets for or against life. At the moment when he wagers (in practice) for life, Mallarmé in *Igitur* tells us how one wagers against life. For it is thus that he conceives his work when he writes, in a letter of November 14, 1869, referring to *Igitur:* "It is a tale by which I want to defeat that old monster

134

Impotence, which, by the way, is its subject, in order to cloister myself in the great work which I have already restudied. If it [the tale] is completed I am cured; *Similia Similibus*." We must beware of the disavowal that Mallarmé thus gives his own pessimistic thought. The mental outlook of Igitur is one the poet shared during his crisis. When Mallarmé recounts it, he has already passed through it. I will not say that his association death—absolute thought was broken. He simply gave up these two extreme terms in order to entertain living ideas more easily.

This evolution was to be followed for many long years. In order to study it, we would have to take up in detail the events and works in Mallarmé's life from 1870 to about 1890. We cannot do this here, but everyone will agree that these twenty years are marked with less anxiety than the preceding years were. We do not find the Paris texts repeating any of the depressive symptoms that were so conspicuous in those of Tournon or Besançon. *Toast funèbre* to Théophile Gautier seems to me characteristic in this respect. A tomb appears as in *Igitur*, but far from associating the ideas of death and of thought, the poem has precisely the aim of distinguishing them. "Niggardly silence and the massive night" are shut up carefully in the sepulcher; lucid thought and the word which expresses it flower in the garden sunlight, the poet's proper place being explicitly on the garden side, not on the tomb side. Worse: the dream must be expelled from Eden. Now, the dream always has for Mallarmé this twin flavor of death and the absolute, of which *Toast funèbre* thus banishes even the memory. If then the fatal association is not broken, it at least appears to be vigorously repressed. I do not have time in this chapter to explain how the Méry Laurent affair at once disperses and subtly recalls it (*Victorieusement fui le suicide beau*). I must come to *Coup de dés* itself.

Let us be specific first as to what the essential terms

135

mean. "Cast of dice" signifies "thought." This is expressly stated in the poem: "Every Thought casts the Dice."[15] We thus find one of the two terms that are so closely associated in *Igitur:* the supreme cast of dice corresponds to an absolute thought. Let us go on to the word "chance" (*hasard*). It also retains the significance which *Igitur* gives it: the unfolding in time of the fluctuations of life and death. The waves of the sea are its natural symbol. Let us recall that, in the game as imagined, death finally triumphs. The word "chance" tends to assume thereafter the meaning "indifferent nothingness": Mallarmé speaks of the "identical neutrality of the gulf" into which everything collapses. The waves formed in it fall back into it, and nothing has happened. What, then, does the principal motif of the poem express? A CAST OF DICE NEVER WILL ABOLISH CHANCE translates as "a thought will never conquer nothingness" (or, if you like, "death"). This assertion is handed us bare of the logic which leads to it, but the steps are easily found by means of inferences from *Igitur.* What thought, if not absolute thought, could overcome death? Now this absolute thought, constituting an element of chance, could only be this chance achieving awareness of itself, of its Idea, of its law, of its totality, that is, of its nothingness. Far from triumphing over chance, absolute thought would return to and disappear in it. Since relative thought could not do what is denied to absolute thought, a thought will never vanquish nothingness, a cast of dice will never abolish chance. Q. E. D. Thus the motif of the 1898 poem reaffirms the thesis of the 1869 story—the apparently indissoluble association between the ideas of absolute thought and of death.

I should now like to go into some detail, though without lingering, and point out, first, a contrast. *Igitur* affirmed crudely: thought leads to death—and the logical conclusion was suicide. *Coup de dés* says: thought will struggle in vain, nothingness has won in advance,

136

and so the only solution is ironic resignation. It is, therefore, fair to say that Mallarmé resumed in 1898 the intellectual attitude he held in 1869, but his emotional attitude had changed greatly. Between the two dates there occurred, after his renunciation of suicide, his struggle for life and work, "chance conquered word by word." This ordeal left basically intact a pessimistic faith which was too tightly bound (as I shall show) to childhood events to be modified by anything; it was this inner fatality which, assuming the form of an unavoidable deduction, imposed itself on Mallarmé as an obvious fact: why expect a cast of dice to abolish chance when it is itself a part of chance? Nothing could break the really inevitable (and irrational) association between thought and death. It grew less inflexible, a little less "black and white," however. Step by step, Igitur descended to suicide, with an inhuman, mad assurance. *Coup de dés*, by contrast, shows in succession scornful pity, irony, horror, a bitter and shuddering hilarity, resignation before nothingness, and hope, in spite of everything, of a constellation rising above the abyss.

This emotional iridescence deserves to be examined from two points of view. On the one hand, it determines the style and movement of the poem which constitute the higher (aesthetic) meaning we are not considering here. But on the other hand it reveals the surface outcropping of the unconscious and subterranean reality of the poem. We will now descend into this sort of hypogeum in order to explore the symbolic structure. Perhaps, however, and for this same purpose, it may be useful to note here briefly the principal external divisions of *Coup de dés*: the reader familiar with the work will pardon these pointers as supererogatory for him.

The title of *Coup de dés*, as reproduced in the text, forms, as we have seen, the dorsal spine. Between the words of this chief motif, three scenes are grafted, in the following arrangement: A CAST OF DICE NEVER

(scene A) WILL ABOLISH (scene B) CHANCE (scene C).
Let us take them one by one:

Scene A. *The shipwreck*

In the tempest, on the ocean of chance, the Master
can shoot the dice which will assure him control.
He hesitates, and a wave carries him off. His fist, still
closed on the Number which he has not thrown, pro-
trudes for an instant above the waves, bequeathing this
supreme knowledge to an indeterminate heir.

Scene B. *Hamlet*

Over the gulf that the shipwreck has just created, a
"vortex of hilarity and horror" suspends the spray. The
highest of the foam flecks comes to serve as the plume
on the toque of an apparition. Hilarity, horror, irony
take shape. The laughter of Hamlet suggests that if
the cast of dice so avariciously held by the old man
were indeed the Number of numbers, absolute thought,
it would have been CHANCE, anyway.

Scene C. *The abyss and the constellation*

Only a ripple agitates the surface of the abyss. Nothing
has actually happened, and the result would have been
equally nil if absolute thought had been uttered. However, above the abyss shines a constellation which perhaps reckons up "some final computation in process of
being formed."

In the preface to *Coup de dés,* Mallarmé declares,
without being more explicit, that the poem involves a
"principal motif, a secondary motif, and adjacent ones."
There is no question about the principal motif: it is the
statement in the title. The secondary motif is, in my
opinion, the one put in italicized capitals which have
the greatest size after the capitals of the principal
motif.[16] Main and secondary motifs, having the same
ending, form a sort of fork, like two rivers which have
the same mouth:

Si c'était le Nombre ce serait

LE HASARD

UN COUP DE DÉS JAMAIS N'ABOLIRA

[If it were the number it would be

CHANCE

A CAST OF DICE NEVER WILL ABOLISH]

Thanks to an extensive use of the most relaxed grammatical methods—appositions, parentheses, suspensions—the adjacent motifs are ranged about almost at will. Thus the pages are designed in such a way that each composes a sort of engraving. If they were printed in a folding album, the poem could be spread out on the wall like a long Chinese painting.

For a psychoanalyst, the Oedipal significance of *Coup de dés* would be unquestionable at first glance. In dreams and myths, the sea is one of the most frequent symbols for the mother. A large part of the analysis devoted by Marie Bonaparte to this theme in Edgar Allan Poe's work would fit here. All mythological heroes who descend to the region of the dead are confronted with seas or funereal rivers. Let us note, in support of the unconsciously sexual character of this symbol, that the Master of *Coup de dés* merges with the sea in a death which is also a marriage. The Number, not thrown into the tempest, is bequeathed by the closed fist of the old man to the shadow of a possible son.

né d'un ébat la mer par l'aïeul tentant ou l'aïeul contre la mer une chance oiseuse, Fiançailles, dont le voile d'illusion rejaillit, leur hantise . . . chancellera, s'affalera, folie!

[born of a frolic, the sea through the ancestor tempting a futile chance, or the ancestor in opposition to the sea tempting a futile chance, Betrothal, whose veil of illusion resurges, their obsession . . . will totter, fall, madness!]

139

The words "frolic" and "Betrothal," as well as the "legacy" to a son who could have been, show distinctly the fusion between death and sexual union with the sea. In *Igitur*, the fusion is complete. Here, on the other hand, death is not voluntary; the cast of dice has not been attempted; the consummation of the act has not taken place, the betrothal appears to be illusory and their obsession to be mad. The two terms are dissociated, the impotent ancestor knows death without having known the mother. Here, I repeat, is what a psychoanalyst would make of it at first glance. The cast of dice which, in Mallarmé's consciousness, is bound to thought ("Every Thought casts the Dice"), would appear to a psychoanalyst as bound in the unconscious to the sexual act, the act par excellence—and particularly, to that supreme act of love which would be union with the dead woman. Leaving this interpretation of universal symbols, let us follow the specific threads that betray themselves in the work.

Igitur flings his dice among tombs; he has descended there by a staircase walled with the brightest and most symmetrical panels, whose alternate succession around him echoes other movements—those of his heart, of a double swinging door above the steps, and of the pendulum clock beyond. These movements, these noises, are those of time, which is about to end. In *Coup de dés*, the descent is made into the cavern of waves, between liquid panels, and the alternating motion is given by this span of billows, at once sail and wing. It is what Mallarmé on page 3 [of *Coup de dés*] calls the "alternating sail," the oblique sliding of which the whole text indicates. One finds nothing in *Coup de dés* concerning the point where this descent began; the poem starts there. But in *Igitur* one discovers a clearly recognizable room, where time grows faint, where work is done under the lamp, on black books with "ancient computations," among furniture, vague monsters, between a mirror and a window. Here each detail is known to the reader of Mallarmé. The "angelic" lamp is the one "which still knows" the poet's agony. The mirror is the one in which the "naked dead girl" appears, that of *Frisson d'hiver* and *Hérodiade*. If one draws the heavy curtains from the window, he will see brightly shining the star of the dead young sister, the moon of the free composition, the one painted by the "Chinaman of limpid heart and subtle," the one Hérodiade again conjures up; and if the moon is absent, it will be replaced by the "septuor" of "scintillations" (found at the end of *Coup de dés*) or by the musical and maternal whiteness of dawn. Now, as to the angelic lamp at the window, we can attach every symbol of it to the dead mother and sister.

In 1868, we have said, Mallarmé reached a critical stage and, faced by the threat of illness or insanity, gave up. It was then that he wrote *Ses purs ongles très haut* and *Igitur*. Sonnet and story have obvious connections, and since they reveal a sequence, which is taken up again under another form in *Triptyque* (I. *Tout Orgueil;* II. *Surgi de la croupe;* III. *Une dentelle*), it is by a comparison of these various pieces with *Coup de dés* that we shall most nearly realize the meaning of this poem. Let me, for the sake of clarity, outline here in a sort of table the correspondences between these four pieces.[17] The principal divisions mark the successive moments of a sort of drama.

A. Anxiety: The room of time
    1. *Sonnet en YX*, first quatrain: anxiety and funereal dreams in the empty room at midnight.
    2. *Igitur:* the room where time dies, at midnight.
    3. *Triptyque I:* the "ancient room of the heir" and its marble chimney like a tombstone, at night.
    4. *Coup de dés:* no scenery; "ancient computations" from which the Master will rise, at midnight.
B. The descent toward death and the empty phial
    1. *Sonnet en YX*, second quatrain: the Master has

descended to the Styx with an empty seashell (dead woman).

2. *Igitur:* descent to the tombs with the "phial of nothingness."
3. *Triptyque II:* the vase of "widowhood" refuses this "most funereal kiss," a "rose in the shadows."
4. *Coup de dés:* the empty hull of a vessel descends into the Maelstrom.

C. The tomb ajar: I. Dream (this side) of union in death
   1. *Sonnet en YX,* first tercet: in the mirror, unicorns assail a nixy, "naked dead woman."
   2. *Igitur:* consummation of the suicide.
   3. *Triptyque III,* quatrains: blasphemous revelation at dawn of what must be a bed; wavering white lights which unite.
   4. *Coup de dés:* lucid and simultaneously nocturnal foam; apparition of an androgynous Hamlet.

D. The opened tomb: II. The birth in the musical and starlit beyond
   1. *Sonnet en YX,* second tercet: "septuor" of "scintillations" replacing the "naked dead woman."
   2. *Igitur:* nothing.
   3. *Triptyque III,* tercets: birth toward a window, outside the "musical nothingness" of the mandora.
   4. *Coup de dés:* the constellation after the shipwreck.

I do not insist on the correspondence between the first quatrain of *Sonnet en YX,* the room of *Igitur,* and that of *Triptyque I.* Absent in *Coup de dés,* it is the room of "ancient computations" and of anxiety, and if we think this anxiety has something to do with a dead past, we are confirmed in the hypothesis by the "cinerary amphora" of *Sonnet en YX,* the theme and innumerable details of *Igitur,* and this marble of a sepulcher that *Triptyque I* delineates and that the "claws" of the past held down. The second quatrain of *Sonnet en YX* treats of this empty vase, "only object with which nothingness honors itself," with which the Master descends to the Styx. Let us recall that, in his descent to the tombs, Igitur bears the "phial of nothingness." Hence the parallelism is quite marked. For a psychoanalyst, every vase is a female symbol; the vase of the phial containing nothingness conjures up, then, a dead woman; to drink of it symbolizes union in death with her. Now *Triptyque II* deals with a vase of "inexhaustible widowhood," which dies without consenting to a "most funereal kiss" (this kiss would produce the "rose in the shadows" which earlier—in the free composition of 1857—overtly symbolized the girl gone from the tomb: the living dead girl). Let us note that the "ptyx" of *Sonnet en YX* is a seashell, a female sexual symbol. In *Coup de dés* the sea has replaced interiors: the descent to the Styx and Igitur's stairway have become an investigation of the abyss (in dreams, the stairway is a classic symbol of the sexual act; here, the descent no doubt adds the funereal note). What new form has the empty vase assumed, then? Probably that of the boat, another female symbol, and its empty hull, vaguely confused with the shadow at the bottom of the swell: "its yawning depth resembling the hull of a vessel bent to the one or the other side." The dice are not cast, just as in *Triptyque* the funereal kiss is refused by the vase. Only in *Igitur* is the act explicitly achieved, for *Sonnet en YX* describes the chamber of the Master—or of Igitur—after the latter has quit it to descend to the dead (Styx or tombs), and one is uncertain whether the act is completed. Inevitably, then, *Igitur* stops at this point: nothing can follow avowed suicide. But in the other pieces something replaces the act which did not occur: the vision. The beyond which has not been achieved will be imagined in some form.

Charles Baudouin, in an article published in *Psyché*,[18] notes, apropos of Easter dreams which he has collected, that the resurrection of the dead, the tomb opened into the beyond, the stone once drawn back, are symbolized by a window's rectangle. I had arrived at this conclusion for Mallarmé, without conceiving the symbol to be so universal. Windows' beyond, let us recall, signifies life's beyond, this "other thing" toward which art tends. It is probable that, on the one hand, the mirror symbolizes the dream in a more conscious, more narcissistic and anxious state. The window's beyond, on the other hand, has itself achieved a sort of definitive truth and peace. This double stage is thus represented in *Sonnet en YX*, at first by the nude female phantom of the nixy in the mirror; and then, after her agony and death, by the reflection of a bright musical constellation proceeding from the window. It is as if the dream itself permitted two conditions: the appearance of the dead one in the open tomb, and her starry resurrection. In *Triptyque III*, correspondingly, it is the curtains before the windowpanes which replace the mirror. The window opens upon an absence of bed; only fleeing lace, joined in pairs, speaks vaguely of white union; the funereal note is given again by the words "abolished" and "entombed." Then there appear, not the constellation or the crescent, but dawn and the sad musicality of an eventual birth out of the womb of a mandora. Different though the tonality may be, one sees that all the elements of the resurrection are present.

What corresponds to them in *Coup de dés?* The constellation rises at the end, with strict fidelity, and, as the two Masters of *Sonnet en YX* and *Coup de dés* descended with an identical impulse toward the waters of death, the two groups of stars rise, one in the "empty Northern window," the other "toward the Septentrion, also North." Like the stars and moon of the free composition, like the crescent of the Chinaman of limpid heart and subtle, like the bright stars in the "cold night of ice and cruel snow" with which Hérodiade identifies herself, these constellations represent a purity that night and death put out of reach. They shine in the beyond of our temporal life: this is why they are exhibited behind the window (outside the room in which time passes and dies), or again, in *Coup de dés,* "as far as a place unites with the beyond," out of space where chance triumphs. All this signifies what is behind the gates of the tomb, in the tomb whose window represents the gaping mouth. There is nothing here that is not perfectly coherent and intelligible.

The second scene of *Coup de dés,* the one that is inserted between the words ABOLIRA and LE HASARD, is a little more difficult to interpret. According to the logic of our correspondences, this episode would have as a parallel the appearance of phantoms in the mirror or the vague union of curtains: the dream in its most anguished, most fantastic, as well as most conscious, state. It is not surprising that the person of Hamlet appears at this instant (the reader would be well advised to return to the résumé given above for the argument of this part of the poem). Hamlet symbolizes the eternal self-questioning of a consciousness in terrible crisis. Such is in fact the meaning of what could be called, in Mallarmé's case, anxiety before the mirror. Furthermore, it is not so much a question of rational investigation as it is of awakened dream and the evocation of phantoms. Recall Hérodiade "desolated with dreams" and seeking memories like leaves in the mirror. Mallarmé sees Hamlet in much the same way. Rereading the pages devoted to Hamlet in *Divagations* is enough to bring conviction:

   . . . il n'est point d'autre sujet, sachez bien: l'antagonisme de rêve chez l'homme avec les fatalités à son existence départies par le malheur. . . . L'adolescent évanoui de nous aux commencements de la vie et qui hantera les esprits hauts et pensifs par le deuil qu'il se plaît à porter, je le reconnais, qui se débat sous le mal d'apparaître: . . . oui, fou en dehors et sous la flagellation contradictoire du devoir, mais s'il fixe en dedans les yeux sur une image de soi qu'il y garde intacte autant qu'une Ophélie jamais noyée, elle! prêt toujours à se ressaisir.

[. . . there is, you must realize, no other subject: the antagonism of man's dream to the fatalities of his existence as they are bestowed by misfortune. . . . The adolescent who has faded from us at the beginnings of life, who will haunt lofty, thoughtful souls by the mourning he is pleased to wear, who struggles under the misfortune of appearing to them, I recognize: . . . yes, mad on the outside and under the contradictory flagellations of duty, but if he, always ready to recover, looks within at an image of himself kept safe like an Ophelia, she! never drowned.]

This inner Ophelia is of extreme importance, for we may naturally suppose that Mallarmé identified himself more or less with Hamlet, as with Hérodiade. And let us not forget that he also possessed an interior Ophelia: this Maria, of whom he writes to Cazalis that she is his "ideal in death." No, by a trick of condensation very common in dreams, where several people merge in one, we see Hamlet not only take on several of Igitur's traits but also borrow the appearance of an adolescent girl who is still a child. Igitur had something feminine about him: "languishing hair," "face lit up with mystery, and vacant, mirror-like eyes," "velvet bust," "frill," "spidery lacework. . . ." But the frail apparition of *Coup de dés,* who is announced as someone "ambiguous," as a "puerile shadow" (Mallarmé in a letter calls his sister "this young phantom"), appears as one shaken with wild, childish merriment from under his toque of "velvet with somber outbursts of laughter." No doubt the wild laughter is "restrained" by a "youth's virile reason," but the aigrette "shades a charming juvenile stature standing in its siren-like torsion." This laughing and mournful phantom, "expiatory and pubescent," thus unites the

146

traits of a young girl with the classic traits of Hamlet. This impression is further strengthened by comparison of *Coup de dés* with the sonnet *A la nue accablante tu*. The ocean, under a lowering sky, hints that a crime has just been committed. Two hypotheses suggest themselves: a ship has just been wrecked in the silence, unless, for lack of such lofty prey, the ocean was content to drown "the infant flank of a siren." The construction is in miniature that of *Coup de dés*. The quatrains suggest a sinister shipwreck; the tercets insinuate ironically: much ado about nothing. It is extraordinary, in this second scene, which corresponds to that of Hamlet in *Coup de dés*, to see the infant siren appear—the child of this sea which stands for the dead mother. It is impossible not to recognize in it, condensed with Igitur and Hamlet—that is, with the conscious Mallarmé, "bitter prince of the reef"—the phantom of young Maria. This condensation of two persons achieves a typical realization of the old desire for union. Hamlet and Ophelia are restored to one another; Stéphane and Maria composed the ambiguous shade that the dead mother hastens to dissolve again in her bosom.

A normal way for the child to resolve the Oedipal crisis is to identify with his father. In this fashion the small boy realizes his desire—by a detour, he avoids the discomfort of an open revolt against the one he fears and admires. I believe that at least a tentative identification of the sort was to be found in the first tableau of *Coup de dés*. Igitur earlier took great care not to cut himself off from his ancestors. The Master in *Coup de dés*, hitherto all-powerful ("formerly he grasped the tiller"), certainly reflects something of the paternal image. But the attitude of the young Mallarmé toward his father and his grandfather, who replaced him, seems to have been very ambiguous and critical under an appearance of respectful submission. The Oedipus complex was certainly involved in this ambivalence. A certain perhaps unconscious scorn for a father who had

147

grown old early, and for a sclerotic grandfather, must have added to this normal hostility in the mind of the adolescent. Identification therefore had little chance and seems to have miscarried precisely to the degree that Mallarmé did *not* believe (as he often repeats in his letters) that he was precociously old and feeble. Let us say, then, that the identification was made in despondency, aggravating the Oedipal situation instead of resolving it; for, in estranging himself from life, Mallarmé resembled his father and at the same time came nearer his dead mother. This aspect of the crisis is well symbolized in the shipwreck of the impotent Master: it is a criticism of the father, a self-criticism (Mallarmé having, like the old man, hesitated before the absolute deed), and at the same time a realization of desire, since in any case sea and death triumph. It will be agreed, however, that arriving at the goal by means of a despondent identification must have been in itself very unsatisfying to Mallarmé's personality. Hence the search for another route, by direct union with his mother or with the sister who alone represented her. I shall not recall the femininity that the portraits and works of Mallarmé reveal: the look of "a loving nanny goat," the movement of a dancer, the taste for interiors, the *Dernière Mode,* and so on. It is one of the irritating sides of Mallarmé; it is also the source of great beauties. I believe it is necessary to put the ambiguous apparition of *Coup de dés,* half-Hamlet, half child-siren, among the numerous manifestations of this inner duality. And as this young and thoughtful phantom with aigrette of foam topples and is dissolved in the same maternal shade in which the old man had already been swallowed up, we have every right to imagine that the first two scenes of *Coup de dés* show the two paths by which Mallarmé's mind symbolically satisfied the obsession with a lost tenderness.

I shall say very little about the constellation. From the philosophic and totally pessimistic point of view adopted by Mallarmé, this hope-in-spite-of-itself represents an absurdity. When a person has demonstrated by an apparently irrefutable abstract reasoning that the triumph of nothingness is inevitable, he does not add: "except perhaps . . ." For this exception and this possibility, if they exist, ruin all the preceding logic. But let us repeat, the philosophic point of view is merely accessory. The unfolding of the ideas is, in fact, dictated by unconscious needs. Now, strong as the poet's impulses to death were, they were always compensated by a taste for living values. These last won out, in the final analysis, since Mallarmé lived, wrote, hoped, and loved. This hope always found its way into expression. It appears to be absent only from *Igitur,* whose unique subject is the denial of life. Logically, suicide closes the book. In all the other equivalent pieces, on the contrary, after the descent toward death we see the image of "the other thing," of the other life, emerge. The reader may give these words a metaphysical resonance, but in quite human psychological reality they have a concrete meaning: the other thing than this life, for Mallarmé, is the dream and the literary work, the only means, in fact, for a writer to conciliate life and his fascination with the dead past—that is, with creation. The constellation (like the musical birth of dawn, but with more austerity) represents childhood that has disappeared, that has been transmuted into future work, Ophelia immortalized. One may prolong this direction "toward Septentrion, also North," but this essay stops with literary analysis and, from this point of view, the constellation has its analogue in Proust's *Temps retrouvé.*

5

The Prisoner

CONVINCED OR NOT, the reader will now agree that our
hypothesis gives us access to strange catacombs underlying Mallarmé's poems. The difficulty is to give an idea
of the whole. One way to do so is to follow the main
themes that run through his entire writing. In the preceding chapter I tried to retrace the most somber of
these motifs, the one in which—from the 1864 poems
to those of his last years—an identical anxiety develops.
I should now like to concentrate on the various states
of a second psychic attitude: that of the prisoner.

In the sonnet *Pour votre chère morte,* the survivor
who waits for the phantom's visit is called "solitary captive of the threshold." What is involved is, of course,
the funereal threshold that the man cannot pass as he
seeks to take his place in the "sepulcher for two which
will be our pride." The same impossible wish, we recall, had already been expressed in *Tristesse d'été:*

Nous ne serons jamais une seule momie . . .

[We will never be one single mummy . . .]

We have just dealt with the taboos and ambivalent
anxieties that result from the dream which wants to pass
beyond. Let us notice that anxiety subsides to the degree that the poet creates a work that manifests this
dream. It does so, first, because an outlet is found in

expression; then, because the personal success which the poem symbolizes when it achieves beauty gives the soul courage to go on living. This problem will be taken up again in the final chapter. Let us note for the moment that when the artist reaps no satisfaction from the awakened dream, his exertion will at times arouse anxiety. The more Mallarmé delved into himself in the course of his poetic, then metaphysical, vigils, and the more he wanted to be profound and sincere, the nearer his consciousness came to the redoubtable, forbidden reality. The higher, therefore, his anxiety rose.

No wonder, then, that the obsessed mind should seek other outlets than dreams or contemplation in the mirror. To end it once and for all, the prisoner may wish to precipitate himself into the void. We have already dealt with that solution. The last strophe of *Fenêtres* elicits it; *Igitur* clearly leads to it. *Pitre châtié* gives a variation of the same idea. "Bad Hamlet,"[1] horrified at his own narcissistic "barnstorming," makes a hole in the canvas wall of his makeshift quarters for a fine plunge into pure waters. Their blue is the blue of Marie Gerhard's eyes; and thus we have the feeling that this flight from the dream's illusion is oriented toward real life. But Marie's eyes are also Maria's, and their living water slyly changes back into the sepulcher he dreamed of entering.

> De ma jambe et des bras limpide nageur traître,
> A bonds multipliés, reniant le mauvais
> Hamlet! c'est comme si dans l'onde j'innovais
> Mille sépulcres pour y vierge disparaître.

> [With legs and arms, treacherous limpid swimmer
> With successive leaps, denying the bad
> Hamlet! it is as if in the wave I invented
> A thousand sepulchers in order to disappear virgin
>   clean into them.]

And, in the final analysis, it is the literary "barnstorming" which is the subject of regret.

Ne sachant pas, ingrat! que c'était tout mon sacre,
Ce fard noyé dans l'eau perfide des glaciers.

[Not knowing, ungrateful one! that it was my
    whole anointment,
This make-up drowned in the treacherous water of
    glaciers.]

The preceding can give us the true meaning of *Brise
marine.* The success of this poem comes in part from
the fact that it can be interpreted merely as the expression of a banal desire to escape toward some distant
Tahiti. The first and last verses should undeceive us.
"The flesh is sad, alas, and I have read all books" can-
cels two of the three evasions suggested in *Fenêtres:*
temporal success and the dream. The third alternative
was suicide, the return through death to the mother's
womb. This explains the violence of the conscious or
unconscious appeal: the abandoning of his art, of his
wife and child, and the hope (usually absent from simple dreams of exoticism) that the boat will shipwreck,
with no chance of escape:

Perdus, sans mâts, sans mâts, ni fertiles îlots . . .

[Lost, without masts, without masts or fertile
    isles . . .]

A la nue accablante tu and *Coup de dés* simply returned
to this theme in more inhuman fashion. Free of the
metaphysical by 1865, he expressed chiefly a shade of
rebellious ennui.

Happily for us, the revolt miscarried. A feeling of
guilt, of madness, or of disgrace halted Mallarmé just
when he was about to leap. If, however, the "harsh vow
—of delving a new grave every vigil" was deemed impossible to resume, the poet did fall back on that "bitter repose" which he also called, with great accuracy,
"Ennui." This state he experienced as soon as he faced
the equally difficult tasks—trying to live and trying to
write—in which his inner conflict enclosed him, that is,

152

almost immediately. By 1864 he could already give a precise definition of his illness, as when he wrote to Mistral: ". . . the affairs of daily life impress me too vaguely for me to love them, and I don't feel really alive except when I am writing poetry. I am bored because I am not at work, and, on the other hand, I don't work because I'm bored. To get out of this! . . ." It is the outlook of the prisoner who, turning his back on life, resting his face against the pane, refuses the dream as equally unhappy whether it is on the far side or the near side of the window. A fatality immobilizes him in this attitude. It is often expressed in Mallarmé's work and letters; but its most perfect symbol is *Cygne.*

It is not known when Mallarmé composed this famous poem. But this does not really matter, since the poem reveals a feeling or rather state which of necessity was repeated every time he felt this bitter repose. The publication of *Cygne* is dated 1885, though the workmanship would make one think rather of the experiments in verbal harmony which belong around the time of *Igitur.* These experiments in style were certainly followed up, as *Prose pour des Esseintes* and *Triptyque* witness, but the subject of these two poems tallies also with the preoccupations of 1869, and it seems that a secret harmony always linked the state of mind of this period with wordplay, as the manuscript of *Igitur* contains conscious traces of such experiments.[2] Nevertheless, I share the opinion of Mme Emilie Noulet, who places the date of the composition of *Cygne* in the 1870–1880 period, and I will add my own reason, because it will allow me to take one further step in the exposition of my thesis.

The first anxiety, after the experience of love, evokes a setting of autumn and sunset, as in *Soupir* and *Plainte d'automne. Symphonie littéraire,* and then *Hérodiade,* have shown us what the night looked like when the anxiety intensified. The room closed then so that time might die there. Midnight in a shut room marks the lowest point of this development and signals the descent to the Styx. Dawn breaking behind the window will bring the musical and lactescent dream of a rebirth.[3] But after 1870, when the desire for literary freedom is affirmed (*Toast funèbre*), light and open air once more occupy a place which has been lost since the sublimation of the *Faune*. I will try to explain, a little further on, exactly what this means. Here I would merely like to stress the fact that of the three terms marking the lowest point of anxiety—the tombstone, the night, and the cold— night at least has disappeared in *Cygne*. The scene is in the open, by day. We shall again find both the morning and the frozen mirror of *Hérodiade*, after the autumnal lions but before the flight toward the inner, subterranean night. Everything considered, it is still a matter of an ennui which is no longer exactly in front of the window but is before the looking glass[4] (we have learned to make this distinction). I speak of an ennui caught in the ice because it cannot detach itself. And as the ice symbolizes the glistening door of the tomb, turned faintly translucent and as though permeable to the phantom, the swan remains the solitary "captive of the threshold." The fatality of an obsessive dream of union and identification with a dead woman has transformed him into a pale specter,

Fantôme qu'à ce lieu son pur éclat assigne,

[Phantom that its pure light assigns to this place,] half-engaged in the tomb, in "the horror of the earth."[5] We are very well acquainted with this fascinated and sterile immobility, unable to live or to die. It satisfies a desire for *white* union with the dead woman, thus realizing the Oedipal dream, but it also punishes him by keeping his wings prisoners, and their loss, we have seen, is always a symbol of disgrace and castration. Creation would, by sublimating them, free these sterilized powers: such is the hope that the first stanza seeks to express, such is the flight that it attempts to make.

But the impotence, the cold, the fascination with the tomb, win out, and the prisoner gives up.

Like all symbols, let us repeat, *Cygne* is susceptible of interpretations at different levels. We give the subterranean meaning here, without denying the others. The advantage of this exploration in depth is that it gives the text its human and true resonance by eliminating the purely intellectual interpretations. Mallarmé's poems reinforce each other. Here, expressions like "lake," "forget," "haunts," "flights," "the swan remembers earlier times," "white agony of death," "inflicted," "horror of earth," "phantom," and "exile" assume their true emotional meaning, because we can tell what branch of the same complex each one is grafted onto. In a more general way the virgin whiteness, the coldness, the *glace* (in the two meanings of the term),[6] the ennui and guilt of the prisoner, thus become much richer themes than if we isolated the poem from the real psychological situation which it symbolically expresses. One final remark, on this subject, will enable us to take a further step. No conscious love inspires the prisoner as he faces his mirror: hence his immobility. He has a horror of the ice imprisoning his wing; he hates the space behind him just as intensely. For, in the symbolism of the poem, space is the equivalent of daily existence. The dream of *Fenêtres* "turned its back on life"; *Cygne* denies space. This denial seems to contradict the hope of the first stanza: if the ice melted and freed the swan, would the bird not fly away in the space it so scorns? This would be the cure for an ordinary neurosis, which, once released from its fixation to a dead past, would resume a life like everyone else's. Poetic sublimation implies a third term: a spiritual space which would not be scorned. The physical allegory of *Cygne* could not provide two spaces, one denied, the other wished for. They must, however, be assumed, in order that the contradiction may be resolved. There is, further, an impossibility at the very core of the poem: if Mallarmé's anxiety had to choose between a life the poet was ill equipped to face and a dream that was a funereal and narcissistic obsession, there would be no escape. Escape is to be found precisely in the other space, the spiritual, the one the *swan* could not fly toward.

We find the same question in another poem that, although apparently very different, is basically quite similar to *Cygne*. I refer to the sonnet *Quand l'ombre menaça*. Again its décor is equivocal. The setting of *Cygne* presented us with coldness without night. Here we have night without coldness. And why, the reader will ask, must this night again be that of the tomb? Because the poem says so: the sky is a funereal ceiling (the tombstone); the constellations are dying; the shadow is fatal; the word "vertebrae" further accentuates the macabre note. Finally, the old dream, distressed at dying, has folded up its wing, punished like all incestuous fantasies of union in the tomb. An emotional difference, which was perceptible in *Cygne,* is again stressed here and differentiates this sonnet from the pure anxiety poems we studied in the preceding chapter. The *swan* was already *against* the tomb which held it prisoner; it yielded only with great suffering to its fate. Here, antipathy toward the sepulcher increases. It is mingled with an old hatred against "this old plumage . . . God" and through this is grafted onto the Oedipal situation.[7] We found a trace of this attitude in the free composition of 1857.[8] In this youthful work, the father was accused of causing the death of the young girl and, no doubt, of the mother. He had possessed her and killed her, as in the old infantile notion we find in *Bluebeard* and *The Thousand and One Nights.* Just something of this oriental tyranny appears in the puerile image that this sonnet gives of the Creator.

> Luxe, ô salle d'ébène où, pour séduire un roi
> Se tordent dans leur mort des guirlandes célèbres . . .

[Luxury! ebony hall, where to flatter a King,
There twist in their death famous garlands . . .]
Naturally, adult consciousness rejects with horror any
dreams of this kind, where, in a night which is but a
vast tomb, constellations—girls—flowers dance for the
sadistic pleasure of a god-the-father Schahriar.[9] Mallarmé, once delivered from suicide and the dream, dis-
carded this macabre paraphernalia of symbols. Indeed,
if symbolism is but the archaic mode of expression of
an infantile unconscious, the adult consciousness sheds
it in favor of a rational view of the world. It is in fact
with this new faith that the "solitary" seems "dazzled."
Space is no longer anything but space; that seems satis-
fying enough. The here below is only the here below.
Does Mallarmé, however, like it the more for that? Dis-
engaged from what he perhaps thinks to be the faith of
Pascal, he nonetheless, contradictorily, retains an ideal-
ist's scorn for the material universe:

L'espace à soi pareil qu'il s'accroisse ou se nie
Roule dans cet ennui des feux vils . . .

[A space unchanged whether it swell or deny itself
Rolls in this ennui vile fires . . .]
We find again, at least in part, the attitude of *Cygne:*
hatred of the dream before the tomb and distaste for
material life. But while the swan resigned itself to an
absurd but fatal immobility in the coldness, a gleam
lights up in the heart of the "solitary." He believes in
the genius of humanity on this planet. The prisoner,
having moved from revolt to bitterness, suddenly sees
hope that earth may provide an escape after all.
The expression of this is found in *Toast funèbre.* It
is a queer poem. Mme Emilie Noulet interprets it as
the height of Mallarméan thought, a magnificent pro-
fession of atheistic faith against the immortality of the
soul. I must admit that I have but small interest in a
free-thinking Mallarmé. Whatever value is ascribed to

rational thought (and this is not the place to discuss it), poetic thought, far from being one with it, is, if I may say so, perpendicular to it: it involves, quite specifically, a new dimension, obtained by rotation on its axis. The unconscious we study lies below rationality; the poetic meaning, above. But unconscious and poetic meanings are thus put on this vertical, which the horizontal—rational and discursive—crosses without understanding it. The beauty of *Toast funèbre* thus has little to do with philosophic thought; it has, on the contrary, a great deal to do with an unconscious psychic attitude.

We have seen in the preceding a confirmation of the revolt against the tomb and its obsessiveness. This revolt is, after all, nothing but the logical result of the 1868 renunciation of absolute suicide. When Mallarmé that summer at Avignon craved for his garden a hammock to idle in, he was already siding with the garden against the tomb. He resolved to live, and his attitude developed logically. Since the dream and the tomb were confused in his mind because of an accident of his psychic life, he declared against the dream. He was to reverse his position later. The phrase written apropos of Hamlet should be recalled:

> . . . car il n'est point d'autre sujet, sachez bien: l'antagonisme de rêve chez l'homme avec les fatalités à son existence départies par le malheur.

> [. . . for there is, you must realize, no other subject: the antagonism of man's dream to the fatalities of his existence as they are bestowed by misfortune.]

He discovered, or rediscovered, to a certain degree (for Ophelia was always present), what I will call a livable definition of the dream. In 1868, on the contrary, the dream had been abandoned as unlivable, and it is precisely this backward movement which reached its limit in *Toast funèbre*. Must it be called rational? Flight from *azur* already showed a dread of the funereal dream in

1864. We have analyzed this fear. It is the product, not of reason, but of a guilt feeling. *Azur* expresses a classic taboo, with its coexistence of desire and interdiction. From 1864 to 1868 Mallarmé came only too near the forbidden object. He felt the punishment in the shape of approaching madness. Now, he recoiled, far from the tabooed object, and rejected the tomb and its fascination. Thus the lovely dream of the first years became the "old dream, desire and sickness of my bones," exactly the one that *Toast funèbre* exorcised and drove from the earthly paradise:

> Où le poëte pur a pour geste humble et large
> De l'interdire au rêve ennemi de sa charge . . .

> [Where the pure poet by humble and generous gesture
> Keeps out the dream, enemy of his office . . .]

And the entire beginning of the poem shows, in support of our hypothesis, that this dream is an obsession in the funereal sense of the term.

> Ne crois pas qu'au magique espoir du corridor
> J'offre ma coupe vide où souffre un monstre d'or!
> Ton apparition ne va pas me suffire . . .

> [Do not believe that to the magic hope of the corridor
> I offer my empty cup wherein a monster of gold suffers!
> Your apparition will not suffice me . . .]

Think of the importance of this word "apparition" in the life and work of Mallarmé. Apparition, Deborah Parrit; apparition, the visit of *Pour votre chère morte;* apparition, the "fairy in the cap of light," the bare phantom or the nixy in the mirror, the constellation behind the window, "heir of many a rich but fallen trophy" which could well "arrive unexpectedly by the corridor." The specters that *Toast funèbre* exorcises by denying, people three-fourths of the poems. And are they really absent from Théophile Gautier's monument? After all, it is still a sepulcher. Therein it is true, is enclosed

> . . . tout ce qui nuit,
> Et l'avare silence et la massive nuit.

> [. . . all that harms,
> Both greedy silence and the massive night.]

The evil is thus prisoner in a derisory beyond, and the poet, rescued from his own silence and his own night, walks in the garden. What does he find there? Recognizable flowers, that is, his dead ones.[10] Doubtless he knew nothing of this, consciously. But there is an irony in the fact that we find again in this space, though supposedly exorcised, as if accidentally near a tomb, and as if accidentally paradisiac and ideal, the corollas of *Apparition,* of *Fleurs,* or of "Chinaman of limpid heart and subtle," the rose-Deborah, the rose-Hérodiade, the lilies of memory once scattered in the dead water of the basins, petal by petal, and so many images associated by so many threads with these phantoms that he had tried to banish. The flowers have become, I realize, words and ideas. The only survival was, for Mallarmé, poetic immortality.

> Moi, de votre désir soucieux, je veux voir,
> A qui s'évanouit, hier, dans le devoir
> Idéal que nous font les jardins de cet astre,
> Survivre pour l'honneur du tranquille désastre
> Une agitation solennelle par l'air
> De paroles, pourpre ivre et grand calice clair . . .

> [I, careful of your desire, I hope to see
> Him who, yesterday, vanished in the ideal
> Duty imposed by the gardens of this star,
> Survived, for the honor of the quiet disaster,
> By a solemn agitation in the air of words,
> Drunken purple and great shining chalice . . .][11]

I do not mean to deny a very definite evolution. The poet has freed himself to a certain extent of his morbid

obsession. That does not prevent poetic survival from
following the pattern of another survival. And as the
latter remains unconscious, it is quite likely that the belief in poetic immortality simply represents it in another
guise. This is, moreover, why there is a continuity of
symbols: the same chalices which spoke of death and
resurrection in 1864 speak, when transposed onto another plane, of death and resurrection in 1873. The very
words of Mallarmé reveal the origin of his idealism.
Look at the definition of "idea":

> . . . Je dis: une fleur! et hors de l'oubli où ma voix
> relègue aucun contour . . . musicalement se lève,
> idée même et suave, l'absente de tous bouquets.

> [. . . I say: a flower! and out of the forgetfulness
> into which my voice banishes any contour . . .
> musically rises, unmistakable and fragrant idea,
> the one absent from all bouquets.]

But we are already acquainted with this forgetfulness
out of which an apparition is born:

> Elle, défunte nue en le miroir encor
> Que dans l'oubli fermé par le cadre, se fixe
> De scintillations sitôt le septuor.[12]

> [She, naked, dead, in the mirror
> While in the forgetfulness closed by the frame, at
>   once
> The septet with scintillations is studded.]

We know that for Mallarmé the mirror is always this
ideal profundity from which memories emerge. A flower
instead of a "naked dead woman" rising from it would
not surprise us after so many analogous associations.
But the most revealing word in the above definition,
after "absent," is "musically." The idealized phantom
is always musical: the septet of the *Sonnet en YX*, the
ancient instruments of *Pénultième*, the seraphim's violas
in *Apparition*, the flute or mandora in *Sainte*, the viola or clavicord in *Don du poème*, the mandora in

Triptyque. Thus the earthly and poetic faith of *Toast funèbre,* apparently freed of ghosts, reproduces the old obsession and consummates in fact the dream it denies. After all, in Deborah Parrit's resurrection, the angel's trumpet had already locked up in the tomb "the greedy silence and the massive night" to lead the girl, her songs and flowers, to the living light. *Toast funèbre* does very much the same thing. In the garden or in the hut, Mallarmé dreams that he is happy near the same rediscovered realities. The important fact remains that he now calls them *ideas* and that in this apparently more intellectual form they seem to evade the fatal interdiction: the guilt feeling disappears, and sublimation becomes possible.

Not that the unconscious is greatly deceived by these transformations and symbolic disguises. I will offer as proof *Prose pour des Esseintes.* In it we again find the flowers—ideas and, still as though by chance, a tomb and a sister. The sister is assimilated to the flowers, those "charms of the countryside." Now *Prose pour des Esseintes* tells the story of 1868 in the language of *Toast funèbre:* threat of madness and renunciation of the absolute. It will be remembered that the pure beauty of Hérodiade had been succeeded by pure thought, its analogue, as the "naked dead woman" was succeeded —in the mirror—by the constellation. If *Hérodiade* is connected with Maria, then the basic progression is sister—poem—idea. In *Prose* and in *Toast funèbre,* the flowers are at once poems (*Toast funèbre*), ideas ("Glory of the long desire, Ideas"), and sister equivalents. Hence, there is no doubt about the chain of associations. Now what does *Prose* say? On an island *on the other side of* a river or a sea[13] (I ask the reader to remember at this point the descent to the Styx) the poet had found again—in the union of a "double unconscious"—the sister herself and her ideal symbols. But the flowers became so huge (read: the obsession grew so strong) that madness threatened:

. . . de lis multiples la tige
Grandissait trop pour nos raisons[14]

[. . . with multiple lilies the stalk
Grew too high for our sanity]
"I have given up this place," the poet says, "out of fear of madness; which doesn't mean at all that the place does not exist." ("And not, as the bank weeps . . . that this land did not exist.") The "wise and tender sister" herself advises departure, resurrection in life ("Anastase!"), before beauty ("Pulchérie!") succumbs to the effect of madness ("the overlarge gladiolus"). Mallarmé thus recounts in *Prose pour des Esseintes* the most crucial adventure of his life, the one he told or was to tell in *Igitur, Sonnet en YX, Triptyque,* and *Coup de dés.* He gave up "hyperbole," which was the absolute leap into the beyond, to return to the work of patient scrawling where the supernatural realm becomes a chart, the idea—flower dried in the herbarium, ecstasy a simple ritual.[15] The first two stanzas of *Prose* explicitly refer to the great decision of 1868–1869. The hyperbolic leap into the absolute, the triumphal ascent, now definitely belong to the past ("Hyperbole! you do not know how to rise triumphantly out of my memory . . ."). He has come back down to patient toil. (In the Avignon letters are to be found the schemes he thought up for this pseudo-scientific work.) I cannot sufficiently emphasize the importance of this crisis, this flight from madness and conversion to life, which separates the Besançon metaphysics from the convalescence of Avignon. Let us cite one more text on this subject, the letter to Cazalis in February, 1869:

. . . Il le fallait: mon cerveau, envahi par le Rêve, se refusant à ses fonctions extérieures qui ne le sollicitaient plus, allait périr dans son insomnie permanente; j'ai imploré la grande Nuit, qui m'a exaucé et a étendu ses ténèbres. La première phase de ma vie a été finie. La conscience, excédée d'ombres, se réveille, lentement, formant un homme nouveau, et doit retrouver mon Rêve après la création de ce dernier. Cela durera quelques années pendant lesquelles j'ai à revivre la vie de l'humanité depuis son enfance et prenant conscience d'elle-même.

Pour susciter l'activité, j'associerai à ces années d'études un but pratique qui sera mon "Egyptologie", mais je ne te parlerai de cela que lorsque je serai sûr d'être tout à fait sorti des griffes du Monstre . . .[16]

[. . . It had to be: my brain, invaded by the Dream, refusing its external function which no longer solicited, was going to die in its permanent insomnia; I prayed to the spacious Night, which hearkened and spread its shadows. The first phase of my life was over. Consciousness, fatigued with shadows, awakens, gradually, forming a new man, and will find my Dream again after the new man has been created. This process will go on for several years, during which I must live through in my turn the life of humanity since its beginnings as it rose to self-awareness.

To stir up some activity, I shall give these years of study a practical goal, which will be my "Egyptology," but I won't tell you about that until I am sure I have entirely escaped the Monster's claws . . .]

The moment of illumination is past, the moment of orderly work arrives. ("The child renounces his ecstasy / And learnèd already along the way.") A series of clues thus tends to put the source of *Prose* in the Avignon period. I will give two others: (1) the siesta atmosphere. The voyage to the enchanted island is told as a dream experienced during a summer's day:

Lorsque, sans nul motif, on dit
De ce midi que notre double
Inconscience approfondit . . .

164

[When, without motive, it is said
Of this noon that our double
Unconsciousness deepens . . .]
(2) Once again, apparently, we find the wordplay[17] belonging to the works which date from this period, or
tally with them. On the other hand, the emotional atmosphere of the story is that of the Paris years, as indicated by the idealism and irony. And, as the flower-
ideas of this beyond match trait for trait the flower-
words of *Toast funèbre*, the conclusion must be, I think,
that *Prose pour des Esseintes* is, like *Triptyque*, one of
those poems that long afterwards, on the banks of the
Seine, tell of the anguish of and convalescence from the
crisis on the banks of the Rhône. Psychologically, in any
case—that is, from the point of view that concerns us
here—*Prose pour des Esseintes* marks a return to the
boldness and earthly faith of *Toast*. The fear of madness made the poet flee from the island Eden. In *Toast
funèbre*, he drives out the old dream and forbids it access to his own garden. In *Prose*, the roles are reversed.
The poet finds himself once again on the side of the
living. The funereal waters, at his feet, play the role
of the window or the sepulcher door.

The emotional atmosphere has, then, changed, but
the drama has remained fundamentally the same. We
must not underestimate the sublimations which were
operative and which in any case lessened the anxiety
tension. Paris not only brought Mallarmé the "burning
glory of the craft"—which, let us note, is again found
to be associated in *Toast funèbre* with the double image
of the setting sun and the tomb[18]—but also with painting, music, friendship, Valvins, and Méry Laurent. Thus,
anxiety at times disappeared almost completely from
the scene. We find again in certain texts—after the troubles of love and everyday life—that innocence which
distinguishes the dream Nick Parrit had by the fire in
his hut. I will take as an example *Mes bouquins refermés*. Whereas in the poems of anxiety the dream remained outside the window, here it has again drawn

close to the hearth with the familiarity of a cat. Behind the windowpanes are reality, cold, and the tomb. For death is present, as the "scythe-like silences" and the funereal song, "dirge," attest. Evidently the dreamer is no longer Nick Parrit; he has learned from books to think subtly; yet in his solitude he still loves an absent one. She comes from antiquity, that is, from childhood. She lived, if one believes books, in Paphos, the island of the Amazons, that is, in the unconscious, the beyond of the waters of death. The "thousand foams" blessing his past ("a ruin") and the hyacinth of his days recall the foam and heavens of *Brise marine* ("Flee! flee out there! I feel that birds are intoxicated / To be amidst the unknown foam and skies!"). In 1865, anxiety pushed Mallarmé to that wild evasion toward the beyond and shipwreck; in 1887, a peaceable beyond returns to take its place before the fire of the satisfied prisoner. Death and cold have been put out of the room; the mother has returned to it. And it is naturally the maternal breast which makes its appearance. "How human and perfumed this one, bursting with flesh."[19] However, Mallarmé, though no doubt he was unaware of this unconscious background, at least knew that he dreamed, and his consciousness had made its peace with phantoms. Like the "child" of *Prose pour des Esseintes*, after having renounced ecstasy, he became poetically "learnèd"; he sublimated the sad absence of a dead woman into an art of absences. The intact bosom of the "antique Amazon" suckled the child of yesteryear; the adult who dreams waking, frankly misses it. The poet reserves to himself the burned breast. Spiritual choice? Self-punishment? Asceticism remains for a long time double-faced.

6

The Spectator

THIRTY YEARS of work have established beyond doubt that art and morality may to a certain extent be explained by psychoanalysis. To what extent? We shall touch on this question apropos of Mallarmé in the course of the next chapter. I raise the problem here merely to let the reader know what is coming, for I intend to delay any discussion of aesthetics, since, if aesthetics were not distinguished from psychology, the argument to follow would at once be falsified. Having devoted the two preceding chapters, first to anxiety, constricted around inner difficulties, and second to boredom, already less acute and dreaming of liberation, I shall now deal with examples of happier sublimation.

When I speak of "happiness," I refer to the impression the work itself leaves. The *Faune* has a happier tone than *Hérodiade;* in fact, even happier than *Toast funèbre,* with its poet strolling in the gardens. The atmosphere of the poems to Méry Laurent is more relaxed than that of *Fenêtres, Igitur,* or *Coup de dés.* A certain emotional attitude may thus be experimentally defined in the texts themselves. We will limit ourselves to specifying their nuances and interrelationships with the rest of his work from our chosen point of view.

Some brief general remarks may be useful here. I see three ways in which a contemplative mind might be led from constricted anxiety to a state of relaxation:

1. Vision can be displaced from the obsessive object —a tomb, in Mallarmé's case. We have seen how the emotion can pass from symbol to symbol by links of association. Nevertheless, the symbol has qualities of its own. Marie can represent Maria; she is nonetheless a living creature who is worthy of a tenderness which may be directed to her personally. By means of the transfer, the obsession is made to evaporate and lose its morbid character.

2. The obsessive object may be split up into images which will symbolize it. We have seen Maria become flowers—constellations—seraphim—autumn—dead water—mirror—snow—moon—Styx—nixy—child   siren, and so on. The emotion thus flies from object to object and diffuses into a veritable network of affective metaphors. In so doing, it loses its force. The cruel *idée fixe* changes into a complex play of resonances.

3. The relationship the obsessed individual has to his obsession, the unhappy person to his misery, can ease if it takes allusive forms. Fantasy can replace sexual possession; the phantom's visit, union with the dead. Guilt will diminish proportionately.

These are three aspects of an identical loosening process. Here and there, in earlier chapters, we have been able to note the effects of displacement and of the multiplication of symbols. The pages to follow will provide other instances of the same sort. Sunsets, for example, will appear in all the poems to Méry. They will keep something of their own meaning, but guilt almost disappears or assumes merely a trifling importance. It is the use of the third method that will particularly engage us in this chapter. It seems to have been far more efficacious than the other two, and the reason is not hard to grasp. Mallarmé was too fixated on his dream to make a transfer readily, as he himself said very clearly: ". . . the affairs of daily life impress me too vaguely for me to love them, and I don't feel really alive except when I am writing poetry."[1]

We have seen how these efforts to transpose the dream into life readily aroused an impression of downfall, and as a result (at least in the short run) favored relapse into the obsession. Grafting is a slow process. Multiplying the symbols seems to have helped Mallarmé greatly by furnishing him with an original poetic keyboard, the instrument of his audacities and his successes. Now Mallarmé was certainly elated with success. On the other hand, so many metaphors focused on the same unconscious nucleus inevitably led the poet back into the same obsessional circle night after night. Poetic labor always increased his anxiety; this is clearly shown in the years of *Hérodiade:* the bitter repose so often observed, Mallarmé's retreats before the "virgin paper," his inhibitions, the enormous quantity of work which he gratuitously devised between conception and realization—all this undoubtedly issues from fear and from an inner taboo. Take *Brise marine.* When for various reasons the garden, the white sheet of paper, and the young mother have all become symbols of the unconscious taboo, the only recourse is to flee from them in the direction of shipwreck. But shipwreck, a new symbol, is in fact equally forbidden. Immobility thus appears inevitable, and the written poem is the only point gained. Such a tearing loose is, to repeat, liberative only in the long run. The immediate effect may be a relapse. Thus, in Mallarmé's case, neither transfer nor symbolism was enough to divert his mind from its fixation. On the contrary, the easing of relations between conscious and unconscious went to the heart of the difficulty.

Hérodiade appears to be the result of such an effort. In writing a scene for the theater Mallarmé broke with normal lyric narcissism. He objectified his inner conflict;

he dramatized it and in this way put it at a distance from him. But in the scene itself, two essential figures are to be distinguished: Hérodiade and St. John. We have equated them more or less with the unconscious and the conscious mind of the poet. Because of this duality, *Hérodiade* provides a contrast with *Igitur*. The hero of the 1869 story is alone. *Igitur* stands lower than *Hérodiade* on the curve of depression. Ambivalence, conflict, anxiety, have disappeared from it because they have been passed by: without hesitation the hero descends toward suicide. Ambivalence, by contrast, is typical of *Hérodiade*. I have noted this fact sufficiently to go on to another point. The look St. John casts at the nakedness of Hérodiade undoubtedly symbolizes a more complete union. It is nonetheless the first sign of a tendency which will play a great role in the further sublimations: the taste for scenes, and at first, of course, for erotic scenes.

Hérodiade presents only the negative side of this taste. Charles Baudouin, in the chapter he devotes to the "spectacular complex,"[2] notes, following Rank, that the taste for nakedness and disapproval of it are satisfied at one and the same time in the compromise of clothes and precious ornaments. The same insistence both veils and points out. This remark applies to *Hérodiade,* where for the first time the Byzantine pomp of all Symbolist princesses is displayed. Besides, psychologically speaking, the heroine's outraged modesty plays the same game. But we have seen the fatality which little by little freezes a *Hérodiade* that Mallarmé composed in winter and which he took too seriously (as a mirror of his own anxious spirit) to permit the least relaxation. St. John's glance had, then, to be a somber one.

Summer, however, came, and with it, the *Faune*. The first version, we know, was written in 1865[3] and was intended for the Théâtre Français. The "spectacular complex" is at work here, then, as in *Hérodiade*. And the subject of the two poems is not so very different, in spite of appearances. The theme is still surprised naked-ness, but here it is transposed into a sunlit tonality. The summer joy which reigns in *L'Après-midi d'un faune* is such that the poem might very well appear to be a suc-cessful sublimation, as against *Hérodiade,* a poem of anxiety. This hypothesis would find support in the famous verses which turn female beauty into musical sinuosities:

> Et de faire aussi haut que l'amour se module
> Evanouir du songe ordinaire de dos
> Ou de flanc pur suivis avec mes regards clos
> Une sonore, vaine et monotone ligne.

> [And to make as high as love modulates
> Vanish from the ordinary dream of a back
> Or pure flank followed by my hooded looks
> A sonorous, vain and monotonous line.]

Closer inspection will change this view. Certainly, the *Faune* is itself a sublimation; but not the poem *of* a sub-limation. On the contrary, the demigod is seen as laying aside his flute, abandoning art, and lazily contenting himself with a daydream, also called "Memories."

We have already said a number of times that in the Mallarmé of this period sensuality and its triumphs al-ways appear to be a thing of the past. The impression of distance is further expressed by means of a historical and fabulous recoil into an autumnal atmosphere: the Latin decadence of *Plainte d'automne,* the galleys of *Fenêtres,* the tawny centuries of the lions in *Hérodiade,* and the ancestors of *Igitur* furnish abundant examples. This technique is not peculiar to Mallarmé: it is com-monly used to express a backward look, that is, into a fabled infancy. The antiquity of the *Faune* obeys the same psychological law, and the word "Memories" con-fesses as much.

The problem of nakedness naturally haunted Mal-larmé's childhood, as it does every other childhood. Let us make no mistake, it is just such highly charged memories, far more than memories of facts, which fill out the poem. It is by no means necessary that young five-year-old Stéphane should have surprised someone in bathing. The water of the fountains and the "tawny hour" put us back into a network of very familiar associations. But why has the anxiety which went with them in other contexts disappeared here? Because of the extraordinary perfection of the camouflage, I think. Pagan eroticism, the animal innocence of a faun, are so well admitted by cultivated minds that in this disguise one can say almost everything and, more important, can dream. The sin is scarcely taken seriously; nor will its punishment be any more important. However, punishment is there:

> Car, à peine j'allais cacher un rire ardent
> Sous les replis heureux d'une seule (gardant
> Par un doigt simple, afin que sa candeur de plume
> Se teignît à l'émoi de sa soeur qui s'allume,
> La petite, naïve et ne rougissant pas:)
> Que de mes bras, défaits par de vagues trépas . . .

> [For, scarcely was I about to hide an ardent laugh
> Under the happy folds of one alone (holding
> By one sole finger, so that her feather-like sim-
> plicity
> Would be colored with the desire of her kindling
> sister,
> The small, naïve, unblushing one:)
> When from my arms, defeated by vague dy-
> ing . . .]

So, when a night dream becomes too revealing for consciousness, it vanishes. The idea of punishment reappears explicitly when the Faun develops the plan of ravishing the "queen," at sunset on Etna:

> O sûr châtiment . . .[4]

> [O sure punishment . . .]

The Faun, instead of dying, falls asleep again, but not before he has indicated that this happy death will unite him with the two he had conjured up:

Couple, adieu; je vais voir l'ombre que tu devins.

[Couple, adieu; I am going to see the shade that
    you became.]
The curve of *L'Après-midi* too is a parabola. The
spirit of the Faun emerges from the unconscious, elabo-
rates a fantasy of desire, and plunges back. The poem's
happy mood derives from this letting go. *Hérodiade* had
two characters: the unconscious and the conscious. And
we set this duality against the solitude of *Igitur*. For
Igitur is the lonely consciousness which no longer has
anything clearly before it but the stairway descending
to the tomb. The *Faune* represents the other solitude,
that of the unconscious playing like a child with its
dreams, between two warm naps. We have asked why
anxiety disappeared from the *Faune*. It is because
anxiety presupposes conflict and struggle—two terms.
Igitur has but one: desperate consciousness; the *Faune*
also has but one: the happy unconscious in its half-sleep,
during which the fantasy rises like a wave.[5]

The *Faune*, in its first form, dates from 1865, in the
high period of anxiety. The later revisions, up to 1876,
bring numerous changes in form, render the poem far
more musical, and delete precisely those elements of a
dramatic monologue which were too harsh to express a
waking dream. But from our point of view, the lesson
of the first version is already clear. Anxiety disappears
from Mallarmé's verses when eroticism can find expression, through the services of an effective camouflage
and various palliations—an eroticism (1) audacious and
witty under its disguise; (2) fleeing before forbidden
conclusions; (3) visual rather than active.

Such a game involves a whole science of veils and
mysteries artfully accumulated and dissipated. In a
contemplative individual, its exercise should lead to an
experience, then to a singular theory of knowledge and
of poetry. In it, reality—a nakedness forbidden and mysterious, behind the veils—becomes the object of desire.

Poetry becomes at once revelation and shame. Such a conception is not peculiar to Mallarmé: it is common to all profound religious or aesthetic thought, mystical at base, symbolic in language. We cannot enter here into such general considerations. Let us merely remark that a correspondence surely exists between the erotic happiness of Mallarmé and his way of thinking or writing. This correspondence establishes a bridge between instinct and style. Such was, for Mallarmé, the chief road to sublimation.

Nénuphar blanc in many ways repeats the theme of the *Faune*. The style is modern; antiquity has disappeared. This proves that in 1885 an actual, viable compromise between Mallarmé's unconscious and conscious had been found. Except for this very important detail, the same estival and aquatic daydream finally leads us to the same mysterious threshold. *Dernière Mode*, the poet's analysis of women's dress, and of course Méry Laurent, helped Mallarmé to avoid this cliché: the glimpsed bather. The "feminine leisures to be surprised" in some watery undergrowth assume the familiar nineteenth-century form:

. . . Subtil secret des pieds qui vont, viennent, conduisent l'esprit où le veut la chère ombre enfouie en de la baptiste et les dentelles d'une jupe affluant sur le sol comme pour circonvenir du talon à l'orteil, dans une flottaison, cette initiative par quoi la marche s'ouvre, tout au bas, et les plis rejetés en traîne, une échappée, de sa double flèche savante. . . .

[. . . Subtle secret of feet which come and go, lead the mind wherever wishes the dear shade buried in the cambric and lace of a skirt flowing on the ground from heel to toe as if to circumvent, waveringly, the initiative by which the step opens for itself, down below, and the folds thrown back as a train, a flight out, through its refined double arrow. . . .]

A happy atmosphere of naïve license, urgently visual, thus brings *Nénuphar blanc* close to the *Faune*, if the transposition into a modern tonality is taken into account. The same prohibition, moreover, by limiting this license, permits it. The "instinctive charm of below, which the most authentically tied of sashes with its diamond buckle does not defend against the explorer," appears, on the contrary, very well protected. The rower, head leaning against the yawl, does not know whether a woman is present, indeed, refuses to check, and, besides, fears more than anything else that a face will be disclosed: ". . . the delight with generality impregnated, which permits and enjoins the exclusion of any face to such a point that the revelation of one (pray, do not bend your own, doubtless, over the furtive threshold, my kingdom) would banish my trouble, alien to it."

This last statement is significant: the exclusion of any specific feminine face sets up an anonymity in whose shadow the unconscious affectivity may be satisfied without reproach. This is what Mallarmé calls "generality"; we have seen[6] the identical sorcery at work in the statement: "I say: a flower! and out of the forgetfulness into which my voice banishes any contour, . . . musically rises, unmistakable and fragrant idea, the one absent from all bouquets." Let us put "woman" in place of "flower" (everything entitles us to this exchange), and we will see what this "delight with generality impregnated" consists of. It is nothing else than a free permission, finally obtained, under cover of an ideal anonymity. Once the "greedy silence and the massive night" had been closed in the tomb in *Toast funèbre*, the poet could stroll through flower-ideas and flower-words. We are much closer here to an enduring sublimation. The tomb has gone, the scene is real; an actual man can taste in it something of the joy that was hitherto reserved for the fabulous pleasure of the Faun. The flower keeps its ideal signification, and I do not deny the subtle symbolism of *Nénuphar blanc*, but the "delight with generality impregnated," which is the equivalent of the "pure pathless delight" of *Eventail,* is given as the avowed harmonic of a specific erotic pleasure. The Rose and Lily of *Toast funèbre* were not to be touched. It goes quite otherwise for the water lily:

Conseille, ô mon rêve, que faire?

Résumer d'un regard la vierge absence éparse en cette solitude et, comme on cueille, en mémoire d'un site, l'un de ces magiques nénuphars clos qui y surgissent tout à coup, enveloppant de leur creuse blancheur un rien, fait de songes intacts, du bonheur qui n'aura pas lieu et de mon souffle ici retenu dans la peur d'une apparition, partir avec. . . .

[Counsel me, o my dream, what to do?

To sum up with a glance the virgin absence scattered through this solitude and, as one gathers, in memory of a site, one of those magic shut lilies suddenly produced, enveloping in their white hollow core a nothingness, made of untouched dreams, of the happiness never to be gotten and of my breath held back for fear of an apparition, fly with it. . . .]

A rape is undoubtedly involved. To make it possible (like Ulysses wishing to escape the glare of Polyphemus) the phantom is called No One: the abduction occurs ". . . without the blow shattering the illusion or the rippling of the visible bubble of foam rolled in my flight, throwing on the unexpected feet of no one the transparent image of the rape of my ideal flower." The absence, in fact, authorizes the absentee. Mallarmé will create his aesthetic out of this success with the perfect disguise.

The symbol, with the partly revealed mystery it admits, forms the normal language of the lower unconscious and of higher spirituality. Our dreams by night express desires that are often infantile in their curious mixture of symbols and plays on words. Now symbols and wordplay also make up the language of poetry and myth. This coincidence, as well as a great number of facts analogous to the ones brought together in this book, naturally induce the mind to confuse dream and poetry. Any true sense of values will oppose this procedure. Knowing the importance of the debate, I refuse to deal with it in a mere few sentences. The correspondences can, however, be noted; we must postpone their interpretation.

Now when Mallarmé, defining poetry,[7] speaks of "stretching the cloud, precious, floating over the inmost gulf of each thought," the reader who has just been admiring *Nénuphar blanc* certainly has the right to at least the shadow of a smile. Erotic obsession is not the issue, since it haunts language and human psychology generally. We are now sufficiently aware of this reality to accept it simply, although with reserve. Between the levels of the human hierarchy there is continuity and resonance; for this reason, moreover, symbols are possible. We have seen in earlier pages how Mallarmé arrived at a true sublimation of his own obsession. A series of transitions and links lead us back from *Nénuphar blanc* to the *Faune*, to *Hérodiade*, to the free composition, and finally to the Oedipus complex. However, every Mallarméan will slip with no effort at all from *Nénuphar blanc* to the strictly aesthetic pages that appear throughout *Divagations*. "The virgin absence scattered through this solitude," the "white hollow core" enveloping "a nothingness, made of untouched dreams," is certainly that of the poems also, or of their margins. Refer to the end of *Mystère dans les lettres:*

Lire—

Cette pratique—

Appuyer, selon la page, au blanc, qui l'inaugure son ingénuité, à soi, oublieuse même du titre qui parlerait tout haut: et, quand s'aligna, dans une brisure, la moindre, disséminée, le hasard vaincu

177

mot par mot, indéfectiblement le blanc revient,
tout à l'heure gratuit, certain maintenant, pour
conclure que rien au delà et authentiquer le silence.

Virginité qui solitairement, devant une transparence du regard adéquat, elle-même s'est comme
divisée en ses fragments de candeur, l'un et l'autre,
preuves nuptiales de l'Idée.

[Reading—
Practice—

To lay, in accordance with the page and on its
opening whiteness, one's own ingenuity, forgetful
even of the title which would speak aloud: and
when, in a chink scattered—the least one—chance
has aligned itself, vanquished word after word,
faultlessly the blank returns, gratuitous a moment
ago, now settled, to conclude (that there is) nothing beyond and to authenticate silence.[8]

Virginity that solitarily, under the transparence
of adequate looking, has, so to speak, split itself
into its own candid fragments, that one and this
other, nuptial proofs of the Idea.]

From Tournon on, it will be recalled, the paper's
whiteness had signified some mysterious interdiction.
This was clearly the prohibition against dreaming too
much, delving too deeply—it was, in a word, censorship. If the difficulty of extraordinary verses alone had
kept Mallarmé from writing, he would not have been
possessed with anxiety, particularly not funereal anxiety. But I have already been too insistent on this point.

Anxiety disappeared, as we saw in the quotation
above, through the grace of a particularly adequate
sublimation. The disguise is so perfect that our whole
network of associations is needed to unravel the mystery. In what respect could "Reading—Practice" dis-
turb an inner censorship? All the precautions of anonymity and secrecy are taken. One even forgets "the

title which would speak aloud"—an effacement analogous to that of the face of the walker in *Nénuphar blanc*. The mystery will be revealed as little as possible, "in a chink scattered (the least one)." Besides, only words are involved, and it may be forgotten that words have been assimilated to flowers, which in *Toast funèbre* sprang up beside a tomb, that this tomb represented an obsession and the flowers a dead woman. Consciousness could forget all that, but not so an unconscious that was charged with emotion. Therefore, words must be revealed in the greatest secrecy, furtively ravished, like the *Nénuphar blanc*, with a vague and delightful sense of guilt, for quickly white returns. Nuptials have, however, taken place: "Virginity that solitarily, under the transparence of adequate looking, has, so to speak, split itself into its own candid fragments, that one and this other, nuptial proofs of the Idea." The "adequate looking" is that of St. John catching sight of Hérodiade, of the Faun taking the nymphs by surprise, of the rower conjecturing "feminine leisures." The spectator, always, remains on this side of the "secret threshold," as he was formerly on this side of the window, the mirror, or the tomb. The sentence which is aligned "in a chink scattered (the least one)" also becomes the easy analog of the constellation which formerly appeared behind the glass and in the mirror, where it replaced the nude phantom. The page is nothing but the window: to the unconscious it represents in its turn the open tomb.

In *Variété II*[9] Valéry speaks thus of *Coup de dés*, the manuscript of which Mallarmé had been showing him:
. . . Il me sembla de voir la figure d'une pensée, pour la première fois placée dans notre espace . . . Ici, véritablement, l'étendue parlait, songeait, enfantait des formes temporelles. . . . Le soir du même jour, comme il m'accompagnait au chemin de fer, l'innombrable ciel de juillet enfermant toutes choses dans un groupe étincelant d'autres mondes, et que nous marchions, fumeurs obscurs,

au milieu du Serpent, du Cygne, de l'Aigle, de la Lyre, il me semblait *maintenant* d'être pris dans le texte même de l'univers silencieux. . . . Au creux d'une telle nuit, entre les propos que nous échangions, je songeais à la tentative merveilleuse: quel modèle, quel enseignement là-haut! Où Kant, assez naïvement, peut-être, avait cru voir la Loi morale, Mallarmé percevait sans doute l'Impératif d'une poésie, une Poétique . . . Il a essayé, pensai-je, *d'élever enfin une page à la puissance du ciel étoilé.*

[. . . It was as if for the first time I saw the form of a thought, put into our space . . . Here, truly, space discoursed, dreamed, begot temporal forms. . . . The evening of the same day, as he accompanied me to my train, the infinite July firmament enclosing all things in a sparkling cluster of other worlds, and as we went, dark smokers, amidst the Serpent, the Swan, the Eagle, the Lyre, it seemed to me that *now* I was taken into the very text of the silent universe. . . . In the hollow of such a night, between the remarks we exchanged, I thought of the marvelous attempt: what a model, what teaching above! Where Kant, rather naïvely perhaps, believed he saw the moral Law, Mallarmé undoubtedly saw the Imperative of a poetry, a Poetic . . . He has tried, I thought, *at last to raise a page to the power of the starry vault.*]
Valéry is magnificent in appreciating the exterior of the problem. We are rejoining him after a subterranean advance. It is not by chance or genius that the words of *Coup de dés* simulate stars in groups. The obscure network of emotional metaphors made the thing possible and almost inevitable. As the man who dreams at the threshold of the tomb or before the window becomes the reader, so the phantom becomes the constellation, the constellation becomes the phrase. The ap-

parition, however, remains taboo. The blank which usurps Mallarmé's pages represents the eternal prohibition, the snow on Deborah's tomb, Hérodiade's "white night of ice," the frozen lake of the Swan—in short, the dead space to which the virgin recedes.

To define clearly here the relations which certainly obtain between these unconscious obsessions and Mallarmé's style, his ideal symbolism, his insistence on absence, his allusions, his use of mystery, and his musicality, it would be necessary to solve the general problem of the relationship between instinct and poetry or, as psychologists say, between functions and values. Now we are far from having hit on this general solution. If the present work has the least merit, it will be due to the fact that it supplies some materials for the investigation of a problem which is in reality the key to human psychology, since man will remain an enigma as long as we do not know what agreements and what oppositions keep animality and the spirit in balance. The word "sublimation" is useful; its content, however, is poorly defined when really superior transpositions are involved. We must gather facts and follow the threads which tie them together. The notion of a "spectacular complex" is certainly most valuable to us in our gropings. Visual enjoyment, "Schaulust," surely forms one of these threads. Taste for the theater, which is manifest throughout his work, from *Phénomène futur* or *Pitre châtié* to the *Ballets* or the *Offices*, going through *Hérodiade* and the *Faune*, has to be added. We have noted apropos of Hamlet, in *Coup de dés*, a number of analogies between Mallarmé's idea of drama in general and the circumstances of his own inner drama. I should like to point out another of these analogies with respect to the dance. Mallarmé is known to have thought of this art as a script, with the dancer becoming a sort of living hieroglyph:

L'unique entraînement imaginatif consiste, aux heures ordinaires de fréquentation dans les lieux

de Danse sans visée quelconque préalable, patiem-
ment et passivement à se demander devant tout
pas, chaque attitude si étranges, ces pointes et
taquetés, allongés ou ballons: "Que peut signifier
ceci" ou mieux, d'inspiration, le lire.[10]

[The unique imaginative training, in the usual
hours when one aimlessly visits the temples of the
Dance, consists of patiently and passively inquir-
ing at each strange step and each strange pose,
toeing, tapping, lunge, or rebound: "What can this
mean?" or better, with inspiration actually reading it.]

What sort of meaning does a dance step have? The
reply is obvious: the same that a musical phrase has.
We cannot examine here what the word "mean" signifies. The point of interest is this: we have elsewhere
established the chain of associations Maria—flower—
idea or words.[11] Since we now have the connection
dancer-idea or hieroglyph, is it not possible to find
somewhere the association Maria-dancer, so as to
form a parallel chain? I believe we can do so by comparing two sentences, one of which, taken from the
free composition, dates from 1857, and the other, from
Ballets, 1885. Here is the first:

Tantôt elle croisait sur sa poitrine ses deux
mains effilées et liliales et, ses cheveux éthérés
ondulant le long de son dos ainsi que deux ailes,
elle semblait, les yeux levés au ciel, s'envoler vers
des régions bleues et mystiques, tantôt la folle
tournait comme un éblouissement et riait sous sa
pâle couronne de morte.

Et quand elle commença sa danse enivrée, elle
cueillit quelques roses de cette couronne, les ef-
feuilla et y mêlant les pistils de la royale rose rouge
avec laquelle elle avait conservé son père, les jeta
en l'air, et, décrochant son tambour de basque

pieusement conservé, y reçut cette neige embaumée et les jeta de nouveau.

Cette fois, son sourire était si céleste que les fleurs, ravies, restèrent à voltiger dans la chambre.

Alors, au sein de cet enchantement, elle s'élança avec un tournoiement vertigineux, et ses cheveux flottaient dans les parfums des roses.

[Now she crossed her two thin, lily-like hands on her breast and, her ethereal hair flowing down her back like two wings, she seemed—eyes raised to heaven—to be flying toward blue and mysterious realms; now rashly she turned like a burst of light and laughed under her pale crown of death.

And when she began her wild dance, she gathered several roses from this crown, plucked their petals, and, mingling with them the pistils of the royal red rose with which she had saved her father, tossed them into the air and, taking down her tambourine which had been so piously preserved, received on it this scented snow and tossed it again.

This time, her smile was so heavenly that the flowers, ravished, remained fluttering in the room.

Then, in the midst of this spell, she shot out with a dizzying turn, and her hair drifted in the fragrance of the roses.]

Here is the second:

Oui, celle-là (serais-tu perdu en une salle, spectateur très étranger, Ami) pour peu que tu déposes avec soumission à ses pieds d'inconsciente révélatrice ainsi que les roses qu'enlève et jette en la visibilité de régions supérieures un jeu de ses chaussons de satin pâle vertigineux, la Fleur d'abord *de ton poétique instinct,* n'attendant de rien autre la mise en évidence et sous le vrai jour des mille imaginations latentes: alors, par un commerce dont paraît son sourire verser le secret, sans tarder elle te livre à travers le voile dernier qui toujours reste, la nudité de tes concepts et silencieusement écrira ta vision à la façon d'un Signe, qu'elle est.

[Yes, she (should you be lost in the hall, Friend, very foreign spectator) if only you will place ever so lightly and submissively at the feet of this unconscious prophetess, not only the roses that a motion of her vertiginous pale satin shoes whisks away and tosses into the sight of higher spheres, but also the Flower *of your poetic instinct,* expecting nothing else to be revealed and in the true light of a thousand secret fancies: then, by an interchange the secret of which her smile seems to shed, without delaying she delivers you past the final veil which always remains, the nakedness of your concepts, and will silently write your visions in the fashion of a Symbol, which she is.]

I come next to Méry Laurent. This affair (Maria—Miss Mary[12]—Marie—Méry: is it pure coincidence?) began in 1883—"the year when father recaptured his youth," Geneviève Mallarmé wrote. The stiff, unhappy letter published by Dr. Mondor[13] apparently marks the end of the intimacy (though friendship remained intact); it is dated 1889. The chronology of the works proves that this same period was rich in publications, articles, or poems:

1884 *Prose pour des Esseintes—Autre Eventail de Mlle Mallarmé.*

1885 *M'introduire dans ton histoire—Victorieusement fui—Quelle soie aux baumes de temps—Le vierge, le vivace—Hommage à Wagner—Nénuphar blanc—Richard Wagner.*

1886 *L'Ecclésiastique—La Gloire—Hamlet—Ballets—Mimique—Le Genre ou des modernes—Parenthèse—Notes sur le théâtre.*

1887 *Triptyque—Mes bouquins refermés—La Che-*

velure vol d'une flamme—Dame sans trop
d'ardeur—O si chère de loin—Crayonné au
Théâtre—Déclaration foraine—Solennité—Ses
purs ongles très haut.
1889 *Rondel II—Chansons bas.*

A selection from these works has to be made. Certain
of them were taken out of desk drawers, perhaps corrected, and published: *L'Angoisse ce minuit,* the three
sonnets of *Triptyque,* and *Cygne* are of this number.
Prose pour des Esseintes also, in my opinion, belongs to
this group. On the other hand, the different pieces that
directly concern Méry (*M'introduire dans ton histoire,*
Quelle soie aux baumes de temps, Victorieusement fui,
La Chevelure vol d'une flamme, O si chère de loin,
Dame sans trop d'ardeur, Rondels, and so on) are properly verses of circumstance. After 1864 Mallarmé had
kept his life separate from his work. But now again the
two curves touched. Was Mallarmé once more going to
try to assimilate life to the dream? living woman to
the phantom? We shall examine several texts from that
point of view. We have cited the tercets of a sonnet unquestionably written for Méry Laurent:

Mon coeur qui dans les nuits parfois cherche à
    s'entendre
Ou de quel dernier mot t'appeler le plus tendre
S'exalte en celui rien que chuchoté de soeur

N'était, très grand trésor et tête si petite,
Que tu m'enseignes bien toute une autre douceur
Tout bas par le baiser seul dans tes cheveux dite.[14]

[My heart that in the night at times seeks to be
    heard
Or by what final, most tender word to call you
Is exalted in the choice of the whispered "sister"

Were it not, huge treasure and head so small,
That you teach me quite another gentleness
Spoken quite low by the sole kiss in your hair.]

185

Marie Gerhard, like Ettie Yapp, had been called sister, we remember: "My sister with the look of yesteryear"—"nevertheless, she was my sister and my wife." The same tender name is now given Méry Laurent, and the first tercet proves that it was not chosen accidentally. "Sister" remains the most tender name, and Stéphane "is exalted" to "whisper" it. This leads us to the sonnet *Pour votre chère morte:*

> . . . Une veille t'exalte à ne pas fermer l'oeil . . .
> Pour revivre il suffit qu'à tes lèvres j'emprunte
> Le souffle de mon nom murmuré tout un soir.

> [A vigil exalts you so that you do not close an
>   eye . . .
> To live again it suffices that from your lips I borrow
> The breath of my name murmured a whole evening.]

A vague and secret assimilation of Méry to Maria seems almost indisputable. Mallarmé's affections all graft onto a single branch. In 1885, however, the sublimations he had already achieved enabled real life to skirt the dream without anxiety. The living woman remained quite real, as the second tercet tells us. We shall come back to the hair image, which has reappeared. I should like first to point out the words "head so small," which will remove all doubt that the sonnet *Victorieusement fui* is addressed to Méry Laurent. A variant of this poem, indeed, includes this verse:

> La tienne, si toujours petite! c'est la tienne

> [Yours, always so small! it is yours]

which later became

> La tienne, si toujours frivole! c'est la tienne

> [Yours, always so frivolous! it is yours]

then

186

La tienne, si toujours le délice! la tienne.

[Yours, always such a delight! yours.]
This detail, joined to the already sufficient indications as to date and subject, establishes the identity of the "child empress." This point is important, since *Victorieusement fui* provides—in my view—the (very awkward) transition between the poems of 1862–1870 and those of 1884–1887.

The new passion, in fact, was bound to evoke the old images used in *Château de l'espérance, Plainte d'automne, Symphonie littéraire,* and others: hair, sunset, faded glory, autumn, blood, tomb, and suicide. When apropos of *Coup de dés* we studied term by term the correspondences of *Sonnet en YX, Triptyque,* and *Igitur,* the image we found throughout was that of the room at midnight. We had already left *Plainte d'automne* and its sunset far behind. But it returns with the Méry affair, and it is to be supposed that, since *Triptyque* was published during this period, the last tawny glare being extinguished in it from the beginning,

Tout Orgueil fume-t-il du soir,
Torche dans un branle étouffée[15]

[Does all Pride smoke out evening,
Torch snuffed out by shaking]
issues from Méry, her hair, and her love. Further, it is Méry who, in the sonnet of *Déclaration foraine,* is likened to a torch:

Ainsi qu'une joyeuse et tutélaire torche.

[As a joyous and guardian torch.]
The links of association in Mallarmé's work are so regular that the hypothesis concerning *Tout Orgueil* may remain undefined. It is not at all necessary that in writing *Tout Orgueil* Mallarmé should have thought consciously of Méry. On the contrary, I am almost sure

that he made the connection unconsciously. In any case, the first quatrain of *Victorieusement fui le suicide beau* lends the most remarkable confirmation to our basic thesis. All the obsessive metaphors associated with love in 1864 emerge again here twenty years afterwards, intact, and manifest themselves under the impulse of the new love. Who forced Mallarmé, in love with Méry Laurent, to refer again to tomb, suicide, sunset, and blood? The difference from 1864 is a quasi-reversal of emotional tone: suicide "victoriously fled," laughing, and absent tomb. Funereal triumph becomes a mild joke.[16]

This is not surprising after *Toast funèbre*, which as early as 1873 represented a victory over the tomb. No matter—the renewed obsession once again forces the arabesque of the poem to pass through the old fixed points. In fact, the sonnet is built on the old plan of anxious nights, as we can see by comparing it with *Triptyque*. Disgrace, punishment, tomb (though in joking fashion), in the first quatrain, correspond to *Tout Orgueil*. The second quatrain is a midnight questioning, but whereas it remained answerless in *Surgi de la croupe et du bond*, in this poem reality asserts itself. However, the living woman is destined in the last verses to undergo the subtle influence of the past:

> Comme un casque guerrier d'impératrice enfant
> Dont pour te figurer il tomberait des roses.

> [Like a martial helmet of a child empress
> From which, to represent you, roses would fall.]

Indeed, "child empress" leads us back to the galleys of *Fenêtres*, the lions of *Hérodiade*, to lost glories, and to childhood. We know the significance of roses. Thus, in spite of everything, this obsession out of the past is shown as filling the tercets of the *Sonnet en YX* and the last part of *Triptyque*.

Do these quests for analogies led us to oversimplification? I do not think so. The image of the "child empress" is a far cry from the "mandolin . . . musician of hollow nothingness." [17] Their difference is that of two states of soul. But diversity of psychological attitudes does not keep the obsession from displaying itself in most insistent fashion. The sonnet *Victorieusement fui* no doubt reveals a certain human joy. In the compromise between life and dream, life has much the better of it. Art suffers to a degree. The two very different versions of the poem reveal an idea that hesitates, as if cramped. The lofty metaphor appears beautiful and simple: the only brightness remaining from the vanished sunset belongs to the hair. But the sunset and its puerile triumph undoubtedly represent a lost glory;[18] if the real woman is only its reflection and is precious only for this fact, it is as much as to say that sunset is missed. But then why call it puerile? Why, as early as the second quatrain, this rather unhappy search?

> Quoi! de tout cet éclat pas même le lambeau
> S'attarde . . .

> [What! of all this brightness not even a shred
> Lingers . . .]

The same reticence is to be seen in another piece to Méry: *Quelle soie aux baumes de temps.* As between the hair, on this side of the mirror, and the flags, on the other side of the window (they are probably still the glorious clouds of sunset), Mallarmé gives preference to the near side. But he does not stop thinking of the glory beyond, its abandonment—unhappily experienced—being the princely price he pays for actual possession. Mallarmé remains obsessed.

The stamp of guilt also persists.

> M'introduire dans ton histoire
> C'est en héros effarouché . . .

> [To introduce myself into your history
> It is as a frightened hero I come . . .]

Mallarmé, it is true, turns the thing into a light joke. It is no less symptomatic that so much pain is discernible in the poem, whether the "innocent sin" has been committed or not. The only complete triumph is still a sunset: [19]

>Dis si je ne suis pas joyeux
>Tonnerre et rubis aux moyeux
>De voir en l'air que ce feu troue
>
>Avec des royaumes épars
>Comme mourir pourpre la roue
>Du seul vespéral de mes chars
>
>[Say if I am not joyful
>Thunder and rubies at the axles
>To see how this fire pierces the air
>
>Scattered with kingdoms
>As if to die purple, the wheel
>Of the only vesperal of my chariots.]

The obscurity of these poems arises in large part from the ambiguity of feeling and the reticent expression that results. Mallarmé did not reach the point of choosing frankly between a real amorous conquest and the heavenly and intangible symbolic triumph beyond the window. We have no doubt, though, of the significance of the glory behind the window, and if we were dubious, we would need only to examine the prose poem which was written at this same period and which reveals what Mallarmé meant by glory in this same year, 1886: "La gloire! je ne la sus qu'hier, irréfragable, et rien ne m'intéressera d'appelé par quelqu'un ainsi." ["Glory! I learned it only yesterday, irrefragable, and nothing that anyone calls by that name will interest me."]

It is the forest of Fontainebleau, in autumn. Let us notice in the text: "bitter and luminous sobs," "daily vigil of immortal trunks bending over one with superhuman pride," and "pass the threshold where torches held high consume bygone dreams." If the "luminous sobs" recall the first seraphic poems, "vigil," "immortals," "pride," and "torches" restore us to the atmosphere of *Triptyque:*

Tout Orgueil fume-t-il du soir,
Torche dans un branle étouffée
Sans que l'immortelle bouffée
Ne puisse à l'abandon surseoir!

[Does all Pride smoke out evening,
Torch snuffed out by shaking
Without the immortal puff
Being able to postpone abandonment!]

and in that of the *Sonnet en YX*, as is confirmed by the torches consuming dreams:

L'Angoisse, ce minuit, soutient, lampadophore,
Maint rêve vespéral brûlé par le Phénix . . .

[Anxiety, this midnight, supports, lamp-bearer,
Many a vesperal dream burned by the Phoenix . . .]

"The royal intruder"—the poet—has only to pass the threshold into this "burst echoing in purple in the skies, the universal rite," in all solitude, letting the train (that is, reality) slip away, reduced "to its proper proportions as a puerile chimera." Such is true glory. It consists, evidently, of abandoning the real for the dream, of entering alive into this beyond (and into the tomb) which—in the sonnets to Méry—gleamed behind the window. For Méry, Mallarmé fled the "royal tomb" spread with purple; in Méry's hair he stifled the cry of glories. But it is in the first loneliness and first autumn that the real triumph is once again to be found—the style leaves no doubt about that.

Thus the second amour of Mallarmé failed, as the first one had, to fuse intimately with his work. Dream and reality remained, at best, tangential. In 1862—we recall *Frisson d'hiver*—the dream paralyzed reality to the point where Mallarmé voluntarily distinguished them. In 1885, the "this side" always made him regret the other side somewhat. All in all, Mallarmé remained the *Apparition* lover, who

S'enivrait savamment du parfum de tristesse
Que même sans regret et sans déboire laisse
La cueillaison d'un Rêve au coeur qui l'a cueilli.

[Intoxicated itself subtly with the perfume of sadness
Which even without regret and without vexation
is left
By the gathering of a Dream in the heart that
picked it.]

Assimilation of the living woman to the dead woman was not easy. Sublimation succeeded infinitely better in the direction of art. "With generality impregnated," the old delight then seemed to emerge into a sort of empty, ideal, detemporalized space where nothing would arrest its development. The most fantastic transpositions met no obstacle. Since the sky of possible creations is not opposed to anything, every impulse (to use the jargon of psychologists) may be volatilized there. Or rather, a single factor resists: the material of the work—language—in the case of poems. But language obeys him who has the key to it, or one of its keys.

7

Orpheus

THE TRUTH OF THE OBSESSION

THE MOMENT has come to stop and cast a critical glance backward. No matter how severe the reader feels about the foregoing, I will join with him in an impartial review. For I will agree that on the plane where we have been functioning, truth alone counts. Is our subterranean explanation of Mallarmé true or false? This is the real question, as long as the word "truth" is used in its scientific sense. In science that hypothesis is "true" which in the present state of knowledge brings together the most facts and gives the best account of them. Since there is no end to experiment, new facts emerge, and it often happens that a new hypothesis must be adopted to include and bind together the experimental materials which have accumulated. This second hypothesis, displacing the first, in its turn becomes truth.

Scientific truth is sometimes thought to be inconsistent because it changes unceasingly before the eye. What is actually growth is taken for chaos. The sage individual learns a great deal from these changes; he finds out how to use theories, their points of view, and their symbols as useful instruments, which for this reason are precious but which are destined some day to be modified. The important thing after each scientific revolution is the new organization that is realized and definitively acquired.

I believe this is the way to look at modern psychological theories. Freud, Janet, Jung, Piaget, Baudouin use different tools. For the general public it is the more or less peculiar appearance of these tools that counts. But often enough the same network of facts can be translated from one terminology to the other without great difficulty. These translations are certainly indispensable in order to eliminate what comes from the specific method, the terminology, the particular theory, and to measure the truth that has been objectively attained.

I must beg the reader's pardon for this long preamble, which I thought was necessary to dispel a number of misunderstandings. In the preceding sections I have used the language I considered most useful—one which was borrowed for the most part from classical psychoanalysis. But I do not hold to it absolutely. A recent work of Doctor Hesnard[1] strives to translate the results of Freudian psychoanalysis into the apparently less mythical language of "behaviorism." Perhaps the day will come when this translation can be readily made. On that day the relationships between conscious and unconscious, infantile and adult thought—relationships which we have tried to follow in Mallarmé's work —may be expressible in terms of behavior, freed of the Freudian mythology. Suppose this does happen? The appearance of the drama will change, but not the drama itself. For the facts will remain the facts; the analogies, the correspondences, the contrasts, will persist. The knots will not unknot.

I say this for the benefit of the reader who may be shocked by psychoanalytic ways of speaking. Let us take a concrete example. One may or may not accept Freudian theory, but the analogies of structure which we have established, by following it, between *Sonnet en YX, Triptyque, Igitur,* and *Coup de dés,* to which must be added poems as different as *Las de l'amer repos* and *Victorieusement fui,* all built on the schema of the famous vigils—these analogies, I say, will persist in any case and will have to be explained in some way that is not too different from ours. I will make the same claim for our chains of symbols. The window, for instance, the obvious threshold to the beyond, will always be related to the tomb. And, since in my opinion it is difficult not to compare this tomb, multiplied as it is by so many specimens in the works—and thus an obvious instance of obsession—with the actual tomb of Mallarmé's sister and his mother, I do not see how the network of relations that criticism will some day establish can differ essentially from the one which has been traced in these pages.

One more word along the same lines. Though I am prepared for a change of language, I would be quite surprised if a future psychological explanation of poetry did not hold onto a great deal of what has been called the "Freudian mythology." It is a question of genius and style. To bring together, as Freud did, worlds as strange and diverse as neurosis, dream, daydream, legend, infantile or primitive morality, myth, and finally religion required an acute, intuitive sense of the thinking that prevails in them and in its modes of expression. As it is difficult to understand poetry without having some poetic bent, so it would appear to be hard to understand myth without being oneself a creator of myths. The farther we move from the physical to the psychological sciences, the less is the distance separating the knowing subject from the known object. There is no psychoanalyst but who must be psychoanalyzed himself, thus combining in himself both patient and doctor. Freud's errors do not arise from the fact that he was too much the poet or metaphysician, but precisely because he was not enough of either. If he had been more the poet, he would not have left the impression that he confused poetic meaning with the expression of a repressed libido, the poem with the symptom. If he had been more the metaphysician, he would not have incurred the objections of Dalbiez.[2] But in the subterranean world, where he so passionately explored the hypogea peopled with strange figures, his way of seeing warrants, I think the truth of his vision. In reading Baudelaire's verses,

> La nature est un temple où de vivants piliers
> Laissent parfois sortir de confuses paroles;
> L'homme y passe à travers des forêts de symboles
> Qui l'observent avec des regards familiers[3]

> [Nature is a temple where living columns
> At times emit obscure words;
> Man passes through forests of symbols there
> Which watch him with familiar looks]

or again,

> J'ai longtemps habité sous de vastes portiques
> Que les soleils marins teignaient de mille
> feux . . .[4]

> [I have long lived under vast porticos
> That sea-drenched suns tinged with a thousand
> fires . . .]

we find truth as well as beauty. Better, we feel that in this realm, truth and beauty could not be far apart. Certainly Freud, aiming at other goals, uses different language from Baudelaire's. But the universe he exposes to us must in the final analysis have a certain beauty, or risk being false. Perhaps I am wrong, but this is my feeling. And if one day the Freudian mythology must be translated into another language, I believe scholars will do well to see that they do not lose in the process what Freud's grand style achieved and not, under the pretext of realism once more, ascribe to petty childhood accidents what will always remain, in the human psyche as in the animal organism, the vast contest between life and death.

To come back to Mallarmé, I wished to indicate, rightly or wrongly, that the subterranean explanation of Mallarmé—barely sketched above—seems to me to contain some truth simply because it is beautiful. The unconscious forms a sort of musical bass to consciousness. Our everyday life is often chaotic, and the unconscious shares in this character. But the substructures of a great idea must participate in the idea's greatness. Mallarmé always had the feeling that he was working toward the completion of a huge project, though he seems actually to have produced only tiny isolated and fragmentary bits. No doubt a person often deceives himself. But may it not also be the case that Mallarmé was better situated than we to understand what he had in mind?

I have not been surprised but pleased to see a sort of underlying unity corresponding to the unity of his intention and therefore to imagine the small poems which *were* written as being so many islands, all links of one broad, submerged shelf. Objectively, too, the importance which is generally accorded Mallarmé's work (an importance always felt but not easily proven because it appears to be out of proportion to the given data), may better be explained in this way. The hypothesis we have set forth certainly accounts for a large number of particular facts, and I said at the outset that conviction on this matter grows primarily from an accumulation of small concordant proofs. But once the accumulation is established, its totality forms a mass whose lines appear to me not unbeautiful. Beneath a Romanesque church it is no surprise to discover a crypt of architectural value. But I have already said enough on this subject, and I shall go on to more general issues.

THE DETERMINATION OF THE OBSESSION

We have used above the words "subterranean explanation." Say that our hypothesis is correct. Does it represent an explanation of Mallarmé? As in the case of the word "truth" at the beginning of this chapter, I shall ask the reader to follow me in a definition. If I am hazy as to why the sum of the angles of a triangle equals two right angles, Euclid explains it to me by having me go back, as along a river, through a series of equivalences: from equality to equality, we arrive at some source of certainty. In experimental science, to explain is also to go back from phenomenon to phenomenon, as in countercurrent.

This is the meaning of the word "truth" in rational or scientific logic. I must stress the fact that value is not involved here. The conclusion of a theorem is no more true or false than its premises: the phenomenon is neither more nor less true than its antecedents. Ideas of value and hierarchy are quite foreign to this logic. When psychoanalysts wondered whether a great work of art could be explained in terms of unconscious phenomena, which are often ludicrously infantile, they naturally ran afoul of this difficulty. There are two ways of dodging the issue: one can deny that value has any objective reality (and in that case there remains little enough of art or morals, whether one admits it or not); or one can concede the reality of value but declare it foreign to the province of science and thus put it aside. This is clearly the attitude taken by Dr. Odier[5] for morals and M. Charles Baudouin[6] with respect to art. The latter, for example, frequently insists that the distinction between value and origin must be maintained. In other words, he remains faithful to scientific logic as defined above.

The average man is not bound by the same scruples. Value and hierarchy are essential for him. Any explanation of art is confused in his mind with an explanation of beauty. And if he is shown that a Mallarmé poem has the same source as a neurotic symptom, he will at once ask where the charm of the poem comes from, and where the imbecility of the neurosis. This sort of explanation will be of little interest to him.[7] Automatically he will seek another, which proceeds, not from phenomenon to phenomenon, but from principle to manifestation, or, if one wishes, from creator to creation. From the standpoint of value, which is basic in this connection, the signifying factor is at the same time higher than the sign and of quite a distinct nature. If I am told that Johann Sebastian Bach is the author of a cantata, I have the explanation of its beauty. It would be worth nothing to the reasoning faculty; it is sufficient in itself. "Because it was he, because it was I"[8] explains nothing to reason but everything to the heart. The logic of the heart is alone adequate when life, love, and creation are involved.

The question "Have we explained Mallarmé?" thus permits two answers. In terms of scientific logic, I believe the answer is yes. Certainly every human creation is a function of numerous variables, and we have studied only one of these. Hence even in this realm the explanation is only partly complete. In any case, though, it would appear difficult to doubt the links between such and such a poem of Mallarmé, on the one hand, and the death of his mother and sister on the other. But if we adopt the other logic? Then the response is different.

An obsession cannot create a work of art, for the simple reason that the obsession belongs to an inferior order of things. The aesthetic irrational is situated above and not below reason. One must admit this as a fact of human experience or give up that hierarchy of mental functions that Janet himself supported with such good sense.[9] Put in another way, the structure of our psyche necessitates two coördinates: the one, which is emotional, vertical; the other, which is rational and discursive, horizontal. This latter line, which is like a threshold of reason, separates the two affectivities, superior and inferior. Aesthetic sensitivity, for example, that is, sensitiveness to style and its variations, cannot be confused with animal emotivity.

In this framework the role that unconscious obsession plays in poetry seems to be clear. It is not a matter of a center of creation but of a load, a fixation, a root. From this point, liberty has to be achieved in the direction of higher things. Mallarmé's obsession with dead mother and sister does not create his work; no more does it explain it; it determines it, it fastens it by the foot.

Obsession and Poem

I would like as far as possible to avoid metaphors in this section and remain close to experience. What has experience revealed about the relations between poems and obsession? The monotony of the unconscious, first of all, is opposed to the freedom of the poems, to their differences in pace and tone. I have given enough examples of this fact; I shall only recall how the major symbols of a single obsession, dividing and multiplying the original fixity, form those motionless constellations through which the arabesque of the poem must necessarily pass. It is what I called, in *Mallarmé l'obscur,* the network of obsessive metaphors. We have just connected this network to its lower center. From this lower center comes a determination—that is, a limitation of liberty, as we have just noticed—but also an armature.

Let us go on to a second feature of our experience. This lower center exercises a sort of magnetism. It creates around it a field of force. Mallarmé experienced it in the form of emotion. We see it otherwise. It counted heavily, I should think, in that impression (shared by so many readers) of a shimmer below. Today I can scarcely think of Mallarmé's windows or his white pages without seeing in filigree the tomb they stand for. The beauty is not diminished by that fact.[10] But let us return to the fascination that the unconscious exerted on Mallarmé himself. It is a marked feature of his works. But let us not deceive ourselves: if Mallarmé had given in to the obsession, he would not have written; he would have committed suicide. We have just mentioned a field of force created by an unconscious center. Its lines converge toward the past and toward death. Life and creation inevitably led him to free himself of this attraction.

Thus we reach the third point suggested by our experimental findings. They led us to an image of unconscious obsession which has much in common with the Fate of ancient times. May one say that the poem escapes this fate? Yes and no. We have amply demonstrated the obstinacy and the irony of such an obsession. The poet, at the outset, seemed to be served by his unconscious: it gave him at first this depth in symbol, these strange, sure correspondences his friends admired. Then anxiety and inhibition developed. Mallarmé had to live counter to his thought. In Paris, he believed the tomb had closed on his obsession. But the flowers in the garden where he strolled were but a new metamorphosis of it. It would follow him behind Méry Laurent's windows, into the forest of Fontainebleau, on the river, at the opera, at Valvins, everywhere. In some respects, though, he evaded it, escaped suicide, lived, and created successful works. How was that possible? We must accept the experimental fact. Without eluding our individual fatality and its obsessive determination, we may—in the direction it has chosen for us—slip out of its magnetic field. I think at this point of Bacon's dictum on nature: "One conquers it only by obeying it." How can our liberty at one and the same time obey and conquer psychological determinism? Mallarmé shows us by his example.

THE TWO SOURCES OF AFFECTIVITY

The miracle of creative liberty will always appear absurd if rational categories are applied to it. To understand anything of it at all, we must—as we have seen—admit that beyond reason there is a higher affectivity, a further irrational magnetic field. The lower irrational has for a center the infantile ego. In the new field, the Other becomes the center of gravity. But, you will say, what is this Other? It takes so many forms that perhaps it is wisest not to name it. Saints call it God; the artist thinks he sees it in the work he undertakes; the mother adores it in her child. I shall not linger over this diversity and the limits it supposes. The main thing is achieved if we admit the existence of this new affectivity, which, over and beyond all reason, is rather a natural gift than an acquisition.[11]

The adoption of this hypothesis would, in my view, be of great help in finally reconciling aesthetics and the particular idea of the development of the human mind which we are using. Modern psychologists agree in ascribing an almost absolute autism to infantile thought. Ego and non-ego are at first confused. They slowly become distinct, but the center of psychic life naturally remains the ego and its instincts. The child's universe contains only a subject, everything else being objects which are more or less at its service. This distinction may seem to be obscured by the animism of the child, who endows objects with wills of their own. But these are always favorable or unfavorable, and hence are oriented with respect to the self. The infantile animation of objects does not change them into independent beings. By a series of adjustments to the real, such as Piaget describes,[12] the child's mind and his universe are transformed. Others cease to appear to him as instruments to serve his egoism; they become independent beings. Material objects, on the contrary, shed their borrowed soul and are no longer considered as anything but instruments. Animals waver between the two categories. Morally, the individual at this same adult stage more or less firmly acquires with regard to other persons what Dr. Odier[13] calls the essential idea of reciprocity. I will add that it is accompanied by an almost absolute idea of superiority with respect to what is non-human. Equality with the animate subject, domination of the inanimate object—such is the ideal of the rational and social consciousness. What does it represent from the spiritual point of view? It is clear that the level thus achieved corresponds to the boundary between the two magnetic fields of ego and Other. Provided that the Other is a human being, I neither take from him nor give him anything, and objects are made to serve us. Such is perhaps the optimum of a closed morality, as Bergson calls it.

But all spiritual life opens up beyond this limit. Let us leave morals for art. What is a work of art if not an animated object? The reader can quarrel with the terms of this definition; I doubt if he can do any more than replace them with equivalent terms. "Animated object" does not fall into any of the categories above. The scholar will naturally be tempted to see in it the same thing as the favorable or hostile objects peopling the infantile universe. He will speak of the animism of artists, thus committing the error of setting below reason what is above it. For the work of art is not favorable or hostile; it is not oriented by its relationship to the ego; it belongs to this new universe, situated beyond reason, where specifically, and as though by definition, objects themselves no longer serve any purpose. Through rational consciousness on the inside, through reciprocity with the outside, the subject (from rational stage on) escapes servitude. The object escapes from that only in the beyond. Thus to a certain degree the poem becomes subject and is animate. Fantasy? No, experience. The artist and the spiritual man cease to consider the objects of the universe as instruments; they renounce them and, so to speak, give them back. Thereupon what we call the soul of things is revealed to the artist. This expression is perhaps defective, but it corresponds to an observable fact. To say that the artist projects his own soul into the exterior universe is a far less adequate way of putting it. False artists, perhaps, do so.[14] The genuine artist looks around him at things with the proper care for their quality, their style. He forgets himself to study them. And inversely, whoever loses himself in the contemplation of an object—were it but for a moment—enters the kingdom of the spirit and makes his apprenticeship in aesthetic life.

But there is more. The artist is not content to perceive the soul of liberated objects; he can create others. Here the word "projection" perhaps is useful. The artist necessarily puts himself at the center of his work. He animates it with his own soul. In this way is created, moreover, a new kind of property, which is acquired not through taking but through giving. To the spiritual universe, peopled with free animated objects serving no purpose (those objects a person encounters during a walk), the artist adds his own, so called because he gives them.

This creation is a wonderful thing, entirely inexplicable in rational logic, of course, but obvious in terms of the other logic. I said just now that the object was freed as soon as we gave up exercising our right of domination over it. Having freed external objects in this way, we gain in return—for a moment, anyway, since we are typically unstable[15]—the power of seeing the uniqueness of things: there remains only to free the ego we have in us. Certainly it will be difficult to detach ourselves from it, to treat it as an object belonging to us, but the operation will offer less difficulty for an ego that is already passé, already dead in us. This we can hold at a distance and look at; love, no longer egotistically, but for itself, in the way we love a tree. This is the reason true poets naturally turn to their past and try, like Proust, to regain their lost time. Let us say, then, that the artist will have objectively at his disposal a fragment of soul detached from himself. Will he project it, as is generally believed, upon external objects? Not at all. He will make the soul of an extraordinary object out of it, and the word "projection" is of value here only if it is understood to mean "gift." The saint pushes this act to its absolute limits; he veritably offers his soul to God.[16] The artist rarely speaks of God.

204

He gives his soul to an ill-defined Other. Precision is, moreover, useless, for the spirit in which the deed is done is all that counts. Now about this spirit there can be no question. Even if the artist upon resuming his ordinary life offers monstrous examples of egotism in daily intercourse, creation remains in itself a free gift.

Unconscious Ego–Conscious Ego and X

The question for those of us who are using aesthetic psychology is to know, not whom the gift is intended for, but who makes the gift. To become detached from the self (unconscious or conscious), we need another personage. Freudian mythology contains a number of entities of the sort: Id, Ego, Superego, and Self, properly speaking. This list is limited to the two psychic layers of the lower unconscious and of the conscious mind. If a superior irrational exists above consciousness, one or several new entities must be considered. Jung realized this aim by developing his thesis of the self and the autonomous centers.[17] To repeat, these are useful terms and no more. But why not adopt them if they exactly reflect the experimental facts?

The personage that gives the world a Mallarmé poem could not belong to the poet's unconscious. We have demonstrated this point at great length. Nor can it be confused with the conscious and rational self. This self speaks in ordinary prose and is by definition ignorant of the unconscious. To remain faithful to the facts, let us say that the true author of the poem was at the same time aware both of Mallarmé's unconscious and of his conscious thought. More, he could reconcile them. Perhaps this hypothesis will seem fantastic to the reader, but I see no alternative. The idea implicit in many psychoanalytic works, according to which the poem was created in the void and effected a sort of compromise between conscious thought and unconscious drives, will not stand up. Besides, we have already refuted it. An intelligent idea, falsified (for this would be the term) by unconscious desires, would be simply a less intelligent idea, not at all a work of art (think, for instance, of the hypocrisy of a biased attorney's address to the court). If beauty, if value, exist, someone has experienced them and longed for them. And since in the poem harmony reverberates as between obsession and clear thought, this combination requires a creator who is aware of the two realities.

Again, only examination of the poems could have suggested to us that this personage existed. Stubbornly, as we have seen, a curve is repeated, that of the vigils: descent to the Styx and reascent to the dawn. This formula exactly retraces the journey of the superior figure we have been speaking of. To write the poem, he had at first to descend toward the dead woman, that is, to the unconscious and its obsession, and then remount to the surface and compare what he had learned below with the means of expression, with the ideas and the idiom, of the conscious personality. For the tomb was ignorant of thought, which in turn was unaware of the tomb. Let us even admit that these two realities do vaguely influence one another, as they do in everyday life; but which one of them could see a way to unite them? Behind the vase or the rose, Mallarmé's conscious mind did not see his dead mother or sister; how then did the idea of a journey to the tomb reach him? But this idea, so foreign to consciousness, must be still more alien to the unconscious. Where, then, did it come from? And how did the poem owe its form to that source? Someone must tell us his story through this imprint (the form) and then, so to speak, sign it.

Orpheus

In his short *Autobiographie* Mallarmé admits that his aim is to give the "Orphic explanation of Earth, which is the sole duty of the poet." Orpheus combines the two figures of singer and mystic initiate. For thousands of years men have amassed spiritual experiences; these experiences are often recapitulated in myths which, if we are to grasp them, we must translate into modern terms without neglecting their higher meaning.[18] Like so many heroes and so many singers—Virgil, Dante—Orpheus must and can descend to the Underworld. Indeed, the beginning of his initiatory journey is there. This is what René Guénon says in *Esotérisme de Dante:*[19]

> . . . Since true initiation is a process by which we take conscious possession of superior states, it is easy to understand why it is symbolically described as an ascent or a "celestial journey"; but it might be asked why this ascent must be preceded by a descent into the Underworld. . . . We will say only this: on the one hand, this descent is like a recapitulation of states which logically precede the human state, which have determined its special conditions and which must also share in the "transformation" to come; on the other hand it permits the revelation (acording to certain modalities) of possibilities of a lower order which the individual still carries within him in an undeveloped state, and which must be exhausted by him before he may arrive at the realization of his higher states.

The point of view adopted by Guénon largely overlaps our own. I have reproduced his text here in order to stress a certain number of correspondences:

1. Recapitulation, Guénon says, of anterior states, which have determined the actual state and must share in the "transformation" to come. This would appear to be the descent toward that obsession to which we have actually given the role of lower determinant and which nevertheless participates in the poetic transmutation.

2. Manifestation of lower possibilities, which have not been realized, thus remaining in a state of virtuality. Here, couched in other language, is the familiar idea

of an emotional potential, to which circumstances (the death of the mother and the sister, in Mallarmé's case) have refused normal expression and which are discharged when the individual, frustrated in this way, may through symbolic forms imitate to a degree what he could not live out in real life. Psychoanalysis has often studied the case of these individuals who because of an infantile fixation are forced to live over and over again the same situation: Poe, as a child in love with a consumptive mother, lost her and, after he grew up, could love only sick women. We have seen Mallarmé live through with Ettie Yapp, Marie, and then Méry, something of a tenderness which remained virtual. On this score we have weighed all the danger the soul runs in its trip to the underworld if it does not reascend; in short, if the passage to superior states does not take place. In the limits to which our study is restricted, it is the beauty of the work that represents this peak for us. And what is the main obstacle to the ascent? That dizziness (seeking its justification in logic) which is the subject of *Igitur* and which would have driven Mallarmé to madness and suicide if it had not been for the intervention of other forces. The myth also includes this idea. Orpheus, rising again from the Underworld, must on no account look back, on pain of returning to death the soul he had wrested from it.[20]

Orpheus clearly represents this third personage we were speaking of just now, endowed as he is with the grace of a vertical liberty (which the flight symbolizes), and can descend into the lower regions in search of a dead happiness, without risking eternal imprisonment there. His essential character is this aerial freeness, which is indefinable but which has been symbolized innumerable times in the various branches of spiritual tradition and is represented for us in the word "spirit." Fénelon calls it "suppleness to life and death." Like Ariel, it is but music, and it would be vain to try to rationalize it. For all that, we are very distinctly aware of it, and we can describe this experience. Such is not, however, my purpose here. I would simply like to recall how important it would be in such a description to stress the growth of freedom which accompanies the experience. From unconscious obsession to work of art, from fixed points to arabesque, from anxiety to dancing, from cubical tomb to birth from the mandora, it is always the same transition from solid to fluid and musical. Our third personage, the Orphic ego, potential in each of us, has this gift of volatilization. Thanks to music and its subtle vibrations, Orpheus can descend to the Underworld and charm the monsters who otherwise would keep him captive. So in the realm of the mind this superior self can pass the barrier of those Cerberi, superego, repression, and censorship, in order to penetrate the dungeon of our unconscious night. So Igitur, with the spidery frill, descending among the tombs. But Igitur wished to die and not to bring back the dead. Orpheus brings them back to life, and the vibrations of his lyre remind us slightly of the ultraviolet rays which in plants create life out of ashes, in that extraordinary carbon cycle whose mechanism is so often taught without its beauty's being revealed. Ashes + light = life. What an equation! The light of art is the music, and the ashes it reanimates belong to Psyche, our soul. But what is this life we are referring to?

Proust reflected long and steadily upon his art. The final volume of his work reveals, at all events, the fruit of a sincere aesthetic experience. It is a well-known fact that at this crossroads of *Temps retrouvé* the novelist-poet felt some little astonishment at coming face to face with metaphysical eternity. This sort of illumination occurs, he tells us, when by accident the present and past mingle in a unique sensation. Thus the taste of a *madeleine,* the unevenness of a stone, surreptitiously reveal to the man of the world that there is such a thing as timelessness. Proust's analysis does not go much further than this. By intuition he passes from this chance synthesis to an idealistic conception of art. But his intuition is valid. The question of time certainly plays as significant a role in art as in mysticism. The problem of affinities between temporal and spiritual is to be found in thousands of forms. Whoever says art says creation, and we are accustomed to think of creation in terms of time; finally, the role of time in art, through movement and musical or plastic rhythm, seems in itself obvious enough. All this would require a special study. I should not be surprised if it led to the following conclusions: art might resemble a transition from a lower immobility to a higher immobility, through time and its rhythms.[21] In spite of the differences between the arts, creative acts must in fact be comparable. But the term-to-term correspondences of music with poetry or painting are still very feebly established.[22]

Nevertheless, the scheme I suggested earlier must have some truth to it. In Mallarmé's poetry, the lower immobility is that of an affective fatalism. The arabesque of creation had no chance to be admitted except by obeying its law. However, a first stage of liberty draws the symbols of this obsession into the flow of conscious thought and mixes the unique idea of death with the external or internal realities of daily life. In brief, window becomes tomb without ceasing to be a window. In the process it acquires depth, while the tomb achieves a participation in life, its movements, its rhythms. We are thus very close to Proust's *madeleine* and the contact it establishes between a dead past and living time. But evidently the flash of eternity which is produced would in itself not so much create a poem as constitute a possible element in the poem. I would compare the words thus charged with a secret potential to men who have suddenly fallen in love. This love will stupefy them or, conversely, refine them, according to whether a general tendency bends this force to the

210

service of the ego or of the Other. A second level of freedom comes into play here. Let us suppose that the free choice does incline to the spiritual side. The movements of time, turned into rhythms, will convey the phrase—composed thus of personal words—toward a form which is the poem and toward a quality which is the style. The form is only the totality achieved by the work. It is therefore composed of continuing rhythms; it is made with time.

However, it does not last. Once completed, it is immobilized, and time passes without changing it. Hence we find in the higher form of the work a fixity which was characteristic of its determinants and, in particular, of its lower obsessions. In short, creation has passed through time from low to high, perpendicularly to its flux. The word "form," however, which is bad enough if it is used in the sense of fixed form, is often taken in its rational or spatial sense, but this meaning must be absolutely excluded in this context. In the spiritual sense, form is almost the same as style. If it marks the poem, it is as a fluid which penetrates and perfumes it through and through. It is to the work of art what life is to an organism. Each part of the body is alive; each part of the work has the form and style of the whole. One can spot Mozart in a phrase. So that what moves in time shares in something that does *not*.

To return to Mallarmé, his unconscious obsession was, as it were, exempt from time because it lay below time's process. His style, emerging from that time, nevertheless escaped it. The poem (for there is only one, many times multiplied) thus seems to join two intemporals together by spanning time and its incessant renewal of figures. Between the inert and the eternal, the spirit would build a metaphorical ascent seemingly by using—in the way that a wing will rest on the wind —this horizontal power of time, whose thread is naturally followed by our discursive thought and everyday prose. Creation is a deed: when one speaks of form, of style, no doubt it is best to think of the "form" of a swimmer, of the "style" of a bird, of the singular way in which they keep themselves up as they go forward, rather than to conceive of the static form of a vase, even though the image of the potter, placing his inert clay on that wheel of time which he is turning and giving it the sort of motionless movement which is to be the form of the vase, suggests another version of the truth I have been trying to express.

The image of Orpheus as a potter who restores movement to life and then to the static grace of the Other, to the soft dead clay which he went so deep in search of—this image has its attraction for me. But I have said that I would avoid metaphors, which lead the mind astray if they are pursued too far. Mallarmé's poem goes from obsession to style, passing through the time of its phrases: this is the experimental fact. Indeed, the text of the poem is confused with this median time. But each of its words now appears to be impregnated with obsession, each of its parts penetrated by style. Thus these fixed elements, which for the convenience of the design we placed above and below time, are really in it, somewhat as the weight and quality of the wingbeat belong to the body of the bird in flight. However, the wingbeat releases the body from its weight. Thus we find something of those fields of force we spoke of in connection with the ego and the Other. They set gravity and liberty in opposition to one another.

Obsession in itself constitutes a form of egoism, that is, attachment to a fixed point. Style is a personal means of escaping it. Do obsession and style nevertheless share a similarity? Quite possibly. In Mallarmé we have seen the page on which the poem is inscribed represent afresh the open tomb, and the poet's highest meditations on his art repeat an unconscious attitude. But we must be careful not to oversimplify things, and another general law invites us to be prudent on this score.

For if spiritual experience always reveals a certain analogy between the Other and the ego, it also shows that through the synthesis of creation the Other resolves contradictions, which opposed the ego and conscious reality, or time. Like the famous arrow, the work of art flies and does not fly, lasts and does not last, is made of time and escapes it, unites subject and object, the ego and non-ego, the irrational and the rational, the unconscious and the conscious, and so on. This resolution of contradictory elements is a trait of the mind, and just as we have defined the work by analogy with time, we could place it, dialectically speaking, by describing it as a peace and harmony in strife. Thus we must not be too hasty to relate Mallarmé's style and form to some higher transposition of his unconscious obsession. Doing so, we would neglect one of the two terms that must be united with each other in a higher synthesis— I mean the unique behavior of the living Mallarmé, the rhythms of his conscious existence in time, his way of thinking and talking (even in prose), to say nothing of the events and external concerns of this same flux, London, his wife, the Rhône, and Méry Laurent. These different elements are the ones that literary analysis usually deals with. They do not form an author's style. A better solution would be to combine these externals with the fascination of unconscious obsessions. The great work would be effectuated by a union of unconscious and conscious in such a way that style would result. But this synthesis is not for us, because it is reserved specifically for the creative mind: to achieve it, one would have to compose the poem.

For our intelligence knows only how to analyze. If, casting a look behind me, I consider what I have been able to do in the way of elucidating Mallarmé, I presume to think that gropingly I have played the chemist, isolating as far as possible the elements of a compound. A poem of Mallarmé's, like any other poem, involves a prose sense. Despite the mysteriousness of certain pieces and the deformations that pressures from below and above, of the unconscious and of style, force upon the line of discourse, the clear sense can be isolated and followed according to its grammatical articulations. In this way something emerges which is not the poem, I realize, but which at least allows the poem to be read as it must be read, not topsy-turvy, by not putting the subject in place of a complement and so avoiding those errors of interpretation which are so often taken for the poetry itself. It is to that sort of elucidation that *Mallarmé l'obscur* tended. The present work again tries to isolate below the horizontal time of the poem an unconscious but manifest rigidity. The work, of course, is more than the juxtaposition of these two elements. They could not be added up in other ways, or be compounded like forces: they do not belong to the same level of reality. Every attempt at a simply intellectual synthesis would face insuperable difficulties in dealing with this problem. Creation is what is involved; and we have sufficiently stressed the fact that it calls for the intervention of a third party. Only a third party can descend among the dead and achieve this miraculous fusion of their strange gloomy fixity with the rhythms of daily life on earth. But once the analysis has been made, there is no ban on finding, in what comes out of the crucible, something of what must have been tossed into it.

I will repeat here, then, apropos of obsession, what I said in *Mallarmé l'obscur* about the intelligible meaning: what do we gain by being ignorant of it? Indeed Orpheus himself sees the near side as Ariel sees the depths of the ocean:

> Full fathom five thy father lies,
>   Of his bones are coral made,
> Those are pearls that were his eyes,
>   Nothing of him that doth fade
> But doth suffer a sea-change

Into something rich and strange.
Sea nymphs hourly ring his knell.
Burden.   Dingdong.
Ariel. Hark! Now I hear them.—Dingdong, bell.[23]
In the great spiritual depths of the Other some transmutation of this sort takes place. Why hide its con-
stituents from ourselves? Corals and pearls can give us,
too, a glimpse of the person who was once loved but is
now dead. I believe that, once we have had the experience, it helps us grasp the beauty of the poems. A work
of art, perhaps because it shares in eternity, as Proust
sensed, and as Boris de Schleuzer[24] in his turn very
finely says, has in the immobility of its form a certain
inflexibility that is reassuring but a bit frightening to
the mind. We hesitate to say it is alive. These animated
objects that appear to us when, upon stepping past the
threshold of reason, we penetrate into the realm of spiritual feeling remain objects rather than beings. But they
are alive. Art alone shows us what another's soul is like.
Proust said as much. But art alone permits us to have
in addition a presentiment of our own intellectual future, that creative liberty a Pierre Janet saw dawning
on our psychological horizon[25] and which spiritual tradition very simply calls the angelic life. True, we
scarcely know these angels of our books, concerts, and
walls except by the traces they have left. The artist
alone can feel, as they pass by him, that they are really
alive. In dedicating our own life to them, we do, however, divine something of theirs. They make use of the
love that we dispense toward our past; they possess
time because they are made out of it. Space has vanished from their lives—time replaces it. This is what
gives them those porous, light, transparent bodies
which are called bodies of glory like immobile rose
windows ordering sensitive thoughts, of which the
flesh of symphonies and pictures gives us the only
image we are able to perceive. Any peaceful room

where masterpieces stand watching will tell the reader much more. As far as I can judge, the angels in their life are not ignorant of ours. "Canticles are not all that they sing," wrote Stéphane at sixteen. Their immobility knows our death.

8

From the Youthful Poems to the Livre

THE APPEARANCE since 1949 of hitherto unpublished Mallarmé texts[1] has made it mandatory for me to complete the present book by the addition of new analysis. What follows will be a brief attempt which, I hope, will broaden the results already obtained and also structure them more completely.

THE MYTH

The network of associations which we established, and which remains the essential point, was centered around the free composition of 1857, and thus around Maria's image. Such simplification may seem extreme; not only is it the result of experimental facts, but it has taken on for me the force of a general law. The example of Mallarmé is but one particular case of this law. Every writer seems to have his basic myth, which is located at the point where the creative ego is grafted to the social ego. Any exchange of energy necessarily passes through this special point. With respect to the work, the myth represents a sort of obligato bass, which is at one and the same time a fatality and a basic structure. The work, being infinitely varied, liberates from this fatality but feeds only through its means on the energy of the personality which in its turn is enriched by this

217

growth. Or more briefly put, exchanges between the man and the work are made through the myth. Hence the myth's psychocritical importance.

For the text of the free composition the reader should consult the publications previously mentioned. Nick represents the ego. At first he is alone and withdrawn in the tiny lighted area of a hut. All around him there is the emptiness of a winter night. The general tone is not sad, as such a setting might lead one to expect. The contrast is nevertheless there, and so is the impression of solitude.[2] Inside the hut, the ego enjoys the comfort of a fire and the presence of small familiar things, a cat and a cricket, and two keepsakes which begin the structuring: the flower and the tambourine. So much for the lighted area of the conscious ego, in which there is no apparent anxiety: a few distinct, well-chosen, charming but rare love-objects against an empty background (no furniture). On the outside the vast zone of cold and shadow is peopled with inanimate or fantastic creatures: snow-covered trees, tombs, a church, a stone angel (we know from *Ange gardien,* an earlier composition, that it is the orphan's mother), three storks associated with the magi, and an owl which guards the cemetery. The myth then in its first form shows us a tiny, delicate ego refusing sorrow in a peaceful but cold and empty world, in between a petrified angel and a petrified tomb, with fantasies of wings and legends.

Nick smells the flower and gives way to an emotional oscillation; he laughs and weeps. This is the beginning. In reality the oscillation passes from the rose to the tambourine (saltarello). Memories of a funereal or pious (paternal) nature are firmly repressed. Memories, with their emotional weight, must be relived, Time "recaptured." The real content of the fantasy is obviously made up of Maria's dances, brotherly affection, and refreshments. But more than anything else Deborah represents a part of Stéphane's personality, the most emotional part, that part which loved a real object, Maria (and behind her, the mother). This ego identified with the sister has also been put away in the tomb through denial of death and sorrow, and losing it has left the remaining ego so impoverished and so forlorn that it appears vitally necessary that they be joined together again. And so in fantasy the personality becomes a couple, the motionless man and the dancing girl.[3]

The central point of the fantasy, when Deborah comes and sits on her father's lap and they look into each other's eyes while "their thoughts bill like doves," corresponds then with a point of blissful immobility and optimum equilibrium. Alexander[4] has emphasized the fact that, in the case of the conscious ego, this stable equilibrium corresponds to a moment when anxiety is at a minimum. In real life Mallarmé sought this kind of happiness and found it in the tenderness of Marie Gerhard, whose glance had "once pierced [his] heart," and then in his "natural, monotonous friendship" with Méry. This level is also marked by a sort of relaxed poetry that is quite close to true tenderness.

But on both sides the structuring of the fantasy is taking place. *Below,* the apparition, then the excitation, the ever more vivid, ardent, colorful, and symbolically erotic dance, the roses whose petals are plucked and scattered to the wind; *above,* the strange, luminous, and musical communion into which the now aerial dance becomes integrated, then dissolves.

The fantasy unfolds in the following order: (1) excitation; (2) tenderness; (3) sublimation. The dance certainly has something to do with the tomb and communion with the angel. But the shadow-and-light boundary comes between them, and we must say rather that the dance is what the ego pulls from the tomb, and the communion what it takes from the angel in order to integrate them into its personal realm, thus finding the desired enrichment and at the same time maintaining the equilibrium of this minimum of anxiety.

It should also be noted that there is a transfer of energy within the fantasy. Deborah pays for the musical communion by renouncing the richly colored flowers (that is, by returning to death). She pities her father in his poverty. In fact, the total personality narcissistically pities itself. But the result is that the energy vested in the revived image of the girl, an energy that has been snatched from the tomb, is caught by the conscious ego and used to reanimate the memory of the maternal communion, which is not only earlier but also more taboo. Furthermore, it is not attainable directly. Thus the anxiety at being abandoned is quieted at its source.

THE BIOGRAPHICAL FRAMEWORK OF THE YOUTHFUL POEMS[5]

Maria died on August 31, 1857. A few months later, Stéphane's grandmother was complaining of the change in his attitude: ". . . I find his heart so dry just now that I hardly dare count on him, whereas his imagination is so strong that it gives him exaggerated ideas about his own merits." This "dry heart" corresponds to his refusal of sorrow at the time of his mother's death, as we have already seen (cf. Introduction, pp. 9–10, and our remark, chap. 3, n. 1). Similarly, on All Souls' Day of 1859, Mallarmé acknowledged that he suffered from not being able to cry. Later on he analyzed this defense mechanism in a letter to Cazalis: ". . . this last vestige of tenderness which I sometimes feel and which, as a result of its lack of restraint, is of a rare—I should say sickly—delicacy" (July, 1862). The ego isolates itself not only from reality but also from a part of itself, the emotional and suffering part whose contact arouses anxiety. Actually the absence of apparent sorrow in the fantasy of the free composition is surprising: one even feels discomfort at seeing this young man of letters so easily transform a recent bereavement into literary effects.[6] In the very course of the narrative the dead girl sacrificed herself, and Nick accepted and therefore sacrificed *her*. The "dry heart" is a defense mechanism against anxiety.

It appears that the year 1858 at Sens was devoted to studies, with no particularly brilliant success. Stéphane read Lamartine, Chateaubriand, and Hugo rather than the assigned Racine. He became interested in a young lady, Em. Sul., whose departure for America inspired the first poem in *Entre quatre Murs. Cantate pour la première communion* was composed the same year. The end of 1858 was distinguished by quite a remarkable scholarly effort. In January, 1859, Stéphane fell sick enough for his family to be worried. During his convalescence (the end of February and the first part of March), he answered the poems from his fellow students with poems of his own. His birthday was on March 18, his dead sister's on the 22nd. He sent flowers from Sens and also visited the cemetery at Passy, that is to say, Maria's grave. At the end of April there came "a night with Emily"; in July the death of Harriet Smyth in England.[7] In November, All Souls' Day rekindled the memory of Maria and caused marked emotional oscillations. All in all, the two great emotional events of that year were, on the one hand, the memory of the dead sister, and, on the other, the amorous initiation.

The spring of 1860 was marked by light, somewhat licentious poems which at least yield an atmosphere. Mallarmé made friends with des Essarts and probably discovered Baudelaire. He failed the examinations for the *baccalauréat* in July but passed them in November. In December the "first step toward degradation" doubtless indicates his entry into the administration of the Registry[8] as a supernumerary. Although his work there was unsatisfactory, he did compose his first Baudelarian poems: *Enfant Prodigue, Galanterie macabre,* and so on. Early in 1862 he left the civil service in order to prepare himself to be an English teacher, published some poems, met Marie, and left with her for London in November.

THE EARLY POEMS

The poems which come under the heading *Entre quatre murs*[9] are arranged in the manuscript by literary types: *Fantasies, Elegies, Reveries, Odelets,* and so on. An examination of this naïvely formal order reveals psychological affinities which will be cleared up when we analyze them. But the first task of criticism is to arrange the poems chronologically from July, 1858, to April, 1860. The densest cluster falls between March and December, 1859, with virtually nothing in August and September.

Thus it becomes clear that a significant number of poems form around outside events whose emotional tonality is reflected in them: (1) the visit to Maria's grave—Harriet's death—All Souls' Day; (2) "a night with Emily"; (3) associations at school; (4) to a far lesser degree, relationship with "Petite Maman," the second wife of Stéphane's father. So much for the real-life external sources. The external literary sources are the great romantics and especially, far ahead of the others, Victor Hugo.

The obsessive persistence of the personal myth, in the form revealed to us by the free composition of 1857, is nonetheless quite marked. It is, in fact, this myth which crosses the field of force of the outside influences. It filters them out (thus, Hugo's sorrow and rebellious attitude [*Contemplations* and *Châtiments*] attune themselves to Stéphane's). It is also modified by them (thus the thrust of puberty eroticizes the myth). The myth persists, chooses, and evolves like a living person undergoing environmental influences.

Solely for the purpose of proving that the personal myth (free composition of 1857) does persist, I shall briefly trace the network of associations for some of the poems, arranged in chronological order.

January–March, 1859:

Chant d'ivresse. Dancing girl—castanet—hair—white breast.

Aveu. Rhythm—laughter and tears—angels—starry wing—pure maiden—prayer.

Vers écrits sur un exemplaire des Contemplations. Shroud—death—angel torn from heaven—girl sleeping under a cross.

Chanson du fol. Dance—castanet—breast—owl—moon.

Hier. Aujourd'hui. Demain. Maria's tomb—kiss—rosy laughter—cold coffin—violet—black—tears—mourning—angel—feather—wing—nest—incense (cloud)—blond locks—father—brother.

Le Nuage. Cloud—(foam)—feather—wing—angels—incense—child—Marie's deep sleep underneath the marble—cypress—death song—dead blond child—mother's breast—wing—shroud.

A P . . . Breast colder than a marble tombstone—silence—coldness—without soul—without warmth—without voice—I pity you.

A Esp. Dying—star—pale Pépita—flying flowers—blond tresses—nun's veil—flower brought back to life by the angel—alarm—refusal of tears—nest—wing—flight—star on forehead.

Sonnet A R . . . Dancing houris—breast—tresses—renunciation—poetry.

Sonnet à M . . . Midnight—moon—black wing—somber raven—voice of fluttering pleasure—laughter, kisses, songs—dancing girl—bells—Stéphane would like to be the flower he offers to Maria and which will fade upon her heart.

April–June, 1859:

Ne riez pas. Tears—eye that is going out—heavenly fire—flower—knell—ill omens—grief—coffin—shadows—azure wing—death—sadness—bitter

smile—roses whose petals have been plucked—
love—kisses—pure fire—heaven.

Lœda. Young flowers—love—tears—purple—lithe
nymphs—ruby and veiled breast—marble—blond
tresses—sleep—solitude—poor Lœda—father and
daughter—hair of gold and snow—tambourine—
awakening—Panpipe—flower—breast—lily—
(swan that prefers love to poetry)—redness—blue
eye—solitude—nest—star—snowy neck—rose-red
breast and undulating whiteness—half-closed eyes
—night hiding ecstasy.

Sourire. Ruby and veiled breast—wintry grief—white
flower crown—pale sleeping violet—sickle—snow
—nests—dancing girl—slim maiden swinging and
admiring herself—cricket—winter—sleeping sister
—blue flowers—blond tresses.

Donnez. Tears—rose—kiss—tear—chilling—wintry
alms to the poor old man—sorrow.

These examples will suffice. The reader may easily go
on with the analysis. In so doing he will note particularly that the metaphors accumulated in the July elegies
(dealing with Harriet) reproduce without any changes
earlier images which will once more be found in the
November and December poems. For instance, in *Sa
Fosse est creusée,* the dancing girl of stanza 5 and
several other images repeat the familiar themes of the
free composition; the death angel carrying off the child
comes from *Nuage* (March); the signs and presentiments of death, the pale halo, and the knell were already to be found in *Ne riez pas* (April) and *Lierre
maudit* (June); despair, depression, and personal fear
of death were present in *Hier. Aujourd'hui. Demain*
(March). The depressive trough marked in the elegies
is quite obvious, since it produces images of persecution. Further on we will establish its place. For the
time being let us confine ourselves to the persistence
of the myth as it is demonstrated by the network of

associations which extends without interruption up to the final poem of *Entre quatre Murs*.

Let us now try to form a clear idea of what is going on. The free composition of 1857 shows us an ego expelling from its hut everything that causes grief (night, cold, death, parental and religious authority) so as to retain on the inside only the good, familiar objects, memories, and dreams. It is this equilibrium that is first so threatened that one may think it is destroyed. For instance, in the November depressive trough, the zinzaris[10] fantasy is obviously superimposed on that of the free composition, except that the hut is destroyed, and the fire sputters and dies out in the open wind in a nocturnal and snowy setting; the cricket has lost all security, the drum is burst, the dresses have holes, the girl (with black hair) dances wildly, and then is buried by malicious gypsies whose mistress (but not sister) she certainly was. The reader may easily go on from here. All I wish to show is that anxiety bursts into the inner circle that was heretofore protected from it.

Such an onrush of darkness naturally leads the heroine back to the tomb and of course the hero to his dismal solitude. On this point the fantasy resumes contact with reality, since Maria is indeed in her grave at Passy among the dead bemoaned by the bells on All Souls' Day. As for Stéphane, he is alone, at night, in his bed (*Minuit au vieux beffroi*, p. 207) or in general, on this earth. And so of the original myth there remains only the form of Nick Parrit in the darkness. He then identifies himself with the dead girl and feels he is entombed, or wishes to be. (*Hier. Aujourd'hui. Demain.* in March, p. 173, and *Larme* in November, p. 178.) This identification with Maria is, to be sure, only one form of the essential communion with the mother through the sister. It will crop up again under various guises. In the present case it is marked with anxiety and is expressed by the idea that Stéphane too might or should die, since he also is a poor abandoned and condemned orphan. Does his sickness in February nourish such dramatized presentiments? In any event, we find them expressed earlier in the poems written during the first half of the year, that is, well in advance of the new shock of Harriet's death: cf. in March *Hier. Aujourd'hui. Demain.* and *Nuage;* in May *Ne riez pas;* in June *Donnez* and *Lierre maudit.* These premonitions of death sometimes involve the hero, sometimes the heroine, through the effect of the identification we mentioned above. Indeed, whenever Stéphane was touched by some distressing reality, he was afraid of dying.

Nevertheless he remained very much alive, and this no less undeniable aspect of reality strengthened an inverse means of defense: the dream of happy and carefree Bohemian existence. The ego decided to enjoy life, and thus the angelic young heroine, who had become Spanish or Moorish under the influence of exterior sources, danced and poured various liquids over her bare breast (*Chant d'ivresse, Chanson du fol,* the sonnet *Quand sous votre corps nu,* etc.). In April appeared the suddenly interrupted dream of a "sister upon the moss," toward the end of a poem full of springtime urges in which Rosette shows her ruby nipple underneath a filmy gown. The nakedness of women bathing also appears, and the vision becomes openly voluptuous with *Lœda,* which comes only shortly before "a night with Emily."

We must pause a moment at the poem *Lœda.* This poem, which is often felicitous in form, offers us without any possible doubt the first embryonic state of an important phantasm that has many metamorphoses (cf. *A une petite Laveuse blonde, Après-midi d'un faune, Cygne, Nénuphar blanc, Quelconque une solitude,* and others). Let us superimpose *Lœda* on the free composition of 1857. At the outset we note in both the same lonely creature waiting. But in *Lœda,* it is the heroine who plays this role and who hopes in vain for the visit, in the water and soon afterwards in the darkness. Like the dancer in the free composition, she tosses a rose. The one who captures the rose will obtain the Panpipe; in other words, we observe the same passage from flower of love to musical sublimation as in the free composition (and in *Après-midi d'un faune,* wherein the feminine curves become melodious ones). A character named Lys (the virginal and poetic double of hero and heroine) attempts to capture the rose but fails. Thus the new fantasy denies and represses the earlier one, which it reproduced in order to show its uselessness. Thereupon the Swan looms up wearing the Promethean spark on his brow; he takes the rose, and Lœda yields to him. The Panpipe is forgotten. Direct instinctive gratification replaces musical sublimation.

The feeling of guilt which ensues is immediately noticeable in *Donnez,* which follows "a night with Emily." Stéphane asked E . . . for a bit of pure love to bring him back to life, for straightway he felt that he was seriously threatened by debauchery. Let us note that the consoling and saving tenderness is exactly what Stéphane asks of Maria. Thus we see appear the antithesis which is well-known in adolescent psychology and consequently in romanticism (beware of inverting this relationship) between the consoling virgin and the impure and fatal beast (in Hamlet's case, Ophelia and the guilty mother). Before leaving *Lœda* I should further point out that in October we again find her under the name of Lycoris (who is also in the water and eager to offer herself). Several typical features link her to the dead girl (yellowed willow, flowering hair that weeps, pale Phoebe, breast compared to the moon, sleep, rose whose petals have been plucked).

Now we shall trace the metamorphoses of the Swan. Clearly we have here Nick's Promethean, and therefore Oedipal, double. He prefers possession to sublimation; he is the son identifying himself with the powerful father. Thus this double prolongs Nick's omnipotence, but in a different direction. If we pass from *Lœda* to *Lierre maudit,* a poem composed at the same time, we again find a lonely wife waiting; a child in the cradle takes the place of Lys (musical sublimation being one form of the mother-child communion). The wife was formerly a nun (that is, both dead and taboo), but her husband had taken her away and they had skirted two dangers, fanatical monks and cruelly lustful Moors. Now abandoned, she is assailed by premonitions of death. The devil suddenly appears in a torn crimson cloak; he awakens her jealousy and rapes her on horseback (she thus abandons the baby). The husband reappears as a retributive ghost and hurls her down while the devil flees laughing. She will be devoured by vultures. It is not difficult to see Lœda in the solitary wife, and the Promethean swan in the devil who takes her. Lucifer, the angel in revolt, star on brow, vying with the Father for omnipotence, and here associated with the vulture, is, like Prometheus, an Oedipal figure. But metamorphosis from Swan to devil suggests ideas of crime and punishment. The emotional tonality has changed from erotic to funereal (premonition of death and tomb) and even sadomasochistic (in this connection one should note the image of the crimson cloak with holes in it, which will have a long line of descendants). The next step in this evolution is furnished by *Colère d'Allah* (December, p. 137). The perverse hero who is the center of attention displays an unrestrained sadism and offers each morning for his beloved tiger's fare his wife of the previous night. Gentle nuns and maidens dancing around a dying fire await their turn to be sacrificed in the same way. But the sadist is stricken at the very moment his cruelty touches the little songster of the hearth, the cricket.

The critic of the exterior sources may perhaps find in the foregoing only romantic commonplaces. For our part, we must consider: (1) that these commonplaces were freely chosen from many possible ones; (2) that a network of personal associations links them to a fantasy that existed previous to all influences (free composition of 1857); (3) that this earlier fantasy, crossing the zone of romantic influences, is to be found again in works deemed original. Thus we have only to follow our own leads.

To come back to the myth of 1857, we observe that the poems of 1859 brutally inject into it a new personage who is amorous, cruel, and dismal. He is a gloomy double of Nick (and therefore of the primitive ego). He denies sublimations and satisfies his impulses directly. He is associated with animal figures: swan, horses, vulture, elephant, boa, tiger. From the analytical point of view, he appears to be the representative of an autonomous complex that superficially is Oedipal but actually is pregenital. The complex, invested with considerable energy and normally repressed, approaches consciousness because of the pressure of puberty. In its charge of energy the death instinct predominates, and in the death instinct, masochism (sadism being only the fear of yielding to passiveness). This diagnosis matters little from the psychocritical standpoint. It suffices for us first to note in the myth the appearance of a gloomy double of the hero, and secondly to realize that this appearance signifies the outcropping of a relatively autonomous ego.

Where in the 1857 fantasy was this double concealed? Certain features mysteriously announce his intrusion into the hut: the symbolically erotic dance[11]—the rose whose petals have been plucked—increasing redness— the girl's sacrifice—oral communion in which the moon may just as well represent a dead woman as the Host—the swaggering licentiousness attributed to the cat—the fear that a shadow may appear on the wall— Nick's doubts about God's wisdom—the wood doomed to the flames of hell, and so on. But the capital fact remains that in the 1857 free composition everything associated with the idea of death remains outside the hut:

cold, dark, tomb, church, parental figures. That is the form the death complex assumes and forces upon the consciousness, in keeping with undeniable exterior reality. In 1859, however, we observe the (more or less personified) eroticizing of this outside shadow as well as its attack on the hut-refuge. The angel becomes the Angel of Death (*Nuage, Sa Fosse est creusée, Viens*); the winter landscape, the sacred places, and the tomb harbor scenes of love and slaughter (*Sourire, Pan, Rêve antique, Colère d'Allah*). It must be added that we know nothing about the amounts of energy that are really involved; unconscious fantasies may unduly exaggerate the impulses they reveal. But I have no doubts about the quality and meaning of these impulses. From inside his hut Nick had control over things outside: the tomb and the angel obeyed his wishes. In 1859 there is a struggle between the earlier equilibrium of the ego and the new disrupting forces. The gloomy double embodies them and demands his share of the personality, if not complete control over it. Further on we shall see just what will be granted and what refused him. This ambivalent state gives rise to perplexities or rapid oscillations, as witnessed by many poems from 1859 (cf. *Ballade, Viens, Causerie d'adieu, Mélancolie*).

I should like at this point to emphasize the origin of the gloomy double, his meaning, and his disappearance. His appearance corresponds to an erotic drive and not to a sorrow. The filiation *Lœda, Lierre maudit, Colère d'Allah* is registered in the texts. The Swan, which seems to be unaggressive, clearly participates in the revolt instinct, and is itself linked to the Bohemian fantasies of the early poems: to Fasco the pirate, to the naked breasts of the dancing girls—in short to a series of boyish readings, conversations, dreams, or experiences which are quite the opposite of meditation on death. If we pass from swan to tomb, it is by way of the Oedipal guilt feeling or pregenital sadomasochism. The memory of Maria definitely has its place in this relationship, since her image is closely associated with that of the mother, who is necessarily at the basis of pregenital and Oedipal fantasies (so that Nick and his double are related through this maternal root). "A night with Emily" just as surely marks a similar evolution. Harriet's image and death, on the other hand, seem to be incidental; without them the development would have been the same, judging from the series *Lœda, Le Lierre maudit, Rêve antique* (Lycoris), *Colère d'Allah*.[12]

The gloomy double is punished by a thunderbolt which obviously corresponds to a brutal repression of the entire fantasy at the moment when Mallarmé's excitement goes beyond a certain level of tolerance. This level is reached at the moment the child (*Lierre*) and the little singer (*Colère d'Allah*), that is, the happy complex, nursing mother—voice—look—food, might be touched by the evil shadow. The gloomy double and his victim, joined as a sadomasochistic couple, are then cast together into the tomb. For reasons of personal defense, the ego gives up the dream, which becomes a nightmare. The visit is stricken with taboo. This repression coincides with total refusal of guilt. But this guilt, in accordance with a well-known mechanism, is then projected onto the Other: "*I*'m not the one who is doing that, *he* is." Thus Prometheus seeks justice upon Zeus; thus Hamlet treats his mother like a prostitute and his uncle like a parricide. The Oedipal son judges his parents harshly. The atheist eagerly and indignantly points out the immorality of the Gods he declares nonexistent: he is projecting on their image the shameful but unsuccessfully repressed side of his own nature. Mallarmé offers a good example of this classic *processus*. The sadistic rape of the roses and the murder of the children are put away in a combined church and grave. The transition is easy from the thunderbolt that strikes the gloomy double to the fantasy *Pan,* which is an embryonic but easily recognizable first draft of *Toast funèbre*[13] and the sonnet *Quand l'ombre menaça* (in which the Creator, a sadistic "King," watches seductive constellations "writhing in death" under the "dismal ceiling" of night). Let us suppose, on the other hand, that the sadistic couple escapes imprisonment and reappears; then it is the child who is in danger, and so we have the fantasy of an ogre-like divinity who gloats over what he is about to devour. Deeply erotic (cf. *Colère d'Allah,* but also *Une Négresse par le démon secouée*), this masochistic fantasy tallies with the obsession of hopeless solitude, the self-pity of the orphan who is in turn carried off to his grave by ill luck.

Let us repeat: we should not be misled by these extremes. Such fantasies would be morbid only if their charges of energy were strong enough to bring on neurotic or perverse outbursts. Now we know nothing about this quantitative side of the problem. Mallarmé's health or neurosis is not at issue.[14]

To sum up, the poems of 1859 show us: (1) that the fantasy of the free composition of 1857 persists, though undergoing changes, because of external and internal circumstances; (2) that the Nick-Deborah couple (the complete personality) tends to dissociate with increasing anguish at being abandoned, feelings of loneliness, and presentiments of death; (3) that the periphery (outside the hut), which is the source of anxiety, loses its iciness and becomes both erotic and hostile; (4) that an invisible sadomasochistic complex (probably centered around a "primal scene"[15]) thus shows signs of coming on; (5) that the appearance of the gloomy double is symbolic of such a complex; (6) that the ego for this reason is subject to oscillations or ambivalent feelings which bring on anxiety, and that, moreover, the ego risks losing again in the unconscious the energy recovered to the advantage of sublimation (the gloomy double wresting the heroine from the conscious ego); (7) that beyond a certain level of anxiety a repression born of a need to mete out punishment rejects and locks up the anxiety-producing sadomasochism in the tomb or in the church, but unfortunately also, to a degree, shuts up dreams and chances of a "visit."

SUBSEQUENT EVOLUTION

We find in *Symphonie littéraire* (1864) the obvious proof that the fundamental myth has maintained its structure throughout this spring storm. The images associated with the two names Gautier and Banville correspond to the center of the fantasy (a tender and calm tête-à-tête), whereas the two parts which frame the center, the dance (erotic) and the communion (musical), are very justly attributed to Baudelaire. As we have pointed out, the center is a kind of optimum for the conscious mind (minimum of excitement, oscillation, and anxiety). Surely this indicates a poetic relaxing and a heading toward conscious, exterior, intellectual, and social happiness. Both the love for Marie and the poems such as *Apparition, Frisson d'hiver, Las de l'amer repos, Toast funèbre,* and *Prose pour des Esseintes* mark the line of escape coming from the center. Cellier suggests that the "Chinaman of limpid heart and subtle" is Gautier.[16] I should rather call it a psychological correspondence. It is set down in the texts. In *Symphonie littéraire:* "the lake, under the motionless blue that even the white moon of summer mornings does not spot"; and in *Las de l'amer Repos:*

Une ligne d'azur mince et pâle serait
Un lac, parmi le ciel de porcelaine nue,
Un clair croissant perdu par une blanche nue . . .

[A line of thin, pale blueness would be
A lake, amid the sky of naked porcelain,
A clear crescent lost by a white cloud . . .]

One notes too in *Symphonie littéraire* that the images associated with Banville[17] are straight from *Toast funèbre* (dedicated to Gautier). Thus there is easy interchange at this level; and *Pan,* long before *Toast funèbre,* attempts to universalize its tranquillity: religion and dream are pushed into the tomb, while poetry enjoys ideal and peaceful gardens.

At a deeper level, however, Mallarmé tends to oscillate below and above this central plane, that is, between erotic dance and communion. The former tends to become perverse, sadomasochistic, and necrophilic; the latter might become religious. Baudelaire goes much further than Mallarmé in both directions; more the feline, a better tamer, he more easily endures dissonances, tensions, and therefore anxiety. But qualitatively the oscillations in the two poets correspond. This is why Mallarmé, when he outlines Baudelaire's psychic structure in *Symphonie*, traces it on the structure of his own myth. However, in order to be faithful, he must let the sadomasochistic complex invade the image of the dance.[18] In other words, everything happens as if the "gloomy double," who turned up in 1859, were a sort of inner Baudelaire who will discover his outer brother the following year in *Les Fleurs du Mal*. Once again we reach the following conclusion: the internal source directs the choice of the external sources.[19] The happy findings of Cellier should, I think, be completed along this path, especially where Hugo, Gautier, and Baudelaire are concerned.

In my own view, Mallarmé's searching for a personal style (throughout his youthful works) denotes an attempt at psychic integration. The Mallarmé of this period is striving for mastery of the emotional surges within his original fantasy without destroying the fantasy itself. This, moreover, is a way of curing oneself and restoring internal ruins.[20] And so Mallarmé will seek marginal compromises.

Thus the "preciousness" of style which begins to appear in 1860–1861 clearly corresponds to a lasting compromise between eroticism on one hand and mourning and ascetic coldness on the other. It was Rodenbach who very keenly defined Mallarmé as "half dancing girl, half priest." Those are the mimic expressions of the two extremities of the fantasy.[21] In the "precious" compromise, the dancer-marchioness and the gallant priest flirt in the winter setting of the free composition now transformed into a park; the predominant colors are silvery white and purple (bishop—amethyst—mourning—purple). The same *processus* can be observed in *A une petite Laveuse blonde.*[22] The heroine yields, but with her eyes closed.[23] Contacts are confined to the lightest touches. Their erotic meaning is given by *Mysticis umbraculis;*[24] their poetico-religious meaning by the finger's grazing the angel's musical wing; and their ordinary meaning by the fan of *Petite Laveuse blonde* and even the series of fans that come later.

But one may well imagine that the gloomy double requires something more than such affectations. And so the "preciousness" slips to *Galanterie macabre,* something a little nearer Baudelaire and Poe. This prose poem deserves a complete analysis. The child has died inside the mother, and she has died inside the wretched hovel whose ragged pall resembles the dress of the zinzari dancer (*Les Trois*) and Satan's cape (*Le Lierre maudit*). The gallant undertaker's mute (gloomy double) tries to get into the hovel. Finding the door too narrow, he climbs a ladder and enters through a window (eyes); he throws away his pipe. He is likened to an angel (flying on the ladder) and is suspected of swindling. In short, cloaked in false airs of elegance, religion, renunciation, and sublimation, the death complex satisfies a necrophilic desire. The poem is like a grotesque and depressed caricature of *Mysticis umbraculis* and *Placet futile.* But that is precisely the forbidden path, the one that leads to the death of the child and the interruption of maternal communion. Mallarmé's Baudelairean friends, who thought most highly of *Galanterie macabre,* were astonished (more than we are) to see him reject this fantasy. Indeed, the macabre, which was so dear to Poe and into which Baudelaire barely ventured, is off limits to Mallarmé.

The mystic and bloody eroticism of *Enfant prodigue* is not acceptable, as such, either. Nevertheless, we may note in this poem that there begins to emerge a compromise between the perverse union, of which the gloomy double dreams, and the mother-child communion, the only one finally sanctioned in Nick's hut. This compromise continues in *Une Négresse* (in which the child has become a girl), and then in the feminine couple of the *Faune*. The Faun's "crime" is that he has (in dream) been a bit too much the "gloomy double." In the darkness of his sleep, comparable to that of the tomb, he tried "to divide the tuft of kisses" of the couple who were still so close to the mother-child communion. By playing the Swan which takes the place of Lys next to Lœda, he tried to substitute for this pure union (or one supposed to be relatively so) satisfactions that were a bit more perverse in a masculine way:

> But scarcely was I ready to hide a burning laugh . . .

Thus the "vague decease" is the echo of the thunderbolt that strikes the gloomy double. The swan turns back into Lys, wins the Panpipe promised by Lœda, sings the story of his sublimation, and returns to the shades whence he came.

In this book I have amply linked *Hérodiade* to the network of the free composition. Obviously Hérodiade comes out of a tomb, "prison of stone and iron," where she had been sleeping among wild beasts that respected her. Her anxious and ambivalent waiting corresponds to Lœda's: in spite of violent and lyrical steps backward, the fantasy passes from icy whiteness to cruel purple. The poem is interrupted just when the sado-masochistic complex is about to triumph, when Deborah is about to become an amorous and murdering Hérodiade.

The passage from *Enfant prodigue* to *Renouveau* is an easy one. In the latter the hero bites into the warm earth and digs his grave. The association debauchery-death, which is pre-Baudelairean in Mallarmé (cf. *Donnez*), the anxiety at being abandoned, the premonitions of death, and finally the acceptance of and desire for suicide—all these constitute the passive aspect of the death complex. It is easily followed throughout the author's works. It is both pre- and post-Baudelairean. Each fit of depression causes it to reappear. In fact, *Le Guignon* and *Le Sonneur* both arrive at the same emotional conclusion as *Igitur* and *Un Coup de dés*.

These few remarks should be enough to enable the reader to follow the course of the myth from the free composition through the youthful poems to the more familiar works. In the earlier analysis we established the network of associations linking Maria and the myth of Nick Parrit and Deborah to all the poems. Our new analysis structures the myth and shows the developments of that structure. Naturally, the goal of the psychic process is still to rescue Eurydice from the Underworld, that is, to reclaim the energy left behind in repressions, an energy that the ego needs for further development of the personality. In Mallarmé's case the mother-child communion represented a supply of energy which the ego reached through Maria's image: hence the imperious necessity for bringing the image back to life in order to link it unceasingly to the present. A second but no doubt less essential source of energy was the complex of the aggressive, sadomasochistic, and Oedipal "gloomy double." The ego is disturbed when it draws near but weakened when it is excluded. This weakening even becomes regressive if the repression of the "gloomy double" entails repression of the "visit." In that case the feminine image is rejected into the tomb, and the hero, who is filled with anxiety at being abandoned, loses no time in attempting to join her in a melancholic and masochistic solution to the problem. The myth therefore constantly outlines compromises, and the free composition is certainly one of them. The death complex is represented by the religious and funereal night scene from which the ego snatches at least the image of Maria. Ardor, revolt, voracious cruelty, desire, and fear of death, all appear thereafter.

We have followed the ego in its efforts to harness the dangerous energy of these feelings. In the series of crises that we have studied at great length in this book, the successes in these attempts mark high points, the failures depressive troughs. Mallarmé seems almost to have given up such effort after *Igitur*. It starts again after 1880. In the poems of that period, setting suns represent the sadomasochistic complex. A reflection of it is caught in Méry Laurent's tresses (and in her nakedness). And so it is that the attempt which failed with *Château de l'espérance* (1863) succeeded twenty years later. After 1890 the setting sun gives way to a storm beyond the windowpane (*Crise de vers*), a musical storm (flashing and streaming), a tempest under heavy clouds (*A la nue accablante*, *Coup de dés*), a turbulent cesspool beneath a brilliant flaming (*Tombeau de Baudelaire*). And so we arrive at the *Livre*, which I shall briefly consider before ending this study, since the text was unknown to us in 1949.

The "Livre"

It is impossible here, in a few pages, to examine either the whole problem of the *Livre* or the solutions Scherer has proposed.[25] Rather let us simply see how the *Livre* appears or what light is thrown upon it if we extend to it the thematic lines of the evolution sketched above.

Materially speaking, it is a manuscript, or rather a dossier, of some two hundred vaguely classified sheets, which impress the reader as disjointed notations (scattered words or calculations) rather than sentences. Perhaps a score of pages deal with the possible content of the work. Fragments of myths with modern overtones are to be found. For instance, the invitation to a party at which the hero will participate in everything but the dinner.[26] All the other manuscript pages deal with the material side of the project: calculations of the number of pages or copies, financing, communicating with the public through reading, customary explanations, and printing.

The disproportion between the two groups of manuscript pages poses a riddle that becomes disturbing at the slightest scrutiny. For there is absolutely no doubt about the almost religious importance that Mallarmé attached to the *Livre* and to the ritual of its revelation. It was Wells who said of Henry James that once he finally admits you to the Holy of Holies, after an arduous and endless journey, you discover an eggshell and a piece of string on the altar. Mallarmé's last text can give the same impression. It is surely a false impression in Mallarmé's case, just as in James'. But the uneasiness remains, and Mallarméan enthusiasts feel "the breath pass by."[27]

These "practical" considerations have little more than a surrealist charm about them: they seem to be lacking in all sense of reality.[28] Mallarmé intended, of course, to write the *Livre, but* refuse its paternity (its creation being attributed to anonymous genius alone). He wanted to be its "first reader" and officiating explicator. The reading would be held before a small group of very carefully chosen guests. The admission price would be enormously high but uncollected. It would accrue to Mallarmé's moral credit, enabling him to have a large number of inexpensive copies printed so as to restore the *Livre* to the masses. On these copies Mallarmé would receive fifty per cent in author's royalties, although the edition was to have been paid for by announcements inserted in the blank pages.

I shall not linger over these calculations nor over the equally surrealist image of the still "half-dancing girl, half-priest" Mallarmé distributing to twenty-four listeners (of whom some eight at times were members of his family) the pages which he, in order to combine them, had to take from a lacquer desk, while the chandelier (probably of his living room) would represent all by itself the theater. Let us pass over all this and behold the no less strange but real genius.

The reader who has a long-standing familiarity with *Divagations* is well aware that the late prose is invaded by two obsessions.

The first concerns new relationships (both wished for and feared) with the body of society, the mob, mere numbers, their unpredictability, and their stark reality. Mallarmé is not content just to attend the theater, concerts, or the ballet. He meditates on them just as he does on religious ceremonies or the techniques of the press. He sees the poet in relation to money, the working man, anarchy, action that his younger companions hope for, and so on.

The second obsession is with the new "instrument of knowledge," *Le Livre, instrument spirituel.* By this he means a new technique of expression that implies a new way of reading, writing, and even thinking.

The two concerns were interrelated: the new art he dreamed about was in fact supposed to "recover its own rights" from the great collective manifestations (religion, music, the dance, the theater) and arrange some future celebration once the "tunnel" of the times had been negotiated.

One may have his doubts about this last dream, but not about the inspired intuitions which illuminate the final prose works. Indeed, everything essential that Mallarmé had to say "about the *Livre*" was to be found in *Divagations* long before publication of the pages of manuscript. In my opinion the great interest of the latter lies in the fact that they allow us to ascertain the final form of the personal myth as it persists in the last prose works.

In this period more than ever Mallarmé refuses to accept any reality, even a technical one, on which a personal myth cannot be projected. In the objective reality of the common consciousness he perceives an intrusion, an indiscretion,[29] or, to the contrary, a screen hiding secret gardens.[30] Briefly put, social man satisfies instinct or submits to censorship: Mallarmé rejects such brutality. The great concern of the new art must be—at once following and opposing the example of music—to play with revelation: to amass mystery, and then tear it apart or dissolve it. Thus ambivalence is still present, but the emotional ambiguity which the conscious would deem turbid, the oscillating between shadow and light, here becomes the supreme aesthetic game. For us, these more or less torn or lifted veils have a long filiation, which runs from snow to the white page, passing through shrouds or batiste lifted with the finger, riddled dresses of dancing gypsies, funeral draperies starred with holes or tears, the clown's wall of cloth, windows, eyes, the devil's purple, tatters, clouds, banners full of holes, and so on. We are hardly surprised then that for the creation of the "instrument of knowledge" the very image of the tomb is projected upon the book,[31] the image of virginity or the shroud upon the paper,[32] that of the dancing girl upon the letters, and that of the dance or communion upon the typographical composition of the page.[33] The newspaper sheet that has flown away covers an "ardent . . . conventicle of roses." The fold of the paper, when the book is cut, protects the mystery: it is barbarous to touch it with the knife suited to slitting a chicken's throat.[34] The book should be manufactured so as to avoid such an attack. The finger lifting the page is enough to reveal aspects which can be reconstructed mentally.

Out of these old themes, however, two relatively new images emerge. We have already noted the first: the storm and its harrowing fulgurations (the last representation of the dangerous complex). The other is the restoration, at a higher level, of a shattered unity. Once again the two are interrelated. The destructive explosion, if one faces it or subdues it, should become the illumination which reconstructs a totality out of scattered fragments. The mystery that was revealed through the cracks comes to an end, because something or someone new and whole appears: the *Livre*, or Self. A prose selection, *Crise de vers* (*Oeuvres complètes*, p. 360), shows us, in a bookcase, books from former times, fragments and distinct musical figures (therefore the results of fugitive "visits") behind the heavy shower of a curtain of pearls. Yet Mallarmé, who is facing the window and the storm, dreams of the flashing Visit which would integrate all these things.

From the psychoanalytic point of view, it would appear that Mallarmé's fantasy, in this storm-filled symbolism, verged on the anamnesis of a primal scene associated with the image of the dead mother and the devouring tomb. On the one hand, we can make all the connections between the setting suns and the storm; on the other hand and at the same period, the *Tombeau de Baudelaire*—which obviously is related to *Symphonie littéraire,* and so to the setting sun—shows us the flaming gas ("darting tongue" in another text)[35] above the idol Anubis rising from a cloacal tomb. To strengthen this hypothesis we could even add certain of Mallarmé's stylistic preoccupations that were no doubt still latent but were becoming noticeable at that period: "alternation and vis-à-vis" causing the "explosion of the mystery" (*Crise de vers*).[36]

But it is time for us to turn at last to the myth fragments discovered in the manuscript pages of the *Livre*. There are five of them, which may be designated as follows: (1) the man listening; (2) women on the shore; (3) the dead city and the beasts; (4) the old man dead of hunger, who (a) eats the lady for twenty francs, (b) gets into the grave and is thus rid of it; (5) the invitation to the party.

Scherer gives a cautious and objective reading of these various fragments. But he is not aware of the networks of associations which will allow us to go a step further. First of all, in a general way, one should note the role of (oral) aggressiveness and ruins: hunger, woman who is eaten, wild beasts, dead city, grave, claustration, tortured person, anger. No such coarseness is to be found in Mallarmé's finished work, with the exception of a few poems in *Entre quatre Murs*. And yet the connection between the pages of the *Livre* and the last prose passages of *Divagations* is quite apparent. This confirms the hypothesis of a separate autonomous complex which barely rises into consciousness during puberty, then becomes subliminal (though still active), and finally reappears in the 1890's in crude form (manuscript pages of the *Livre*) or aesthetically elaborated (*Divagations, Coup de dés*).

Now to return to the myth fragments.

The man listening (sheet 12A) gives way to invectives against the "realist" writers (a theme already dealt with in *Solitude* and *Le Mystère dans les lettres*).[37] Mallarmé accused his "contemporaries" of not knowing how "to read." Doubtless he is showing here how to listen to words when, as he puts it, we "give them the initiative." The writer hears the word "as it comes from above him, and falls into the depths." This word calls him in a personal way and commands him to obey; he makes as though to leave, exaggerating the "defiance," but without moving ("it will not be he"). This is the contemplative attitude that curbs all action ("restrained action"). It is also the position of the patient in psychoanalysis who listens and talks but is kept from acting out. If we go even deeper, it is the experience of the very young child listening to its mother's call that "comes from above him" and not being able yet to give it a motor response. We find once more the complex of the nursing mother (voice—eyes—food) and poetic sublimation.

Women on the shore (sheet 16A). They are dancing and trying to reach one another from a great distance but do not succeed. They could do so only through the mind of the hero. He leaves them in order to seek the unique Fiancée and comes upon them at every turn. This kind of ballet with its "alternation and vis-à-vis" brings us back to *Divagations:* it is a question of separate themes or poems, "nuptial fragments of the Idea" which the *Livre* would at last bring together. Since the latter is the "Orphic explanation of the earth," its discovery merges with that of the "Fiancée (or earth)." All this is already in *Quant au livre* and *Crise de vers.* But from the psychological standpoint it is clear that these forms, which are vainly trying to join one another and are multiplying, represent the various facets of the personality that are to be integrated. Furthermore, they are dancers and lead us back to the free composition. Each one of them is a Visit. The hero speaks ungraciously to them, since he has gone beyond this stage of fragmentary illuminations; they, however, join each other in a "cunning embrace," which Scherer rightly compares to that of the nymphs in *Après-midi d'un faune.* Our network of associations linked the latter couple to presentiments of some primal scene; if we refer back to note 36 for chapter 8, we observe that there is definite correlation in this.

In my view all the other fragments, more or less, deal with the hero's descent into Hades to seek the unique Fiancée. Indeed, the ballet is followed by a sort of entr'acte during which the foreground is doubled with another, deeper one (sheet 20A). The curtains become torn and the description of the dead city begins with several metaphors whose persistent vis-à-vis Scherer quite rightly emphasizes. The struggle of the wild beasts follows immediately. Scherer speaks of these descriptions as if they were infernal visions. The city (or palace) in ruins "lies in the shadowy past . . . unless it lies in the future." A note indicates (22A) that it could be a ship ("floating city—rocking") which could become the "city of the future poet." It is no difficult matter to link this ruin to the image of the dead mother. Through an atmosphere at times reminiscent of *Igitur* we go all the way back to the cemetery of the free composition. The "double fountain" no doubt represents two eyes, the dead girl's or, by identification, those of the hero, in which "his dream cursed people—who [? which] sleeps—no longer comes to look at itself—in the stare of its immense pride" (cf. *Igitur* and *Triptyque*).

What has happened? The manuscript (24A) tells us that for the answer we must ask the "tamer," and this word introduces the wild beasts. At once we are back to *Colère d'Allah:* we find the boas, the elephant, and the great cats. The animals do not dare come near the light (apparently a campfire, the traveler's campfire, separated from the city or ship by the shadows). Therefore we see only the shadows of the animals playing on a "curtain background." They have "lunged twice—as it were one against the other," whereas "serpents hiss them hate" and also "through the mobile rings" of the latter. In a note the elephant is given as being a combination of the two most dangerous beasts: the white bear and the black panther. The connection between such a scene in Mallarmé's work and the imagery of *Colère d'Allah* can hardly be denied, especially if we remember that in the latter the tiger devours the wife and that we are about to witness the reappearance of the lady who is eaten. Here again, as in *Colère d'Allah,* or in the zinzaris fantasy (*Les Trois*) or the free composition itself, the fire's glow is a precarious protection against the shadows where aggressiveness and death are lurking. All this is just so much proof of the hypothesis of nocturnal and traumatic infantile excitations.

The three remaining fragments must be considered together. Several important elements (hunger—torture —devoured lady) are to be found simultaneously in the old man dead of hunger (27A) and the invitation (169A). These two fragments are pure myth. On the contrary, the one in which the old man descends into the tomb with the child worker (28A to 33A) takes on almost explanatory form, with characters (the priest, the comrade) who are also to be found in *Divagations* (*Action restreinte, Catholicisme*). The descent into the tomb is therein exposed as a "trick," a literary fiction used by the man who has died of hunger.[38] But the absolute necessity for this descent is strongly emphasized: "it is only there in the tomb that he can find it [the mystery]" (30A) and "because death is necessary if mystery is to be known" (32).

The following episodes, however, seem to occur:

1. The old man pretends to descend into the tomb and attempts to demonstrate "what would happen if" (we glimpse the possibility of a development analogous to that in *Coup de dés*). But he is the victim of his own trick: the door comes to behind him ("is it the wind or the priest?"), which amounts to a fall from heaven, and the old man has to experience a claustration that makes him like a priest, but "deprived of everything." It is the situation of the contemplative person without religious faith (one incident seems to indicate the possibility that the inside of this tomb is also the castle of an old count, in which case the claustration would become that of *Igitur;* but the incident, with its wind, also brings to mind the dead city). The state of priest implies sexual frustration: "priest must, for human glory, remain in ignorance of woman's mystery—from which (child between the legs) all will be resolved by that —" (29A). This forced claustration brings on revolt and anger.

2. Deliverance requires, moreover, the intervention of a child worker, who is willing "to put the great machine into motion" and wants to learn the mystery "before getting married" (30). It becomes apparent from the text that both the child and the priest are confused with the old man; but no doubt it is a matter of one of his other selves, the one that craves action (cf. the young comrade in *Action restreinte*), and in the present case sexual action, that is to say, aesthetic creation.[39]

246

The child also shuts his Fiancée up in the tomb. It is difficult to say just what goes on. But it does seem clear that deliverance stems both from revolt against claustration (on the part of the man dead of hunger) and desire for creation (on the part of the child worker).

As we have seen, it still remains for us to show the close ties between the invitation (169) and sheet 27. The analogy of these two fragments indicates that we are still dealing with the same adventure of the man dead of hunger. The tortures involved in the two cases could thus be a building into story form of the burial, another form of which might be commitment to a prison, factory, or school. The hero seems to be invited to a sumptuous party, but "to everything except the *meal*, hence his hunger," the only law being to eat, "eat the lady—20 francs for her." Since the man dead of hunger in sheet 27 has only one louis (20 francs) left, little doubt remains about the use he intends to make of it ("hunger for your flesh thirst for your eyes") unless he should turn toward the "trick of death from hunger," that is, toward a sublimation that replaces direct satisfaction. On sheet 169, the lady herself issues the invitation "perhaps without her [?his] realizing it." Indeed, she has "given herself to him." To accept all this without saying anything is in itself a "theft" (cf. *Nénuphar blanc*). On the other hand, the "exploit which was supposed to bring him glory [as a result of the invitation] is a crime: he stops this Operation in time." Here again one can hardly deny the existence of erotic desire in an oral expression (eating the lady), since the only crime possible would then be incest or sadism. An overtone of light humor is noticeable in the expression, but the network of associations is nonetheless present underneath these appearances, and all the links with *Divagations* or with the other sheets prove the importance of the subject. How does the episode end? It would seem that the hero "covers" the lady symbolically with his hat and that an explosion occurs ("hat, he

covers her within self" and further on: "hat bursts sun").
Another half-humorous, half-serious text[40] shows that
at that period Mallarmé had made the hat the symbol
of a kind of divinity: "The world will end, not it."[41] In
any event, the denouement is ambiguous ("so that no
one has ever found out that—"). The last prose selec-
tions of *Divagations* offer us so many explosions, fulgurations, and outbursts that we are tempted to attribute
a meaning of revelation to this ending of the myth. Thus
the invitation to the party would be a kind of rough
sketch of what is going on within the tomb, that is to
say, the manner in which hunger and revolt combined
lead to deliverance and resurrection.

Psychologically, one may call to mind the frustrations
of the analytical situation entailing regression, and then
the achievement of conscious awareness with the liberation of a great amount of emotional energy. Elsewhere
I have emphasized at great length the dynamic analogies between aesthetic creation and self-analysis. Mallarmé's quip about an anarchist bomb during this same
period—"The only explosion is a book"—clearly points
out that, for him, the *Livre* would have been a tremen-
dous liberation of energy. On the other hand, this explosion interrupting the criminal deed reminds us so
clearly of Satan's thunderbolts in *Lierre maudit,* those
of Siben in *Colère d'Allah,* and also of the "vague decease" of the Faun, who also is ready to commit a
"crime," that we have some doubts about the positive
meaning of the explosion. *Coup de dés* ends with a shipwreck, and the *Livre* was never written. From this negative point of view, the explosion, at the end of the myth,
could once again signify the brutal repression of a fantasy that was deemed dangerous by the conscious mind.
This would be one of the causes which prevented Mallarmé from completing his work. We can go even further: it is not impossible that Mallarmé, through his
spasm of the glottis, completely forbade himself to pursue his dream. Before the second attack, which cost him

his life, he wrote the letter ordering the destruction of the manuscript sheets.

However this may be, it seems to me that our network of associations, as completed by the foregoing analysis of the youthful works, affords the only means of connecting the Mallarmé of 1898 with the Mallarmé of 1857 throughout the entire series of the works known to us today.

Notes

INTRODUCTION TO THE AMERICAN EDITION.

[1] Chapter 8 is a new chapter, added to the American edition. [Trans. note.]

[2] (Paris: Denoël, 1941). [Trans. note.]

[3] Henri Mondor, *Vie de Mallarmé* (Paris: Gallimard, 1941).

[4] Cf. Mme Adile Ayda, *Le Drame intérieur de Mallarmé* (Istanbul: Edition La Turquie Moderne, 1955), p. 232:

"But it is the critic André Rousseaux who, in his article 'Mallarmé tel qu'en lui-même,' has most magnificently defined the attitude of Mallarmé to women:

'. . . His taste on the one hand for ambiguous forms of chastity, fierce, intangible but naked and very close to desire, precisely the chastity of a Hérodiade; on the other hand for beloveds who have turned maternal and to whom one can "whisper" the name "sister." This ambiguity constitutes in fact a magnificent keyboard passing from the most carnal sensuality to the most subtle ideality' (André Rousseaux, *Le Monde classique*, Vol. II, Albin Michel, Paris, 1946)." [The passage is identical with the one given above in Mauron's preface dated 1941.—Trans. note.]

[5] I call *personal myth* (or *fundamental myth*) in psychocriticism the obsessive and hence constant fantasy which appears when one superposes the works of an author. Cf. [Charles Mauron's] *L'Inconscient dans l'oeuvre et la vie de Racine*, Annales de la Faculté des Lettres d'Aix-en-Provence (1957), and "La Méthode psychocritique," *Orbis Litterarum* (Copenhagen, 1958).

[6] W. Ronald Fairbairn, *Psychoanalytic Studies of the Personality* (London: Tavistock Publ., Ltd., 1953). [Trans. note.]

[7] *Narration française à sujet libre,* written by Mallarmé as a normal exercise in the fourth or fifth year of the *lycée*—hereafter referred to as the "free composition."

[8] ". . . This tale is of the poet's seraphic period. All the religious fervor that his grandmother, Madame Desmolins, had inspired in him was still intact.

"Provided one does not read these pages with sarcasm at finding

251

in them only childish games, or with impatience to discover extraordinary gifts, one may range them in the very first exercises which may properly instruct us as to the beginnings of a schoolboy, great-writer-to-be, and as to a sensibility which was later to become so squeamish and proud.

" 'That adds nothing to his glory!' some will say. 'Why didn't he always have this transparence?' others will ask. But this is reading especially for those who are led to meditation by roses, snow, angels, *azur*, lilies, winter laments, dreamy songs, and an experimental vocabulary" (Mondor, *Mallarmé plus intime* [Paris: Gallimard, 1944], p. 22).

[9] As if the incestuous feeling were not of necessity repressed at that age, hence unconscious, hence inexpressible directly in a letter; and as if the true Oedipus complex, which emerges toward the third or fourth year, were such an extraordinary and scandalous thing! Where should the affective structure of an individual be formed (heredity being given) if not in early childhood, that is, in relation to the parents? And who is not aware, on the other hand, that the imaginative fantasies of young children are truly eroticized and aggressive, under the most fantastic forms? The Oedipus complex is simply one among several consequences of this factual situation.

[10] ". . . à travers des forêts de symboles / Qui l'observent avec des regards familiers" (Baudelaire, "Correspondances," in *Les Fleurs du Mal*). [Trans. note.]

[11] Cf. p. 23, where Dr. Mondor, referring to Mallarmé as well as to Dante and Baudelaire, speaks of an "essential emotional frustration," and p. 93, "Perhaps . . . he prescribed to himself a duty which called for extreme fidelity to the pure phantoms of his dead mother and Maria. . . . The 'blank of lost attachments' imposed on Mallarmé little by little, no doubt, as on others, a precocious inner song" (*Mallarmé lycéen* [Paris: Gallimard, 1954]).

[12] Publications de la Faculté des Lettres et des Sciences humaines, Université de Grenoble, Presses Universitaires Françaises (1959).

[13] Mme Ayda believes in "psychological determinism, as the disciples of Freud conceive it," and hence in the "unfortuitous character of the association of human ideas," in "the bondage of the imagination to the Unconscious and in individual complexes," and in "the possibility of recognizing them behind disguises and symbols" (*op. cit.*, p. 52).

On the other hand, she rejects what she calls the "principles of psychoanalysis" (that is to say, the results of all the clinical labor of this same Freud and these same disciples). "We confess that certain typical Freudian conceptions appear suspect to us. Thus we mistrust complexes such as the Oedipus complex or the castration complex . . ." (*op. cit.*, p. 9). So she thinks it is possible to separate from the "principles" the "method," which she admits has received official sanction in practice.

[14] Camille Mauclair (1872–1944), author of *L'Art en silence, Les Princes de l'esprit, Mallarmé chez lui,* and other works. [Trans. note.]

[15] Ayda, *op. cit.*, p. 270.

[16] *Narration française*   January, 1858(?)
    Cantate pour la première communion   June, 1859
    Sa Fosse est creusée   June, 1859
    La Prière d'une mère   July 7, 1859
    Sa Tombe est fermée   July 11, 1859
    Symphonie littéraire   April, 1864
    Plainte d'automne   May, 1864

This choice of texts, involving the exclusion of *L'Ange gardien* of 1854 and the addition of *Symphonie littéraire* and *Plainte d'automne* (why not works of the same period?) appears somewhat arbitrary. It would be even more so today, since we now know the whole series of works composed around 1859; I shall analyze them below.

[17] ". . . The baby experiences depressive feelings which reach a climax just before, during and after weaning. This is the state of mind in the baby which I termed the 'depressive position,' and I suggested that it is a melancholia in *statu nascendi*. The object which is being mourned is the mother's breast and all that the breast and the milk have come to stand for in the infant's mind: namely, love, goodness and security. All these are felt by the baby to be lost, and lost as a result of his own uncontrollable, greedy, and destructive phantasies and impulses against his mother's breasts. Further distress about impending loss (this time of both parents) arises out of the Oedipus situation, which sets in so early and in such close connection with breast frustrations that in its beginnings it is dominated by oral impulses and fears. The circle of loved objects who are attacked in phantasy, and whose loss is therefore feared, widens owing to the child's ambivalent relations to his brothers and sisters. The aggression against phantasied brothers and sisters, who are attacked inside the mother's body, also gives rise to feelings of guilt and loss. The sorrow and concern about the feared loss of the 'good' objects, that is to say, the depressive position, is, in my experience, the deepest source of the painful conflicts in the Oedipus situation, as well as in the child's relations to people in general. In normal development these feelings of grief and fears are overcome by various methods" (*Contributions to Psychoanalysis, 1921–1945* [London: Hogarth, 1950], p. 312). [Trans. note.]

[18] See chap. 2.

[19] Edmund Bergler, *The Writer and Psychoanalysis* (New York: Doubleday, 1950).

[20] "Some days after the event, his grandmother called him to the parlor where she had a visitor, and as this person spoke of the sorrow that had befallen them, the child, embarrassed by his lack of grief, which did not produce the expected expressions of sorrow, chose the expedient of rolling on the carpet, shaking his long hair, which beat against his temples . . ." (Henri de Régnier, *Nos Rencontres* [Paris: Mercure de France, 1907], p. 192). Cf. my comment, chap. 3, note 2.

[21] "His childhood letters reveal Stéphane Mallarmé as a typical boy at play, never as the 'sublime' or repressed child who is incapable of having a good time." Mondor, *Mallarmé lycéen*, p. 52.

[22] Mondor, in *Mallarmé lycéen*, sustains, on the contrary, the thesis

that the boarding school life the poet led from his tenth year on made young Stéphane "very unhappy" at times (p. 27). "The boy who later accused himself of having waited a humiliatingly long time before feeling the sorrow of his first bereavement could have been reminded of the cruel loss of his mother by nothing so much as by boarding school life. More and more he would miss this essential, if not infallible protection, this charming face and incomparable tenderness" (p. 19). "Finding that he was perhaps more obligated to believe in a providential protection than any of those whose young mothers sparkled during their visits in the parlor not far from his austere grandmother, he wrote in September, 1854, at the age of twelve, a short narrative, *Ange gardien*. . . . In this child's leaf, perhaps a simple exercise . . . a sigh tells us of his deep sorrow" (pp. 28–29). Mondor thinks, all in all, that Stéphane especially felt the practical inconveniences of being an orphan. I believe rather that there was a shock which was never resolved: at any rate, the contrast (which is basic to Mme Ayda's thesis) between the pre-1857 happiness and the later wound is obliterated by the new Mondor material.

[23] His sister's death must have constituted a trauma that re-evoked the earlier one caused by his mother's death. Cf. Otto Fenichel: "If a person has developed a certain amount of castration anxiety over loss of love, and subsequently has overcome this anxiety by certain inner reassurances . . . , the experience of a trauma is apt to upset these reassurances and to remobilize the old anxieties. Persons who, for example, have hitherto denied their fears by partial regression to the security of primitive narcissism and omnipotence are forced by the trauma to admit that they are not omnipotent after all, and the old anxieties reappear. This is especially true in one type of anxiety over loss of love. Some persons have the capacity for hanging on to the belief that fate will protect them, just as their parents had protected them before in their childhood. Such persons experience a trauma as a betrayal by fate which refuses to protect them any longer" (*The Psychoanalytic Theory of Neuroses* [New York: W. W. Norton, 1945], p. 123).

"The degree in which a trauma is experienced as a loss of the protection of fate or as castration is dependent, of course, upon the pre-traumatic history of the patient. . . . What is most characteristic in the reaction to a trauma is that associative connections are immediately established between the trauma and the infantile conflicts that become activated. . . . The trauma may be experienced as a mere repetition of other older traumata of childhood" (*ibid.*, p. 124).

This outline can be useful to us as a guide in Mallarmé's case. If, in particular, we replace the word "fate" with the expression "guardian angel," we find once more the essence of Mallarmé's religious crisis and of the paranoid mechanism of defense (punishing indignation) which appears to form its essence; but many other defense mechanisms come into play, and it is the whole of the picture which is expressed in the fantasies and which we must therefore consider.

[24] The first is accepted as living and associates sister with mother

in the idea of oral and musical communion. The second is rejected as being associated with death. Cf., in the free composition, Nick, that is, the ego, who refuses to let the angel (the mother) sing the sister's saltarello in its funeral mode. Later, and as a continuation of an agreement, the angel brings the communion object and leaves. The ego and the young girl then celebrate the communion with fragments of a lunary cake, which become a melodious light in which the sister dissolves. The association "food—music—light" represents the milk-giving mother: breast—voice—eyes.

[25] See chap. 7, "Orpheus."

[26] For example, Ayda, *op. cit.*, p. 90: "Again and again he related those events which caused the crisis and modified his psychic and moral evolution, veiling them with symbols and images." ["Ces événements qui engendrèrent la crise et donnèrent une direction nouvelle à son évolution psychique et morale, il n'a cessé de les raconter, en les voilant de symboles et d'images."]

In the same way, on p. 94, Mme Ayda adopts Mauclair's judgment, " 'his writings are those of a man confessing,' with this reservation, which only heightens the voluntary aspect of the process: 'Mallarmé told his story in the hope no one would listen, confessed with the desire not to be understood. He concealed his stories and disguised his confessions with images and symbols.' " [" 'Ses écrits sont des confidences d'homme,' sous cette réserve qui ne fait qu'accentuer l'aspect volontaire du processus: 'Mallarmé s'est raconté avec l'espoir de n'être point écouté, s'est confessé avec le désir de n'être pas compris. Il a voilé ses récits et masqué ses confidences d'images et de symboles.' "]

[27] "On sait que le système d'images symboliques, qui caractérise l'Inconscient d'un individu, est d'autant plus compliqué que les refoulements subis ont été plus puissants et que ceux-ci obéissent à une énergie d'autant plus grande que le sentiment ou l'événement, qui les a nécessités, est plus proche des aspirations intimes de l'individu."

[28] Thus "breast" is associated with Harriet's tuberculosis by "analogy" ["raisonnement analogique"] (*op. cit.*, p. 195). "Rubies" signify God's crime, according to a deduction ascribed to Mallarmé: God killed Maria, since the sky was red on the day of her burial. Let us add more generally that in a network of associations, each point can be joined to any other one, so that the classification of symbols Mme Ayda proposes appears entirely arbitrary. Thus, "corridor" is attributed to Harriet because of association with time and a quotation from *Igitur*, "corridor du temps." But it may be associated, with much greater certainty, with the apparition (*Toast funèbre, Triptyque*) and therefore with Maria, since Harriet's apparition is not the subject of any text. "Thunder" and "rubies" are attached, by Mme Ayda, to God's wrath; but in direct fashion (*La Chevelure vol d'une flamme,* where "flashing" and "rubies" are found) or indirect fashion through all the sunsets they are associated with woman's hair and, finally, with Deborah Parrit's. If I am told that erotic pleasure and God's wrath are associated through the Oedipus complex, I will agree.

[29] I add that the fireless hearth and the dismally absent rose are

255

signs of a deeper depression in the *Triptyque* than in the free composition.

[30] René A. Spitz, *La première Année de la vie de l'enfant: Genèse des premières relations objectales* (Paris: Presses Universitaires Françaises, 1958). [Trans. note.]

[31] *Mallarmé* (München: C. H. Beck'sche Verlagsbuchhandlung, 1938). [Trans. note.]

[32] Mme Ayda indicates (pp. 61–62) that Kurt Wais in his first work, of 1938 (who Harriet was, was not then known), had formulated the hypothesis that Mallarmé loved the dead girl, and that this feeling had inspired other poems. She adds that in his new book of 1952, the author abandons this hypothesis, no doubt "under the influence of Charles Mauron," whose work "makes the poet's psychic and even erotic life gravitate around the image of Maria." She regrets that a fecund hypothesis was thus relinquished and she limits herself to discussing what Kurt Wais has nonetheless retained of this, and in so doing confuses Harriet (who was still not yet identified as Harriet *Smyth*) with Ettie Yapp. But one may read in Mondor's *Vie de Mallarmé*, published in 1941: "In Kurt Wais' view . . . the death of a friend, Harriet, must have troubled him deeply and broken the links that bound his soul to his Catholic education. Henceforth he was never to mention God's name . . ." (*op. cit.*, p. 18, note 3). Here are the essentials, it seems, of Mme Ayda's thesis.

[33] According to M. Cellier, Mme Ayda was acquainted only in part with these works of Mallarmé's youth which he himself studies and which I shall analyze in my turn in the Appendix. They were published in 1954 by Dr. Mondor.

[34] *Mallarmé et la morte qui parle*, p. 118.

[35] Ayda, *op. cit.*, p. 97.

[36] The ciphered message is mysterious to the reader; the true poetic symbol is mysterious to the writer.

[37] See chap. 8.

CHAPTER 1.

[1] Camille Soula, *La Poésie et la pensée de Stéphane Mallarmé* (Paris: H. Champion, 1931). [Trans. note.]

[2] Albert Thibaudet, *La Poésie de Stéphane Mallarmé* (Paris: Gallimard, 1912). [Trans. note.]

[3] Emilie Noulet, *Etudes littéraires: L'Hermétisme dans la poésie moderne* (Mexico City: Talleres Gráficos de la Editorial Cultura, 1944). [Trans. note.]

[4] Charles Mauron, *Mallarmé l'obscur* (Paris: Denoël, 1941).

[5] Charles Chassé, *Lueurs sur Mallarmé* (Paris: Editions de la Nouvelle Revue Critique, 1947).

[6] Bibliothèque de la Pléiade (Paris: Gallimard, 1945).

[7] Because Thibaudet did not have the documents made available later by Mondor. [Trans. note.]

[8] A chronology given in such minute detail, however, that even the death of Canon Agricol Aubanel, uncle of the Provençal poet, is to

be found in it. Maria Mallarmé died on August 31, 1857. The chronology gives for this same year: "July 15: death of Béranger. August 10: awarding of prizes at the Lycée de Sens. Stéphane Mallarmé, of Paris, boarding student: 4th place in French composition; 2nd place in Greek translation. October 5: Mallarmé returns to the Lycée de Sens as a boarder in the 4th year."

[9] *Plainte d'automne* was first published in 1864 (Mallarmé was twenty-two) at the same time as *Pauvre Enfant pâle,* a prose poem which later becomes, in my opinion, the *Cantique de Saint-Jean.*

[10] Cf. Charles Baudouin, *Psychanalyse de l'art* (Paris: Félix Alcan, 1929), p. 4: ". . . the complex is a system of media of reaction (of tendencies), more or less mutually entangled because of more or less intimate associations."

[11] Marie Bonaparte, *The Life and Work of Edgar Allan Poe: A Psychoanalytic Interpretation,* trans. by John Rodker (London: Imago Publishing Company, 1949). [Trans. note.]

[12] René Laforgue, *The Defeat of Baudelaire,* trans. by Herbert Agar (London: Hogarth Press, 1932). [Trans. note.]

[13] Mauron's italics. [Trans. note.]

[14] In the first version of *Pitre châtié,* the association eyes—lake—lashes is given directly:

> Pour ses yeux—pour nager dans ces lacs dont les quais
> Sont plantés de beaux cils qu'un matin bleu pénètre.

> [For her eyes—to swim in these lakes whose quays
> Are planted with splendid eyelashes that a blue morning penetrates.]

[15] See notes 11 and 12 above.

[16] Cf. Emilie Noulet, *L'Oeuvre poétique de Stéphane Mallarmé* (Paris: Librairie Droz, 1940), pp. 102–103: "After citing the last verses of *Hérodiade,* R[obert] de Montesquiou added: 'It is indeed the supreme avowal, the ultimate sob, the final harmony: but their reverberation survives them; it outlines the secret, which—and I have this from the poet himself—is none other than the future violation of the mystery of her being by a glance from John, who will see her, and pay with his life for this single sacrilege.'"

[17] Henri Mondor, *Propos sur la poésie* (Monaco: Editions du Rocher, 1946), pp. 58–59. Here we find the indication that the use of repetitions, with which the *Ouverture* is systematically sown, was suggested by Poe's repetitions. They are artificial, and Mallarmé gave them up in time.

[18] The reader should be reminded that the evidence for this association comes from ten other related associations interpretable in the same sense as here: the flower of infancy, snow, moon again, cold water, the blue of the eyes, and so on. Conviction is born of this convergence.

[19] Cf. *Fleurs:*

> Qui roulant sur des mers de soupirs qu'elle effleure
> A travers l'encens bleu des horizons pâlis
> Monte rêveusement vers la lune qui pleure!

[Who rolling on seas of sighs which she glides over
Across blue incense of horizons grown pale
Mounts dreamily toward the weeping moon!]
[20] Roland Dalbiez, *La Méthode psychanalytique et la doctrine
freudienne* (Paris: Desclée de Brouwer, 1936). [Trans. note.]
[21] Charles Odier, *Les deux Sources consciente et inconsciente de
la vie morale* (Neuchâtel et Paris: La Baconnière, 1943). [Trans.
note.]

CHAPTER 2.

[1] Dr. Jean Fretet, *L'Aliénation poétique* (Maîche [Doubs]: J. B.
Janin Editeur, 1946). The references in the text are to this edition.
[2] Letter to H. Cazalis, May 14, 1867, in Henri Mondor, *Propos sur
la poésie* (Monaco: Editions du Rocher, 1946). Cited by Dr. Fretet,
p. 79.
[3] The italics are Mauron's. Fretet's words are "Entre tant, il
s'éprend de Marie," no doubt a misprint for "Entre temps." [Trans.
note.]
[4] *La Carte du Tendre*, an allegorical map introduced by Mlle de
Scudéry in her long-winded heroic romance *Clélie* (10 vols., 1654–
1660) representing the route to the three cities Tendre-sur-Inclination,
Tendre-sur-Estime, and Tendre-sur-Reconnaissance. The terrain was
fraught with obstacles (Lake of Indifference, Mount of Pride, and
so on) but was also dotted with such encouraging towns and villages
as Petits Soins, Billet Galant, Exactitude, and Grands Services.
[Trans. note.]
[5] Henri Mondor, *Vie de Mallarmé* (Paris: Gallimard, 1941), p. 55.
[6] Letter to Cazalis quoted by Mondor, *op. cit.*, p. 84.
[7] Letters to Cazalis of February 3 and March 5, 1863; *ibid.*, pp.
82, 84, 85.
[8] *Ibid.*
[9] Letter of Lefébure, April 15, 1864; *ibid.*, p. 120.
[10] Letter to Aubanel, November 27, 1864; *ibid.*, p. 150.
[11] Letter to Mme Desmoulins, November 20, 1864; *ibid.*, p. 148.
[12] *Ibid.*, p. 160.
[13] Letter to Cazalis, March, 1865; *ibid.*, pp. 160–161.
[14] Letter to Catulle Mendès, spring, 1866; Henri Mondor, *Propos
sur la poésie*, p. 62.
[15] *Ibid.*, p. 82.
[16] Henri Mondor, *Vie de Mallarmé*, p. 259.
[17] *Cantique de Saint-Jean.* [Trans. note.]
[18] Henri Mondor, *Vie de Mallarmé*, p. 259.
[19] *Ibid.*
[20] The sea does not appear in *Igitur*, but the fact that it was associated with it is not, perhaps, irrelevant to its appearance in the
Coup de dés, when Mallarmé again, at the end of his life, passed
through an emotional and mental state analogous to the one revealed
in *Igitur*. Cf. on this subject the chapter below, on *Coup de dés*.
[21] Henri Mondor, *Vie de Mallarmé*, p. 268.
[22] *Ibid.*, p. 270.

[23] Chapter 7 of this book develops the idea of this second alienation. The word "other" will there be taken, consequently, in exactly the opposite sense from Dr. Fretet's.

CHAPTER 3.

[1] See pp. 3 and 31 above.

[2] If the reader refuses to accept this hypothesis because it is not sufficiently proven, the elements of this awakened dream which go to make up the free composition of 1857 must then be directly connected with the Oedipus complex proper and the wound caused by his mother's death. Thus almost nothing would have to be changed, for his sister's death was, all things considered, only a relay stage between the subsequent conscious life of the poet and the shock he sustained in early childhood. We have proof (*Plainte d'automne* and his correspondence) that the second wound grieved him to the depths, and also reverberated, no doubt, as an echo of the first. Let us recall the story reported by Henri de Régnier (cf. H. de Régnier, *Nos Rencontres* [Paris: Mercure de France, 1907], p. 192), in which the young Stéphane, five, reproaches himself for being unfeeling at the death of his mother. Pierre Janet has shown that such lack of apparent feeling often accompanies a very deep wound. Whether the free composition is placed before or immediately after Maria's death makes no essential difference for our thesis as a whole. It nevertheless seems very likely that the composition came after this death.

[3] *Nuit blanche* also means "sleepless night." [Trans. note.]

[4] I have cited elsewhere (p. 32) the two youthful poems–*Sa Fosse est creusée . . . Sa Fosse est fermée*—which date from 1859 and which therefore fall with several others between the free composition and *Apparition.* What concerns us here is not the chronological but the psychological sequence.

[5] Letter of Stéphane Mallarmé to Henri Cazalis, December 30, 1862, quoted by Henri Mondor, *Vie de Mallarmé* (Paris: Gallimard, 1941), p. 78.

[6] Letter of Mallarmé to Cazalis, December 2, 1868; *ibid.*, p. 275.

[7] Letter of Mallarmé to Cazalis, July 1, 1862; *ibid.*, p. 54.

[8] *Ibid.*

[9] See note 4, chap. 2.

[10] Henri Mondor, *op. cit.*, p. 78.

[11] *Oeuvres complètes,* Notes et Variantes, p. 1390.

[12] *Fenêtres.* [Trans. note.]

[13] *Mes bouquins refermés.* [Trans. note.]

[14] *Las de l'amer repos.* [Trans. note.]

[15] Letter to Aubanel, October, 1864 [cited in Mondor, *op. cit.*, p. 144—Trans. note].

[16] Cf. pp. 27 and 48.

[17] We shall find the "sister reasonable and tender" again in *Prose pour des Esseintes,* in which the child who "renounces her ecstasy" finds, moreover, her charms compared with those of the surrounding countryside. Méry Laurent, in her turn, is treated as a sister:

Mon coeur qui dans les nuits parfois cherche à s'entendre
Ou de quel dernier mot t'appeler le plus tendre
S'exalte en celui rien que chuchoté de soeur

[My heart which by night at times seeks to hear its own voice
Or by what final word to call you most tender
Delights in the scarcely whispered word of sister]
and it is known that she was not passionate; see *Dame sans trop d'ardeur* and "hostile glaciers."
    [18] Cf. *Fenêtres:*
        . . . m'enfuir, avec mes deux ailes sans plume—
        Au risque de tomber pendant l'éternité

        [. . . flee, with my two unfeathered wings—
        At the risk of falling for all eternity].

Chapter 4.

    [1] Letter to François Coppée, April 20, 1868; Henri Mondor, *Propos sur la poésie* (Monaco: Éditions du Rocher, 1946), p. 81.
    [2] This network of associated ideas could be expressed by a poor play on words in Latin: "Quos vult perdere Jupiter dementulat."
    [3] Henri Mondor, *Mallarmé plus intime* (Paris: Gallimard, 1944), p. 35.
    [4] In *Oeuvres complètes,* the *Ouverture ancienne, Scène,* and *Cantique* are parts I, II, and III, respectively, of *Hérodiade.* [Trans. note.]
    [5] See chap. 7. [Trans. note.]
    [6] This gesture, let us recall, has already appeared, free of any feeling of sin, in Deborah Parrit's childish dance.
    [7] ". . . Ta tête se dresse toujours et veut te quitter, comme si d'avance elle savait. . . ." [Trans. note.]
    [8] "Tu vins probablement au monde vers cela et tu jeûnes dès maintenant. . . ." [Trans. note.]
    [9] The reader will immediately recall the revolt against God the father, "The Son will do better," which appears in the free composition, and the hand-to-hand struggle in which "God, this old plumage" (in the famous letter of May 14, 1867, to Cazalis), is at last overcome.
    [10] See pp. 111–113. [Trans. note.]
    [11] Emile Borel, *Le Hasard,* new edition (Paris: Librairie Félix Alcan, 1938). [Trans. note.]
    [12] The miracle of the typewriting monkeys consists in this: suppose that a multitude of monkeys strike at random on the keys of typewriters, what is the chance that one of them would in this way tap out the text of *The Odyssey?* [Trans. note.]
    [13] The physicist Guye (Charles E. Guye, *L'Evolution physico-chimique* [Paris: Etienne Chiron, 1922]) demonstrated the point at which this thesis was difficult to maintain for the order shown in living organisms.
    [14] Most of the letters we possess date from the first period. Mallarmé seldom confided in others; thus the work furnishes almost the only evidence as to the thought of his last years.

[15] The words *Coup de dés* may easily be given the broader meaning of *event* or *act*, and we should add at once that for mankind, as Mallarmé certainly believed, thought constitutes the event or act par excellence.

[16] M. Claude Roulet, who has devoted two books to *Coup de dés*, adopts as a secondary motif, on the contrary, the one in Roman capitals and reads it thus, correcting the inversion: "When indeed . . . the Master is cast into eternal circumstances, etc." From this he reaches a theogonic and cosmogonic interpretation which I believe to be, unfortunately, beside the point. M. Roulet's two works [*Elements de poétique mallarméenne* (Neuchâtel: Editions du Griffon, 1948), and *Elucidation du poème de S. Mallarmé: Un coup de dés jamais n'abolira le hasard* (Neuchâtel: Aux Ides et Calendes, 1943) —Trans. note] are nonetheless rich in intelligent insight and full of interest for the devoted solver of Mallarméan enigmas.

[17] *Sonnet en YX* was composed in 1868, *Igitur* in 1869; *Coup de dés* is dated 1897. The date of composition of *Triptyque* is unknown; its publication date is January, 1887. As the three sonnets reproduce a temporal succession (evening—midnight—dawn) and a spiritual curve which never ceased to haunt Mallarmé, it may readily be conceded that the basic idea of *Triptyque* is, in fact, contemporary with that of *Sonnet en YX* or *Igitur*. I will show in a later chapter that their form confirms this hypothesis. This naturally does not exclude the possibility that they were reworked much later. I have limited the table of correspondences to four pieces. The reader will see that I could have added at least *Las de l'amer Repos* (February, 1864), in which the four stages have already appeared: anxiety at the quest for the dead one; the vase, here the cup of the Chinese artist; the evocation (the flower); the sudden appearance of the crescent moon. At this period the reality of the "vigils" had thus already furnished a mold for poetic expression, but Mallarmé does not seem to have been aware of it until later, and the different phases of the vigil are not fully delineated until *Triptyque* and *Coup de dés*, that is, very late.

[18] *Psyché* (Revue Internationale de Psychanalyse et des Sciences de l'Homme), vols. XIII–XIV (November, 1947), pp. 1291–1306.

CHAPTER 5.

[1] "Mauvais Hamlet" = "Hamlet who plays his role inadequately." [Trans. note.]

[2] Cf. Preface to *Igitur* by Dr. Bonniot, p. 17. It is also the moment of the "abolished bibelot."

[3] Cf. *Don du poème* and the third sonnet of *Triptyque*.

[4] *Glace* (which translates as "ice" or "mirror"). [Trans. note.]

[5] Here is remarkable confirmation of our hypothesis equating the mirror (*glace*) with the stone of the sepulcher.

[6] *Glace* as "mirror" or "ice." [Trans. note.]

[7] Vaguely assimilating the tomb to the father, who possesses the mother and forbids any such possession to the son. In *Toast funèbre* the son will triumph. Cf. pp. 157–159.

[8] Cf. pp. 125–126.

[9] The word "garlands" veils what "seduce" reveals. Mallarmé always avoided the macabre, which Poe so easily yielded to. In the unconscious, associations are cruder; the association of the young dead girl with the flowers and with the constellations is undeniable.

[10] He thus overcame the interdiction of the tomb-father and could enjoy freely what he stole. This "rape of an ideal flower" will be found again in *Nénuphar blanc.*

[11] We are indebted to Roger Fry's translation in *Mallarmé: Poems* (New York: New Directions, 1951). [Trans. note.]

[12] *Sonnet en YX.* [Trans. note.]

[13] The idea which most naturally comes to mind is "river" because of the word "bank" ("And not, as the bank weeps"). But *Prose à Cazalis,* published in the *Oeuvres complètes,* inclines us to the choice of "sea." This droll poem, in which it seems that Anastase is Mallarmé himself, Pulchérie his wife, and Anastasie their daughter, appears to have been addressed to the unreliable friend who departed for Cette instead of accompanying the Mallarmés to Bandol in the summer of 1869. This hypothesis fits in nicely with the idea—for me, at least, now obvious—that *Prose pour des Esseintes* tells the spiritual adventure of 1868–1869. In the *Prose à Cazalis,* Anastase and Pulchérie are at the seaside: "Blossom, Pulchérie, beside the sea." In a letter of this period Mallarmé treats the Mediterranean as a lake, and the lake has a bank.

[14] ". . . I have almost lost my wits and the meaning of the most familiar words." Letter to Coppée, April, 1868; *Correspondance, 1862–1871* (Paris: Gallimard, 1959), p. 270.

[15] Recently I have seen another absurd explanation of the word "Prose" by a commentator on Mallarmé. It is useful to remember that *proses* were specifically the religious works of the decadence, when rhyme was introduced into Latin verse. *Prose pour des Esseintes* is so called because of the extraordinary richness of its rhymes, each of which is, in fact, a play on words ("Gloire du long désir, Idées— . . . la famille des iridées").

[16] Henri Mondor, *Propos sur la poésie* (Monaco: Editions du Rocher, 1946), p. 87.

[17] Cf. p. 153.

[18]   Si ce n'est que la gloire ardente du métier,
Jusqu'à l'heure commune et vile de la cendre
Par le carreau qu'allume un soir fier d'y descendre,
Retourne vers les feux du pur soleil mortel!

[Unless it be that the burning glory of the craft,
Until the common, vile hour of death,
Through the window that an evening proud to descend to it
Illuminates, returns to the fires of the pure mortal sun!]

[19] *Mes bouquins refermés.* [Trans. note.]

CHAPTER 6.

[1] Letter to Mistral, December 30, 1864; quoted in Henri Mondor, *Vie de Mallarmé* (Paris: Gallimard, 1941), p. 149, note 1.

[2] Charles Baudouin, *Psychanalyse de l'art* (Paris: Félix Alcan, 1929).

[3] In May, 1865, Aubanel was a juror at the Court of Assizes, when a case was tried involving the rape of a girl by a shepherd from Ventoux. M. Léon Teissier, in a thin volume (*Aubanel, Mallarmé et le faune* [Aiguesvives (Gard): Editions Marsyas, 1945]) suggests this news item as the source of the *Faune* by Mallarmé, the *Pâtre* by Aubanel, and a canto in Mistral's *Calendal*. The friendship of the three writers at this period, the general role of such external factors in literary creation (as in dreams), and finally the dates of composition and certain analogies between the texts give high probability to a thesis which is ably defended by Teissier.

[4] In the first version, the Faun fears he will be struck down by a thunderbolt. It is not, therefore, a question of the satyr's dreaming of subjecting the queen to a "punishment" as revenge for the two nymphs' flight. This interpretation, which is admissible when the second text is considered by itself, no longer holds when the first version is known.

[5] It is the happiness of animality that precedes consciousness.

[6] See chap. 5, p. 161. [Trans. note.]

[7] See *Le Mystère dans les lettres.*

[8] The parenthetical phrase here is the translators'.

[9] Paul Valéry, *Variété II* (Paris: Gallimard, 1929), pp. 169–175.

[10] *Ballets.* [Trans. note.]

[11] *Toast funèbre* and *Nénuphar blanc.*

[12] Henri Mondor, *Vie de Mallarmé* (Paris: Gallimard, 1941), p. 55.

[13] Mallarmé to Méry Laurent; quoted in Henri Mondor, *Mallarmé plus intime* (Paris: Gallimard, 1944), pp. 247–249.

[14] *O si chère de loin et proche.* [Trans. note.]

[15] *Tout Orgueil.* [Trans. note.]

[16] This same light tone appears again in *Quelconque une solitude:*

Au regard que j'abdiquai
Ici de la gloriole
Haute à ne la pas toucher
Dont maint ciel se bariole
Avec les ors de coucher

[In the look which I turned
Here, away from the vainglory,
Really too high to be touched
With which many a sky paints itself
Together with sunset golds.]

[17] *Une dentelle s'abolit.* [Trans. note.]

[18] Or a dream of glory betrayed in favor of love. Cf. the "cry of glories which it stifles."

[19] This interpretation, which is made obvious by the fact that sunset never fails to appear, is reinforced by the word *royaume* (kingdom), which recalls the verses of *Eventail:*

Le sceptre des rivages roses
Stagnants sur les soirs d'or . . .

[The scepter of the rose-red shores
Stagnant against gold evenings . . .]

CHAPTER 7.

[1] A. Hesnard, *Freud dans la société d'après-guerre* (Geneva: Editions du Mont-Blanc, 1947).

[2] Roland Dalbiez, *La Méthode psychanalytique et la doctrine freudienne* (Paris: Desclée de Brouwer, 1936). [Trans. note.]

[3] *Correspondances.* [Trans. note.]

[4] *La Vie antérieure.* [Trans. note.]

[5] Charles Odier, *Les deux Sources consciente et inconsciente de la vie morale* (Neuchâtel and Paris: La Baconnière, 1943). [Trans. note.]

[6] Charles Baudouin, *Psychanalyse de l'art* (Paris: Félix Alcan, 1929). [Trans. note.]

[7] It will also be asked whether the scholar can remain faithful to his scientific logic indefinitely and not sooner or later adopt the viewpoint of the average man on this question. All phenomena are of equal value to the physicist; but a doctor puts life above death, and the psychiatrist sets adult consciousness above infantilism. If he goes on explaining life in terms of physicochemistry, or superior mental functions in terms of inferior, he will end in a real philosophic trap.

[8] Montaigne, "On Friendship," *Essays*, XXVIII. [Trans. note.]

[9] Pierre Janet, *De l'Angoisse à l'extase* (Paris: Félix Alcan, 1926–1928). [Trans. note.]

[10] This is the answer to the question I have often asked myself: does a psychoanalytic study risk ruining the poetry it takes as its subject? If I can trust my own feeling, poetry stands up to this test very well. True beauty has no fear of intelligence; its errors do not harm beauty, still less its truths.

M. Charles Baudouin, who wrote *Psychanalyse de Victor Hugo* (Geneva: Editions du Mont-Blanc, 1943), comes to the same conclusion.

[11] This distinction is often replaced by the one between the active and the contemplative life. The latter contrast appears to be hazier and more subject to various confusions because the artist and the spiritual man *act*. Better, they create. With a little care, though, correspondences could be set up between the two pairs of terms.

[12] Jean Piaget, *La Formation du symbole chez l'enfant* (Neuchâtel: Delachaux et Niestlé, 1945). [Trans. note.]

[13] Charles Odier, *op. cit.*

[14] More or less false art, which is much more common than the real thing, is the analogue of tartuffery. Dr. Odier gives two sources of morality: instinctive functions, and values. He is thus drawn to a consideration of numerous cases in which functions seek a natural satisfaction under the aegis of borrowed values. In human intercourse there is almost always a mixture, and this fact should be accepted as normal. There is no abrupt shift from egoism to generosity, nor from daydream (centered in the ego) to creative dream (centered in the Other). The Other must at first have something of the self in it; so many parents love themselves in their children. The gift and the value nonetheless exist and are purified through exercise.

[15] If this instability were lost sight of, the hierarchy of mental functions would become absurd. We put aesthetic creation above reason. It does not follow that an artist is always superior to a reasonable man. The same remark applies to the hierarchy established by Janet [Pierre Janet, *De l'Angoisse à l'extase*—Trans. note]: a great scientist in his laboratory may go astray when his passions are involved. Great fluctuations in mental level are of common, not to say psychiatric, observation. The mind lives, furthermore, on several levels, at the same time or through quick vibrations.

[16] This takes place in a world which is the higher equivalent of the infantile universe: ego and non-ego again mingle; but the Other has replaced the ego.

[17] Carl G. Jung, *Essais de psychologie analytique* (Paris: Stock, 1931). [Trans. note.]

[18] To take an example from my own experience, it was years before I realized that a concert hall is the image of a communion service (one in which the god remains intact), and that in general the truths of art are easily expressible in mystic language, as the reader can discover for himself in the transpositions of that genre. The myth of Orpheus, who is both singer and initiate, would have revealed this to me much sooner if I had only thought.

[19] (Paris: Les Editions Traditionnelles, 1939).

[20] This taboo on looking back is found in various mythical legends. In the Biblical tradition there is Lot's wife, changed into a pillar of salt for having committed the same mistake in the course of that reascent from the underworld which was represented in the flight from Sodom. Lot's entire history then calls for a symbolic interpretation, which would no doubt lead to an image of the principal figure as the artist or sage rather than the saint, as the curious dialogue with the angel attests: "And it came to pass, when they had brought them forth abroad, that he said, Escape for thy life; look not behind thee, neither stay thou in all the plain; escape to the mountain, lest thou be consumed. And Lot said unto them, Oh, not so, my Lord; behold now, thy servant hath found grace in thy sight, and thou hast magnified thy mercy, which thou hast shewed unto me in saving my life; and I cannot escape to the mountain, lest some evil take me, and I die: behold now, this city *is* near to flee unto, and it *is* a little one: Oh, let me escape thither (*is* it not a little one?) and my soul shall live. And he said unto him, See, I have accepted thee concerning this thing also . . ." (Genesis 19:17–21).

[21] Among moderns, at any rate, Albert Gleizes is, to my knowledge, the first to rediscover this idea and to follow out certain of its consequences. Our analysis of Mallarmé, which has been pursued independently, seems to lead—in a field that is separate from that of the plastic arts—to results that confirm Gleizes' [Albert Gleizes, *Tradition et cubisme* (Paris: Editions La Cible, 1927)—Trans. note].

[22] This is one of the greatest sources of the confusion which reigns in aesthetics. In my opinion, the analogies must be sought according to the following plan: to the emotional magnetic field creating the fixed element in poetry correspond (1) in music, the fields of force in harmony; (2) in painting, the transition from black to white, through

the scale of tone colors. By contrast, to the second element, which is mobile and which in poetry is mingled with the verbal expression of our conscious time, correspond (1) in music, the flow of rhythm; (2) in painting, the movement imposed on our attention by plastic form. A rhythm that crosses fields of harmony becomes melody; a form crossing fields of color composes the picture; a conscious sentence crossing the emotional field of force creates the poem. Hence one descries the two elements—horizontal and vertical—which are so obvious in musical notation. The combination of these two seems precisely to comprise the mystery of all creation.

²³ *The Tempest*, Act I, scene 2, lines 397–404. [Trans. note.]
²⁴ *Introduction à J.-S. Bach* (Paris: Gallimard, 1947).
²⁵ Cf. *De l'Angoisse à l'extase*, p. 232: "To take cognizance of progress, of its possibility despite determinism, to understand the ideas of freedom and evolution—all this seems to me a new stage which humanity appears to be entering."

CHAPTER 8.

¹ Henri Mondor, *Mallarmé lycéen* (Paris: Gallimard, 1954); *Eugène Lefébure* (Paris: Gallimard, 1951). Jacques Scherer, *Le Livre* (Paris: Gallimard, 1957); Mallarmé, *Correspondance, 1862–1871* (Paris: Gallimard, 1959).
² This solitude is characteristic. From a letter to his sister (April 22, 1856, *Mallarmé lycéen*, p. 48) in which Stéphane describes his school, one would gather that there were no students. In the story of Nick Parrit there is no description of a village, despite the allusion to a church and a cemetery.
³ In Baudelaire the corresponding instances are the Cat-Prince and the Prostitute.
⁴ Franz Alexander, *Fundamentals of Psychoanalysis* (London: Allen and Unwin, 1949).
⁵ The elements of this concise framework are borrowed from Dr. Mondor's works.
⁶ It is noteworthy that Mallarmé hesitated about the right dating of his text. "Much later," Dr. Mondor tells us, "Mallarmé wrote on the carefully preserved manuscript the words: 'Free composition—in his third or fourth year at the Lycée de Sens.'" Now Maria's death occurred precisely during the vacation period between his third and fourth years. The presumption in favor of the hypothesis placing this composition after Maria's death is overwhelming if one considers both what Mallarmé says about this death and his work as a whole. One naturally thinks of a memory block which refuses to connect the event and the text. This instance should, moreover, be compared with an error of the same type made by Mallarmé in his *Autobiographie* addressed to Verlaine: in it he states that he lost his mother when he was seven, whereas he was really five when Elizabeth Mallarmé died. However, when his own daughter Geneviève was born on St. Elizabeth's day, he was genuinely moved.
⁷ Dr. Mondor, in *Mallarmé lycéen*, indicates "that on the last page of this rhetoric notebook there is, in six short penciled lines, a sort of

266

autobiography which is a bit less chaste than it is laconic." Mondor then gives the following information:

June 18, 1854   first communion
August, 1857   Maria's death
April, 1859   I spent a night with Emily.
. . .   alone with J. F. (date not specified by Mondor)
November 8, 1860   *baccalauréat*
December 14   first step toward degradation

[The words "Maria's death," "I spent a night with Emily," and "alone with J. F." are in English in original.—Trans. note.]

Thus Mallarmé, writing for himself, put the accent on a bereavement, Maria's death, and two erotic events. This indication, along with others, convinces me that Harriet was above all a charming image, an episodic double of Maria, like Em. Sul. No more is said about her later, whereas Maria's image recurs insistently in the texts and seems to be associated much more closely with Ettie Yapp. In the grouping of the 1859 poems made by Mallarmé himself, Harriet is associated only with Em. Sul. and Béranger, under the title *Elégies*, whereas the *Rêveries* bring together poems directly inspired by Maria's tomb, All Souls' Day, and his anti-religious revolt.

[8] Office where official acts and documents are put on record. [Trans. note.]

[9] *Mallarmé lycéen.*

[10] *Les Trois*, p. 143. "Zinzaris" is probably a hybrid word from "Zingari," Italian for "gypsy," and "Zinzar," an inhabitant of Macedonia or northern Greece, speaking a language akin to Rumanian.

[11] M. Cellier, whose point of view is not psychoanalytic, nevertheless says of Deborah's dance: ". . . it is as though it were the sketch of a sexual ritual" (Cellier, *Mallarmé et la morte qui parle* [Publications de la Faculté des Lettres et des Sciences humaines, Université de Grenoble, Presses Universitaires Françaises, 1959], p. 192).

[12] Detailed analysis of the elegies clearly shows Stéphane's thoughts irresistibly wandering from Harriet's death to the fear of his own. In *Sa Fosse est creusée*, starting from the same position as in *Nuage*, he adds the idea that God interrupts love (*Lierre maudit*). Next the ego attempts to maintain the defenses noted in the free composition but must give in to reality; past experience (part II) and a dialogue with a persecuting reality (part III) denote a situation which is the same as Stéphane's: the mother's absence ("—Her mother, she has none . . .") and the sister's departure (". . . She takes flight to the heavens"), the brother's solitude "in the dormitory," the father's indifference to that solitude (he has remarried). In *Sa Tombe est fermée* Mallarmé builds on the Smyth family's situation, but once more he drifts toward himself. He projects his own refusal of reality on the father and his premonitions of death on the mother. He proposes Nick's consolations to the family (rose, memory, and visits). Then through the image of the distant, lonely sister in America he returns to his own position, equates Harriet and Maria, sees death approach, and accepts it. The anxiety over being abandoned thus recalled is superimposed on the guilt feeling, which antedates the

267

elegies (cf. *Donnez, Lierre maudit,* and also *Prière d'une mère,* an occasional piece renewing the 1858 *Cantate,* and thus perhaps written before July, in which the parental figure-guardian angel—mother of the orphan, that is, no doubt, the grandmother—expresses her concern: "If he should betray the faith his mouth has confessed . . ."). The double grief creates the depressive trough and the revolt with its attendant feeling of persecution.

[13] Perhaps it is not without interest to note that chronologically *Pan* follows *Lœda,* just as *Toast funèbre* (Paris period) follows *Après-midi d'un faune* and *Hérodiade* (Tournon-Avignon).

[14] Many misunderstandings stem from a confusion on this point. Thus Dr. Mondor always seems to reject the thesis of any hypothetical psychoanalyst who would make of Mallarmé a consciously morbid person. Such an attitude indicates ignorance of the patent fact that a person does not have the same innocence or even logic in his dreams as in real life. The less chance his fantasies have of being realized, the cruder they are likely to be. With this reservation, we must accept what Mallarmé dreamed. His atheism was the repression of a dream that projected on God a sadomasochistic complex which was within him and caused him to suffer. His fear of aggression and his sadness at being alone released this mechanism of the persecuted person becoming judge and jury; we should not mistake this for a philosophy. The great interest of this mechanism for us is that it protects poetic sublimation. Siben kills the cricket (*Colère d'Allah*) at the end of the dance just when it has fallen into a childlike sleep and is dreaming of a fairy—obviously the "fairy with the cap of light." By striking Siben down, the ego protects this moment of inner bliss. We would point out that in real life the same adolescent Mallarmé demonstrated the greatest inflexibility when he had to defend his poetic creativity.

[15] A very confused memory or fantasy of a parental embrace deemed cruel by the very young child.

[16] Cellier, *op. cit.,* p. 109.

[17] ". . . he strides like a king through the Edenic enchantment of the age of gold, celebrating for all time the nobleness of the rays of light and the redness of the rose . . ." (*Oeuvres complètes,* p. 265).

[18] The text passes through a series of metaphors from shaken tresses and roses to rouge, blood (sunset), Satan, and then on to Crime and Remorse.

[19] Dr. Mondor quotes a fine passage from Mme Marie-Jeanne Durry, a professor at the Sorbonne, which helps bear out this thesis: ". . . A work of art worthy of the name is not created solely by reaction against influences, but also by welcoming them, as someone has admirably put it: 'No influence is ever more than a wish fulfilled.' The process is not one of accumulating elements that are foreign to oneself, but rather of discovering, through others, what is already one's own" (*Jules Laforgue* [Paris: Seghers, 1952]). Daniel Mornet had already demonstrated that the number and variety of possible influences canceled each other out, as it were: "the principle of choice was then to be sought in the living imagination" of the

creator (*La Littérature française classique de 1660 à 1700* [Paris: Colin, 1947]).

[20] I cannot here go into detail about a subject which I have treated at length elsewhere (cf. *Orphée* and *La Méthode psychocritique*). If Cellier had more exactly understood my thoughts on this point and if he had consulted psychoanalytic literature dealing with it, he would not have reproached me with seeing evidence of morbidity in the "visit of the dead girl," unaware as he is of redemptive value, which he seems to limit to sacred matters. Actually the symptom is evidence of a defense mechanism as much as it is of sickness. The signs of healing are everywhere. The important thing is how much it succeeds. Each sublimation worked in its own way.

[21] As a child Baudelaire wanted to become a military pope and an actor. I have shown that these "vocations" corroborate the structure of the Baudelairean myth. As a child Mallarmé wanted to be a bishop and fancied his sister in a convent (because the mother she represented was already in the grave); the tender union of these two images corresponds to the center of the myth.

[22] If the washerwoman, who was blond in the sunlight, had been transferred to the gallant past, she would have encountered cold, frost, and snow. Sadly she would have danced and made love in the woods; she would have made the roses weep. She would have played with the swan (stroked him with her fan) in a symphony of whiteness; she would have dragged aged lovers behind her purple and silver robe; she would have been a statue of Eve in a bishop's garden. In a word, we find winter, angel, death, and religion in this elegant affair.

A series of associations links this text to *Sourire, Lœda, Ballade,* and *Au Bois des noisetiers,* which are in *Entre quatre Murs,* and, through them, not only to the free composition but also to some poems of the period: *A un Poète immoral, Placet futile,* and *Soleil d'hiver.*

[23] Cf. the variants of *Placet futile:*

Et qu'avec moi pourtant vous avez succombé . . .
Et que sur moi, pourtant, ton regard est tombé.
Et que je sais, sur moi, ton regard clos tombé

[And that with me, however, you have succumbed . . .
And that upon me, however, your glance has fallen.
And that I know your closed eyes have fallen upon me]
to be compared with the *Faune:* ". . . with my eyes closed"; and the free composition, in which Deborah "drowned her blue stare in Nick's eyes."

[24] In it we find that the snow, the nest, the finger lifting the cloth, and mourning (purple-amethyst), all from the free composition, have been eroticized.

[25] Jacques Scherer, *Le "Livre" de Mallarmé* (Paris: Gallimard, 1957).

[26] The corresponding pages of the manuscript bear either groups of words (for example, "hunt—yacht—ball—fireworks—factory—

school" or "burial—marriage—baptism") or else sentence fragments (for example, "The exploit which was to bring him glory is a crime: he stops this Operation in time . . . ," or "and that the lady may have been afraid of what she had come to do to him. Perhaps without her [his?] knowing it. Agree. hat he cover her in oneself," or "but . . . it has never been ascertained that [illegible word] hat bursts sun"). MS pp. 169A and following.

[27] Mme Emilie Noulet, reconsidering her own disappointment ("Réponse à moi-même. A propos du 'Livre' de Mallarmé" in *Revue de l'Université de Bruxelles*, October, 1958–February, 1959) suggests that the poet wanted to set up the cult of a nonexistent Book, along the lines of a religious cult, adoring (according to Mallarmé) a nonexistent God with piousness and rites that are as admirable as they are effective. In my view such a thesis will not stand up. One simply does not make minute calculations about the future printing of a nonexistent book, nor does one decide on its price.

[28] Scherer adds to their surrealism and not to their realism by bothering with (in their connection) non-Euclidean geometry, combinative analysis, and electronic computers. Mallarmé's imagination is just as astounding as his mathematics is elementary.

[29] ". . . exposing our Lady and Protectress to exhibiting her dehiscence or lacuna . . . ," *Le Mystère dans les lettres, Oeuvres complètes*, p. 383.

[30] ". . . the unending blindness [of walls running along suburban streets], without shaded fountains or greenery rising above, bottle bottoms, and wretched potsherds. Even advertisements are posted there with hesitancy . . . ," *ibid.*, p. 384.

[31] "The folding is . . . a quasi-religious token; which does not strike so much as does its compressing, in thickness, offering the minute tomb, to be sure, of the soul." *Le Livre, instrument spirituel, Oeuvres complètes*, p. 379.

[32] *Ibid.* The folding is responsible for the fact that "a closed leaf contains a secret, silence remains there. . . ." "Yes, without the refolding of the paper and the under parts which it creates, the shadow diffused in black letters would not offer a reason to spread out like the breaking of a mystery, on the surface, in the spread opened with the finger."

[33] *Ibid.*, p. 380: "The book, total expansion of the individual letter, must draw from the latter . . . a mobility and spaciousness . . . institute a game. . . ."

[34] *Ibid.*, p. 381.

[35] In *La dernière Mode*.

[36] Otto Fenichel, *The Psychoanalytic Theory of Neuroses* (New York: W. W. Norton, 1945), p. 264: "In psychoanalytic practice, we have the habit of stating, when sensations of this kind come up, such as unclear rotating objects, rhythmically approaching and receding objects . . . , that 'primal scene material is approaching.' "
Let us remember that the primal scene may have been purely imaginary; in fact, the dance is hereditarily a sexual manifestation.

[37] *Oeuvres complètes*, pp. 405 and 387.

[38] This calls to mind Bergler's theory, which, it seems to me, is too limited; it makes of literary creation a specific defense against moral masochism. See *The Writer and Psychoanalysis* (New York: Doubleday, 1950).

[39] This child then would correspond rather to the gloomy double, whereas the old man and the priest combined would correspond to Nick Parrit.

[40] *Sur le Chapeau haut de forme, Oeuvres complètes,* p. 881.

[41] In dreams the hat often has a sexual meaning. But here it is also a question of wit: one calls to mind Poe's *Raven.* Another very closely related symbol, it seems to me, is that of the fanciful head of hair, whose metamorphoses I have analyzed in my psychocritical study of Baudelaire.

Index

Numbers in parentheses are note numbers; 266 (4) refers to note 4 on page 266.

Alexander, Franz, 219; *Fundamentals of Psychoanalysis*, 266 (4)
All Souls' Day, 221, 222, 225, 267 (7)
Amazon, 97, 166
America, 221, 267 (12)
Annabel Lee, 45
Anubis, 242
Ariel, 214, 266 (23)
Art as psychosis, 58–59; role of time in, 209–210, 211, 212, 215, 266 (22); work of (defined), 203
Astarte, 43
Aubanel, Théodore, 256 (8), 258 (10), 259 (15); *Le Pâtre*, 263 (3)
Avignon, 61, 69, 70, 75, 77, 88, 103, 129, 158, 163, 164, 268 (13)
Ayda, Adile, 5–22 *passim*, 251 (4), 252 (13, 15), 254 (22), 255 (26, 28), 256 (33, 35); *Le Drame intérieur de Mallarmé*, 5, 251 (4), 252 (13, 15), 255 (26, 28), 256 (35)

Bach, Johann Sebastian, 80, 199, 266 (24)
Bacon, Francis, 201
Bandol, 74, 77, 262 (13)

Banville, Théodore de, 233
Baudelaire, Charles, 26, 36, 41, 42, 96, 105, 106, 108, 124, 221, 233, 234, 235, 252 (11), 266 (3), 269 (21), 271 (41); *Correspondances*, 5, 196, 252 (10), 264 (3); *Les Fleurs du Mal*, 234, 252 (10), 264 (3, 4); *La Vie antérieure*, 264 (4)
Baudouin, Charles, 143, 170, 194, 198; *Psychanalyse de l'art*, 50, 257 (10), 263 (2), 264 (6, 10); *Psychanalyse de Victor Hugo*, 264 (10)
Beatrice, 28
Bechet, Dr., 69, 77
Beethoven, Ludwig van, 57
Béranger, Pierre Jean de, 257 (8), 267 (7)
Bergler, Edmund, 9, 19; *The Writer and Psychoanalysis*, 253 (19), 271 (38)
Bergson, Henri, 203
Bernard, Claude, 57
Besançon, 61, 70, 77, 111, 135, 163
Bluebeard, 156
Boileau-Despréaux, Nicolas, 54
Bonaparte, Marie, *The Life and Works of Edgar Allan Poe*, 36, 41–45 *passim*, 139, 257 (11)
Bonniot, Edmond, 261 (2)

273

Borel, Emile, 128; *Le Hasard*, 260 (11)
Brussels, 63, 94

Cannes, 70
Carbon cycle, 209
Carte du Tendre, La, 258 (4)
Cazalis, Henri, 28, 29, 30, 42, 48, 61, 62, 65, 69, 73, 74, 77, 87–95 *passim*, 146, 163, 220, 258 (2, 6, 7, 13), 259 (5, 6, 7, 8), 260 (9), 262 (13)
Cellier, Emmanuel, *Mallarmé et la morte qui parle*, 5–6, 18–22 *passim*, 233, 234, 256 (33), 267 (11), 268 (16), 269 (20)
Cerberi, 209
Cette (Sète [Hérault]), 262 (13)
Chassé, Charles, 24; *Lueurs sur Mallarmé*, 24, 256 (5)
Chateaubriand, René de, 221
Chimène, 28
Coppée, François, 70, 260 (1), 262 (14)
Coquelin, Benoît, 68

Dalbiez, Roland, *La Méthode psychanalytique et la doctrine freudienne*, 50, 196, 258 (20), 264 (2)
Dante, 207, 252 (11)
Debussy, Claude, 6
De Lisle, Leconte, 69
Descartes, René, 57
Des Essarts, Emmanuel, 93, 95, 221
Desmolins (maternal grandparents of Mallarmé), 8, 9, 29, 47, 100; André-Marie (grandfather), 85, 147, 148; Mme André (grandmother), 220, 251 (8), 258 (11), 268 (12)
Durry, Marie-Jeanne, *Jules Laforgue*, 268 (19)

Emily, 221, 222, 227, 231, 267 (7)
Em. Sul., 13, 221, 267 (7)
England, 221
Etna, 172
Euclid, 198, 270 (28)

Eurydice, 116, 124, 237
Eve, 269 (22)

Fairbairn, W. Ronald, *Psychoanalytic Studies of the Personality*, 3, 251 (6)
Fénelon, François, 208
Fenichel, Otto, *The Psychoanalytic Theory of Neuroses*, 254 (23), 270 (36)
Fontainebleau, 74, 88, 93, 190, 201
Fretet, Jean, *L'Aliénation poétique*, 9, 12, 46–47, 49, 53–80, 110, 111, 258 (1, 2, 3), 259 (23)
Freud, Sigmund, 37, 41, 42, 46, 50, 75, 119, 194, 195, 196, 252 (13); *The Psychopathology of Everyday Life*, 48
Freudian mythology, validity of, 194–196, 252
Fry, Roger, 262 (11)

Gautier, Théophile, 6, 135, 160, 233, 234
Genesis, 265 (20)
Gerhard, Marie (Mme Stéphane Mallarmé), 13, 14, 61–66 *passim*, 74, 77, 81, 88, 91–95 *passim*, 100, 104–109 *passim*, 151, 168, 184, 186, 208, 213, 219, 222, 233, 258 (3), 262 (13)
Gleizes, Albert, *Tradition et cubisme*, 265 (21)
Guénon, René, *Esotérisme de Dante*, 207
Guye, Charles E., *L'Evolution physicochimique*, 260 (13)

Hamlet, 145–151 *passim*, 158, 181, 227, 261 (1)
Hegel, Georg Wilhelm Friedrich, 133
Hérodiade, 2, 65, 69, 86, 98, 114, 115–127 *passim*, 144, 145, 146, 160, 170, 179, 181, 236
Hesnard, A., *Freud dans la société d'après-guerre*, 194, 264 (1)
Hindu mystic, 58

Homer, *The Odyssey*, 260 (12)
Hugo, Victor, 221, 222, 234; *Booz endormi*, 99; *Châtiments*, 222; *Contemplations*, 222

Icarus, 124
Igitur, 98, 117, 123, 124, 132–146 *passim*, 209
Infantile thought, autism of, 202

James, Henry, 239
Janet, Pierre, 194, 259 (2); *De L'Angoisse à l'extase*, 199, 215, 259 (2), 264 (9), 265 (15), 266 (25)
Jesuits, 54
J[eune] F[ille], 267 (7)
John the Baptist. *See* St. John the Baptist
Juliet, 28
Jung, Carl, 194, 265 (17)

Kant, Immanuel, 180
Klein, Melanie, 9, 19; *Contributions to Psychoanalysis, 1921–1945*, 253 (17)
Kronos, 124, 125, 126

Laforgue, René, 36, 41; *The Defeat of Baudelaire*, 259 (12)
Lamartine, Alphonse de, 221
Laurent, Méry, 14, 26, 107, 110, 112, 130, 135, 165, 167, 168, 174, 184–191 *passim*, 201, 208, 213, 219, 238, 259 (17), 263 (13)
Lautréamont, Comte de, 54
Lecques, 77
Lefébure, Eugène, 29, 42, 61, 64, 70–71, 73, 74, 106, 115, 258 (9)
Lombroso, Cesare, 53
London, 62, 63, 65, 75, 76, 77, 87–95 *passim*, 100, 103, 109, 110, 124, 125, 213, 222
Lot, 265 (20)
Lot's wife, 265 (20)
Lycoris, 227, 231

Mallarmé, Anne-Hubertine (stepmother), 100, 222

Mallarmé, Elisabeth (mother), 8–10, 12–13, 19–20, 22, 29, 33, 35, 47–48, 60, 75, 91, 112, 115, 123, 141, 148, 219, 225, 242, 252 (11), 254 (23, 24), 259 (2), 266 (6), 267–268 (12)
Mallarmé, Geneviève (daughter), 62, 64–65, 69, 102, 104, 184, 262 (13), 266 (6)
Mallarmé, Anatole (son), 130
Mallarmé, Maria (sister), 2–5, 8–9, 12–13, 17, 19, 21, 26–48 *passim*, 60, 63, 75, 81–82, 86–88, 91–92, 96, 100, 104–107, 115, 118–119, 123–125, 141, 146, 148, 151, 168, 181, 184, 186, 195, 217–223, 225, 227, 230, 237–238, 252 (11), 254 (23, 24), 255 (28), 256 (32), 257 (8), 259 (2), 266 (2, 6), 267 (7, 12), 269 (21)
Mallarme, Marie (wife). *See* Gerhard, Marie
Mallarmé, Numa (father), 9, 29, 85, 94, 147, 222, 267 (12)
Mallarmé, Stéphane: atheism, 128, 129, 231, 256, 267 (7); biographical data, 26–27, 220–222, 253–263 *passim*; contemplative mind, and relaxation from anxiety, 167–168
Works: *A Ésp.*, 223; *A P*, 223; *A la nue accablante tu*, 130, 147, 152, 238; *Ange gardien*, 9–11, 218, 253 (16), 254 (22); *Angoisse*, 101, 109; *Apparition*, 19, 43, 87–88, 96, 108, 160–161, 192, 233, 259 (4); *L'Après-midi d'un faune*, 6, 64, 67–68, 77, 86, 154, 167, 170, 171–176, 181, 226–227, 236, 244, 263 (3), 268 (13), 269 (23); *L'Assaut*, 95; *Au Bois des noisetiers*, 269 (22); *Aumône*, 125; *A une petite laveuse blonde*, 226, 235; *A une Putain*, 64, 77; *A un Poète immoral*, 269 (22); *Au seul souci de voyager*, 130; *Autobiographie*, 52, 206, 266 (6); *Autre éventail de Mlle Mallarmé*, 184;

Mallarmé, Stéphane (*Continued*)
Aveu, 223; *L'Azur*, 64, 77, 101,
109, 159; *Ballade*, 230, 269
(22); *Ballets*, 181–182, 184,
263 (10); *Brise marine*, 68,
122, 130, 152, 166, 169; *Cantate*, 268 (12); *Cantate pour
la première communion*, 221,
253 (16), 268 (12); *Cantique
de Saint-Jean* [*Hérodiade*], 41–
42, 71, 102–103, 112, 116, 123–
128, 130, 257 (9), 260 (4);
Causerie d'adieu, 230; *Ce que
disaient les trois Cigognes* (*see*
Free composition); *Chanson
du fol*, 223, 226; *Chansons bas*,
185; *Chant d'ivresse*, 223, 226;
Château de l'espérance, 64, 95–
96, 107, 126, 187, 238; *La
Chevelure vol d'une flamme*,
118, 184, 185, 255 (28); *Colère
d'Allah*, 228, 230–232, 245,
248, 268 (14); *Conférence à
Oxford*, 78; *Correspondance*,
1862–1871, 259 (2), 262 (14),
266 (1); *Coup de dés*, 112–
114, 123, 128–132, 135–148,
152, 163, 167, 179–181, 187,
194, 237–238, 243, 246, 248,
258 (20, ch. 2), 261 (15, 16,
17); *Crayonné au Théâtre*, 185;
Crise de vers, 238, 242, 244;
Cygne, 153–157, 185, 226;
Dame sans trop d'ardeur, 185,
260 (17); *Déclaration foraine*,
185, 187; *Démon de l'analogie*,
48, 102; *La Dernière Mode*,
148, 174, 270 (35); *Divagations*, 42, 102, 106, 118, 145,
177, 240–248 *passim*; *Don du
poème*, 20, 34, 49, 161, 261
(3); *Donnez*, 224, 226–227,
237, 268 (12); *L'Ecclésiastique*, 184; *Enfant prodigue*,
221, 236; *Entre quatre Murs*,
221–222, 225, 243, 269 (22);
Eventail, 176, 263 (19); *Fenêtres*, 49, 95–99, 102, 107,
109, 118, 151–152, 155, 167,
171, 188, 259 (12), 260 (18);

Fleurs, 77, 102, 106, 109, 114–
115, 160, 257 (19); *La Folie
d'Elbehnon*, 69, 72; Free composition (*Ce que disaient les
trois Cigognes*), 4–5, 13–15,
18, 31–32, 38, 43, 48, 81–91
passim, 96, 108, 114, 123, 156,
220–232 *passim*, 236, 244–245,
251 (7), 253 (16), 256 (29),
259 (2), 266 (6), 267–268
(12), 269 (22, 23, 24); *Frisson
d'hiver*, 92, 102–103, 105–107,
109, 120, 123, 141, 191, 233;
Galanterie macabre, 221, 235;
Le Genre ou des modernes,
184; *La Gloire*, 118, 184; *Le
Guignon*, 61, 237; *Hamlet*, 184;
Hérodiade, 41–47 *passim*, 64,
66–71, 75, 77, 81, 86, 102, 104–
106, 110–124 *passim*, 129–130,
141, 153–154, 162, 167–173
passim, 177, 181, 188, 236, 257
(16, 17), 260 (4), 268 (13);
Hier. Aujourd'hui. Demain.,
223–225; *Hommage à Wagner*,
184; *Igitur*, 69–70, 72–73, 77–
78, 99, 110–117 *passim*, 123–
124, 128–136, 140–143, 149,
151, 153, 163, 167–173 *passim*,
187, 194, 208, 237–238, 244–
246, 258 (20), 261 (2, 17),
Larme, 225; *Las de l'amer
Repos*, 36–38, 40, 45, 101, 109,
194, 233, 259 (14), 261 (17);
Lierre maudit, 224–231 *passim*,
235, 248, 267–268 (12); *Le
Livre*, 238–244, 248, 270 (31,
32, 33, 34); *Lœda*, 224, 226–
231 *passim*, 236, 268 (13), 269
(22); *Mélancolie*, 230; *Mes
bouquins refermés*, 165, 184,
259 (13), 262 (19); *Mimique*,
184; *M'introduire dans ton histoire*, 184–185; *Minuit au vieux
beffroi*, 225; *Le Mystère dans
les lettres*, 177, 243, 263 (7),
270 (29); *Mysticis umbraculis*,
235; *Une Négresse par le
démon secouée*, 68, 232, 236;
Le Nénuphar blanc, 174–177,

179, 184, 226, 247, 262 (10), 263 (11); *Ne riez pas*, 223–224, 226; *Notes sur le théâtre*, 184; *Le Nuage*, 223–224, 226, 230, 267 (12); *Offices*, 181; *O si chère de loin*, 185, 263 (14); *Ouverture ancienne* [*Hérodiade*], 116, 119, 260 (4); *Pan*, 230–231, 233, 268 (13); *Papillon*, 61; *Parenthèse*, 184; *Pauvre Enfant pâle*, 42, 48, 102, 124–125, 257 (9); *Pénultième*, 102–109 *passim*, 161; *Phénomène futur*, 102, 181; *Pipe*, 102; *Le Pitre châtié*, 40, 102, 151, 181, 257 (14); *Placet futile*, 86, 235, 269 (22, 23); *Plainte d'automne*, 27–28, 40, 42, 48, 96, 100–101, 104–107, 109, 118, 124, 153, 171, 187, 253 (16), 257 (9), 259 (2); *Pour votre chère morte*, 29–30, 88, 150, 159, 186; *La Prière d'une mère*, 253 (16), 268 (12); *Prose à Cazalis*, 262 (13); *Prose pour des Esseintes*, 153, 162–166, 184–185, 233, 259 (17), 262 (13, 15); *Quand l'ombre menaça*, 75, 130, 156, 231; *Quand sous votre corps nu*, 226; *Quant au livre*, 244; *Quelconque une solitude*, 226, 263 (16); *Quelle soie aux baumes de temps*, 184–185, 189; *Renouveau*, 236; *Rêve antique*, 230–231; *Richard Wagner*, 184; *Rondels*, 86; *Rondels II*, 185; *Sa Fosse est creusée*, 224, 230, 253 (16), 259 (4), 267 (12); *Sa Fosse est fermée*, 32; *Sainte*, 34, 49, 161; *Sa Tombe est fermée*, 253 (16), 259 (4), 267 (12); *Scène* [*Hérodiade*], 116–124 *passim*; *Soleil d'hiver*, 269 (22); *Solennité*, 185; *Solitude*, 243; *Sonnet à M.*, 223; *Sonnet A R.*, 223; *Sonnet en YX* [*Ses purs ongles très haut*], 73, 78, 111–113, 128, 130, 141–144,

161, 163, 185–191 *passim*, 194, 261 (17), 262 (12); *Le Sonneur*, 61, 237; *Soupir*, 39–40, 100–109 *passim*, 117–123 *passim*, 153; *Sourire*, 224, 230, 269 (22); *Surgi de la croupe et du bond* [*Triptyque*], 17, 188; *Sur le Chapeau haut de forme*, 271 (40); *Symphonie littéraire*, 96, 104, 106–108, 126–127, 153, 187, 233–234, 242, 253 (16); *Toast funèbre*, 75, 111, 130, 135, 154–167 *passim*, 175–176, 179, 188, 231, 233, 255 (28), 261 (7), 263 (11), 268 (13); *Tombeau de Baudelaire*, 238, 242; *Tout Orgueil* [*Triptyque*], 17, 117, 187–188, 263 (15); *Triptyque* (*Tout Orgueil fume-t-il du soir; Surgi de la croupe et du bond; Une dentelle s'abolit*), 17–19, 49, 73, 113, 117, 128, 130, 141–144, 153, 162–163, 165, 184–191 *passim*, 194, 245, 255 (28), 256 (29), 261 (17), 261 (3), 263 (17); *Tristesse d'été*, 68, 102, 150; *Les Trois*, 235, 245, 267 (10); *Une dentelle s'abolit* [*Triptyque*], 17, 20, 49; *Vers écrits sur un exemplaire des Contemplations*, 223; *Vers et proses* [of E. A. Poe, transl.], 43; *Victorieusement fui le suicide beau*, 127, 135, 184–189, 194; *Viens*, 230; *Le vierge, le vivace, le bel aujourd'hui*, 184

Maspéro, Gaston Camille, 29–30, 97

Mauclair, Camille, 6, 255 (26); *L'Art en silence, Mallarmé chez lui, Les Princes de l'esprit*, 252 (14)

Mauron, Charles, 256 (32), 258 (3); *L'Inconscient dans l'oeuvre et la vie de Racine*, 251 (5); *L'Introduction à la psychanalyse de Mallarmé*, 1, 5–7, 17; *Mallarmé l'obscur*, 2–3, 23, 33–35, 51–52, 200, 214,

Mauron, Charles (*Continued*)
256 (4); *La Méthode psycho-critique,* 269 (20); *Orphée,* 269 (20); *La Personnalité affective de Baudelaire,* 271 (41)
Mendès, Catulle, 258 (14)
Miss Mary, 184
Mistral, Frédéric, 153, 262 (1); *Calendal,* 263 (3)
Mondor, Henri, 4, 24–27 *passim,* 35, 87, 92, 252 (11), 256 (7, 33), 266 (5), 268 (14, 19); *Amitié de Verlaine et Mallarmé,* 24–25; *Eugène Lefébure,* 266 (1), 267 (9); *Mallarmé lycéen,* 5, 10, 252 (11), 253 (21, 22), 266 (1, 2, 6, 7); *Mallarmé plus intime,* 3, 24–25, 31, 252 (8), 260 (3), 263 (13); *Propos sur la poésie,* 25, 257 (17), 258 (2, 14, 15), 260 (1), 262 (16); *Vie de Mallarmé,* 2, 21, 24, 26, 60–61, 74, 184, 251 (3), 256 (32), 258 (5–13, 16, 18, 19, 21, 22), 259 (5–8, 10, 15), 262 (1), 263 (12), 266 (6)
Montaigne, Michel de, 59; *Essays,* 264 (8)
Montesquiou, Robert de, 257 (16)
Mornet, Daniel, *La Littérature française classique de 1660 à 1700,* 268–269 (19)
Mount Ohara, 83
Mozart, Wolfgang Amadeus, 211
Mysticism, 11

National Observer, 75
Nerval, Gérard de, 54
Nietzsche, Friedrich, 54
Noulet, Emilie, 27, 153, 157, 270 (27); *Etudes littéraires: L'Hermétisme dans la poésie moderne,* 23–24, 256 (3); *L'Oeuvre poétique de Stéphane Mallarmé,* 257 (16); "Réponse à moi-même. A propos du 'Livre' de Mallarmé," 270 (27)

Nurse (in *Hérodiade*), 47, 119–120

Odier, Charles, 50; *Les deux Sources consciente et inconsciente de la vie morale,* 198, 202, 258 (20, chap. 1), 264 (5, 13, 14)
Ophelia, 146–149 *passim,* 158, 227
Orpheus, 22, 206, 208, 212, 214, 265 (18)
Orphic ego (of Mallarmé), 15
Ouranos (father of Kronos), 125

Paphos, 97, 166
Paris, 69, 75, 77, 100, 111, 135, 201, 268 (13)
Parnasse contemporain, 69
Parrit, Deborah, 82, 85–86, 97, 107, 116, 119, 121, 159–160, 181, 218, 220, 232, 236–237, 255 (28), 260 (6), 267 (11), 269 (20, 23), 271 (39)
Parrit, Nick, 82–86, 91, 96–97, 103, 165–166, 218–221 *passim,* 225–237 *passim,* 255 (24), 266 (2), 267 (12), 269 (23), 271 (39)
Pascal, Blaise, 157
Passy, 100, 221–222, 225
Personal myth, 3–4, 217–218, 222–248 *passim,* 251 (1), 269 (21)
Phoebe, 227
Phoenix, 191
Piaget, Jean, *La Formation du symbole chez l'enfant,* 194, 202, 264 (12)
Plato, 58
Poe, Edgar Allan, 36, 41–49 *passim,* 75, 96, 126, 257 (11, 17), 262, (9), 271 (41); *Annabel Lee,* 44–46; *The Raven,* 138, 208, 235; *Ulalume,* 43–49 *passim,* 126; *Vers et proses* [translations by Mallarmé], 43
Poe, Elizabeth (mother of Poe), 45

Poet, and relationship to world about him, 240, 265 (15)
Poetic creation: answer to death, 78–80, 98–99, 154, 160, 161; anxiety in, 67, 71–72, 112, 153–154, 166, 188, 219; and impotence, 64–67, 73, 87, 135, 153–154; and narcissism in, 57, 91, 98, 105, 134, 169; Orphic explanation of, 206–212, 237, 244, 265 (18); psychology of, 4–6, 22, 91, 203; for sake of "the Other," 54, 201–206, 210–215, 231, 259, 264 (14); synthesis of, 213, 265 (22)
Poetic thought vs. rational thought, 158, 198–199, 204, 208
Poetry, layers of meaning in, 33, 40, 155, 214
Poincaré, Jules Henri, 57
Polyphemus, 176
Port-Royal, 26
Prometheus, 124, 228, 231
Proust, Marcel, 53–54, 204, 209–210, 215; Le Temps retrouvé, 149, 209
Psyche, 44, 49, 209
Psyché (periodical), 143, 261 (18)
Psychiatry, use of, in literary interpretation, 53–54, 78–79
Psychoanalysis: use of, in literary interpretation, 36, 46–52, 167, 181, 194–195, 208, 232, 252, 254, 264 (10), 268 (14)
Psychocriticism, 1–7 passim, 13–15, 20, 22, 264 (10), 269 (20)

Racine, Jean, 36, 54, 221
Rank, Otto, 170
Régina, 28
Régnier, Henri de, Nos Rencontres, 253 (20), 259 (2)
Rhône River, 69
Rimbaud, Arthur, 53–54
Rodenbach, Georges, 234
Roulet, Claude, Eléments de poétique mallarméenne, 261 (6); Elucidation du poème de S.

Mallarmé: Un coup de dés jamais n'abolira le hasard, 261 (6)
Rousseau, Jean-Jacques, 54
Rousseaux, André, Le Monde classique, 251 (4)
Rue de Rome, 29

Sadomasochism, 228–232, 234–238 passim, 247, 268 (14)
Sainte-Beuve, Charles Augustin, 26, 36
St. John of the Cross, 58
St. John the Baptist (in Hérodiade), 41–42, 47, 114, 119, 123, 125, 170, 179, 259 (16)
Satan, 126–127
Schahriar, 157
Scherer, Jacques, Le "Livre" de Mallarmé, 238–244 passim, 266 (1), 269 (25, 26), 270 (26, 28)
Schleuzer, Boris de, Introduction à J.-S. Bach, 215, 266 (24)
Scudéry, Mlle de, Clélie, 258 (4)
Sens, 62, 94, 100, 221, 257 (8), 266 (6)
Shakespeare, William, The Tempest, 215, 266 (23)
Smyth, Harriet, 8, 13, 17–22 passim, 221–226 passim, 231, 255 (28), 256 (32), 267 (7, 12)
Socrates, 57
Sodom, 265 (20)
Soula, Camille, La Poésie et la pensée de Stéphane Mallarmé, 23–24, 27, 256 (1)
Spitz, René A., 19; La première Année de la vie de l'enfant, 256 (30)
Styx, 73, 143, 154, 162, 168, 206
Symbols, 16–22, 252, 255 (26–28)

Tahiti, 152
Teissier, Léon, Aubanel, Mallarmé et le faune, 263 (3)
Thibaudet, Albert, 256 (7); La Poésie de Stéphane Mallarmé, 23–27 passim, 256 (2)

Thousand and One Nights, 156
Tournon, 26, 30, 37, 62, 64, 69–
  70, 77, 100, 103, 123, 135, 178,
  268 (13)

Ulysses, 176

Valéry, Paul, *Variété II,* 179–180,
  263 (9)
Valvins, 69, 165, 201
Ventoux, 263 (3)
Verlaine, Paul, 266 (6)

Villiers de l'Isle-Adam, Philippe,
  117
Virgil, 207

Wais, Kurt, *Mallarmé,* 21, 256
  (32)
Wells, H. G., 239

Yapp, Ettie, 13, 28–30, 39, 74,
  87–93 *passim,* 186, 208, 256
  (32), 267 (7)

Zeus (son of Kronos), 125, 231